The
Peace Pursuit
Handbook

The Peace Pursuit Handbook

JOHN SHINDELDECKER

Biblical, practical, and accessible tools for resolving interpersonal conflicts

PeacePursuit.org

ISBN 978-1-7327003-0-7

DISCLAIMER
This guide is meant to help the reader resolve relational problems between individuals. I do not offer legal or financial advice, and I accept no responsibility for legal, relational, or financial consequences that arise from your use of what I write here in your own life or the lives of others.

Cover design and illustrations:Tessa Taylor, cornercube.co.uk/
Book layout: Karisma Design, karispratt@gmail.com

Published by John Shindeldecker.

To Laura

My precious wife and soul mate who has patiently read, listened to, and improved on my ideas as this handbook has taken shape over the years. She has been a sacrificial and loving partner especially when helping others resolve their conflicts has interrupted our family rhythms. It is no cliché to say that without her faithful encouragement, this handbook would never have been completed.

CONTENTS

HOW TO USE THIS HANDBOOK

This is a practical, how-to guide to help you navigate your biblical choices to resolve a relational problem. It is designed so you can easily access just the material you need when you need it.

You might not need to read every chapter or section every time. Skim through the headings, find what you need at the moment, and go there. To make it possible for you to follow your chosen role to resolve a conflict without reading the whole book, I have repeated some important concepts in various sections.

If you want to have a broad view of the Peace Pursuit process, read through the whole book and highlight sections that might address a specific relational problem you have a part in resolving.

Chapters 2 through 7, which include Stage One and Stage Two, are the sections that apply to most people most of the time:

Chapter 1. Introduction. Feel the effects when Christians don't resolve their conflicts and discover how the Peace Pursuit Model™ can help you and others reach peace.

Chapter 2. Biblical Foundations. As you read the Five Pillars of Peace Pursuit and the P.E.A.C.E. Principles, you can find biblical motivation to resolve interpersonal conflicts and learn the values on which the Peace Pursuit Model is built.

Chapter 3. Decide what you mean by peace. How do you know when you have reached peace with another person? Decide what you are making before you start peacemaking.

Chapter 4. Choose your primary role. Choose from the basic Peace Pursuit role descriptions to identify your appropriate role in a relational problem and/or its resolution.

Chapter 5. Embrace your role. After you choose your role, accept the options and responsibilities of fulfilling your role.

Chapter 6. Stage One: Meet with God. Prayerfully and sincerely meet with God before you talk to another party in the conflict. Follow your role icon and complete the appropriate steps for your role.

Chapter 7. Stage Two: If appropriate, meet with the other person. Depending on your role and what you decided when you met with God at Stage One, you may decide it is appropriate for you to communicate with another party in the conflict. Stage Two shows you how to communicate so that your interaction feels more like a conversation than a confrontation.

Chapter 8. Stage Three: You and the other person meet with someone else. There may be occasions when you and another party don't reach peace at Stage Two and you need some help from a third person in the Peace Pursuit role of witness or mediator. Or, in a different situation, two people might ask you to help them reconcile with each other in the role of witness or mediator.

Chapter 9. Extraordinary situations: a brief introduction. The vast majority of conflicts between two people can be resolved at Peace Pursuit Stage One, Two, or Three. In unusual cases, you may need to proceed further.

Chapters 10–12. Stages Four, Five, and Six. These stages are only for those rare occasions when a person has not understood or accepted wisdom from godly and loving sisters and brothers who have appropriately processed the first three stages of Peace Pursuit. Stages Four, Five, and Six demonstrate a special commitment of love, patience, and an investment of valuable resources for that person by his or her community to reconcile him or her to God and others.

PREFACE

The personal back story

While I was growing up, members of my family frequently had stressful verbal exchanges which resulted in emotional distance between my parents, and between my parents and us children. The atmosphere in our home wavered between tension and awkward silence.

The summer before my final year of high school, my parents decided to move to a different city. This meant I had to attend a new school where I knew no one.

Three months before my graduation, my father announced that he and my mother were getting a divorce. To be honest, my first feeling was relief. At least I wouldn't have to endure the stress from both parents living in the same house.

Looking back, I see God's providential hand in my school transfer. He introduced me to a new kind of family.

I had gone to church until I was about thirteen, and I had even been a leader in the youth group. But church didn't seem relevant to my life as a teenager, so I stopped going when I started high school. That's why I was surprised that some of my classmates at the new school were intelligent, fun-loving, and sincere about living for Jesus. Up to that point, I didn't know that combination was possible.

They explained that through Jesus I could be forgiven and reconciled to God. I was self-aware enough to know that I needed to be forgiven by God—and by many people—for many things. I accepted God's forgiveness and committed my life to follow him.

I soon learned that to be a disciple of Jesus meant doing whatever I could to be at peace with all people. I initiated a series of conversations in which I apologized to my parents, my teachers, other adults, and schoolmates I knew I had offended. It felt awkward to be humble and honest to confess my wrong attitudes and actions to so many people. I admit I secretly hoped that each one would not understand what I was apologizing for and dismiss my confession as unnecessary.

However, my eyes were opened to a deep spiritual lesson when it turned out that each person actually remembered my offenses, took my confession seriously, and forgave me specifically. And not all were believers in Jesus.

Those were amazing experiences of God's grace. I still remember the fresh joy I had from a clean heart and clear conscience, forgiven both by God and by people.

Since those early days, I've observed that many of Jesus' family members aren't very good at making peace with each other. As I've listened to people from many cultures share with me about relational problems in their marriages, families, friendships and churches, I've felt the same feelings of strife and tension I experienced when I was growing up in my biological family.

I've also seen first-hand the tragic results when spiritual families don't purge their relational poisons. Angry people leave one church and just take their anger to the next. Wounded people don't get healed and are hindered in their relational and spiritual growth. Some even reject Jesus altogether when they don't see his so-called followers practice the love, humility, and forgiveness that he taught.

Of course, all of this dishonors God, his word, and his other children. There are practical consequences as well. I've witnessed the abominable waste of time, energy, and money when disciples of Jesus avoid resolving conflict in healthy ways. Those wasted resources could have been invested in bringing people God's love.

My passion is to transform this sad picture one relationship at a time. I am not naïve; I know that Jesus' disciples are always going to offend each other. We are going to have conflicts because we are not all perfectly like Jesus yet. Still, faithful followers of the Prince of Peace should not leave relational problems unaddressed. Making peace is such a priority for the Body of Christ that Jesus included it in his famous teachings known as the Beatitudes: "Blessed are the peacemakers, for they will be called children of God" (Matthew 5:9, NIV).

I believe that most Jesus followers already know they should be peacemakers. And, I believe that many sincerely want to resolve their relational problems with other Christians. So, why do they let so many conflicts persist in their homes, churches, schools, and work places? Why do so many leave their church or ministry team and go to another one (or none at all) without resolving their conflicts? Why do some abandon family members or friends without doing their part to make peace and wrongly think that doing so is acceptable to God?

I used to think the answer to these questions is that people are proud or just plain stubborn. Over the years, I've observed that while pride certainly does keep some people from making peace, it is not true for everyone. I am now convinced that most good-hearted disciples of Jesus want to make peace, but they simply don't know how. Some are afraid they'll make mistakes in the process. Or, they have no hope that whatever they try will "work." For others, their past attempts at making peace turned out so poorly they feel it is too painful to try again.

I am fully aware that an interpersonal conflict can be complicated. But, I am convinced its resolution doesn't have to be.

This handbook is a step toward my goal to give Christians Bible-based, practical, and user-friendly tools to reconcile with one another so they can fulfill Jesus' plan for them to demonstrate his love to the world with integrity. It is the distillation of decades of experience in helping resolve conflicts. Along with fellow peacemakers, my wife Laura and I have collected biblical principles and practical tips that we have seen bring peace in the most common, real-life situations and in difficult, complicated ones. I address a number of "What if?" scenarios and I offer answers to more than 100 questions we've been asked over the years. Much of what you read here comes from upgrades we have made after we reflected on peacemaking conversations that didn't go as well as we had hoped. We are still learning from God and other peacemakers.

My greatest desire in preparing this handbook is to provide you with tools so you can be encouraged, strengthened, and prepared to do the spiritual and practical work it takes to do everything you can, as much as it depends on you, to be at peace with all (Romans 12:18).

1. INTRODUCTION

HOPE LOST

Unresolved conflict threatens the spiritual life and witness of Christians all around the world. It also grieves God's heart. The true story below is just one example of what can happen in a church or ministry. To protect identities, names and non-essential details have been changed.

William, Sarah, James, and Deborah were bright, young, passionate Jesus followers. They gave up promising careers in their home country to bring the good news of Jesus to a community overseas where there were no followers of him. William was their team leader.

Before they went abroad, they prayed together, worshiped together, studied together, trained together, planned together, and recruited others to join their team. Their faith and commitment built up the faith of their friends and family in churches at home. Everyone anticipated how God would be glorified through the lives and witness of these ambassadors for Jesus among people who had not heard of him. They arrived in their new country full of faith, hope, joy, and trust in each other. All was good.

Less than a year later, they were empty of faith, hope, joy, and trust in each other. James and Deborah wanted to resign from the team. They had come to dislike, resist, and complain about William's leadership. At the same time, William was ready to dismiss James and Deborah from the team. Sarah and Deborah's relationship had built up mutual pain from a cycle of criticism and withdrawal. Each woman said that she did not feel emotionally safe to be in the same room with the other one.

Sadly, this same story happens more often than you might think.

Eventually, William asked for outside help. Mediators were called in. The two couples in conflict put their ministry on hold for a week to work on their relationship problems. Teammates lovingly served by watching the couples' children when needed.

Deborah told the mediators that she would not meet in the same room with Sarah until she felt emotionally safe to do so. Sarah said the same thing about Deborah.

James announced to the mediators, "I don't understand why we have to spend all this time and energy on this conflict with William and Sarah. I just want to get out and share Jesus with these dear people in our community who haven't heard of him."

Which Jesus?

When I first heard this part of the story, a question came to my mind. I wondered which Jesus James wanted to share with the local people. Was it the Jesus who tells us to postpone our acts of worship until we reconcile with someone who we know has something against us (Matthew 5:23–24), and the Jesus who tells us to forgive others while we are praying (Mark 11:25), and the Jesus who tells us that others will know we are his disciples by the love we have for one another (John 13:35)? Or, did James want to introduce a different Jesus to his local friends?

Maybe that question came to your mind, too.

How could it get this bad?

I had another question as I heard more of the story. These were four committed, passionate, biblical, and spiritual ambassadors for Jesus who were approved, commissioned, and sent out by their churches. How was it that these two couples got this far in life and this deep in their conflict without applying basic biblical principles to pursue peace?

By asking a few questions, I learned a number of sad facts.

I learned that William had been advised to have his team trained in biblical peacemaking before they went overseas, but he had declined. "I didn't think we would need it," he confessed later.

I learned that their theological and ministry training did not include any course on how to resolve conflicts biblically.

I also learned that their churches did not teach or model for them how to pursue peace. At least one of their sponsoring churches had been through a nasty split that was never reconciled. Sadly, that also happens more often than you might think.

Finally, I learned that William, Sarah, James, Deborah and their churches did not understand that their unresolved conflict was an aspect of spiritual warfare. They let Satan use their unresolved conflict as a tool to attack their individual relationships with God and damage their testimony as representatives of the Prince of Peace to the very people they moved across the world to share his love with.

A tragic story, isn't it? I'll come back to it a little later.

HOW THE PEACE PURSUIT MODEL™ CAN HELP YOU

The Peace Pursuit Model™ gives you field-tested, practical, clear, and accessible tools so you can know the biblical choices you have and positive steps you can take to honor and obey God when you encounter a relational problem.

The Peace Pursuit Handbook focuses on how to fulfill your role in four common situations you will likely encounter in your family, your workplace, your church, your small group, or in whatever context two people have a relational problem. Your problem doesn't have to be as serious as the conflict between William, Sarah, James, and Deborah for this handbook to help you. In fact, if you use this handbook regularly, you most likely will never find yourself in a conflict like theirs.

Here are the four most common Peace Pursuit scenarios:

- You feel offended by someone. You feel hurt, angered, disappointed, or something similar.
- It appears you have offended someone. Apparently you have hurt them, angered them, disappointed them, or something similar.
- You consider helping a person do their part to resolve a problem they have in their relationship with God or with another person. You are not a party in the conflict.
- A person wants to talk or pray with you about a relational problem that doesn't involve you. They either have a personal problem with another individual, or they want to talk about a problem between two other people.

There's a folk proverb that says, "If your only tool is a hammer, you see everything as a nail." For some Christians, Matthew 18:15–17 is their hammer, and the supposed offender is the nail ("If your brother sins against you, go and tell him his fault..."). Peace Pursuit is not built on just this one passage. It is a craftsman's case full of biblical tools you choose to use according to the need of each person at any given moment.

Peace Pursuit takes into account that people are unique, that relationships can be complicated, and that the resolution of one conflict can look very different from another. It is not a one-size-fits-all checklist. It is a comprehensive model based on biblical principles widely accepted by sincere Jesus followers. The model is designed to help you avoid two extremes: the rigidness of "everyone must do it this way" and the chaos of "everyone does what is right in their own eyes."

Churches and ministry teams who have adopted the Peace Pursuit Model have given us this feedback:

- Their unity and trust in each other has grown.
- They have a common vocabulary so that every person involved in the peacemaking process is "on the same page."
- They can spot some potential conflicts before they happen.
- They are able to resolve their relational problems in a shorter time and with less emotional energy than before.
- Their faith in the Prince of Peace has grown as they have experienced his love and power to reconcile individuals to each other.
- They are resolved to make peacemaking an essential part of their walk with the Lord as individuals and as a community.

How well does it "work?"

Over the years, we have heard many testimonies from those who regularly use the Peace Pursuit Model to resolve conflicts. Based on those testimonies and our personal experience, we believe that if each party fulfills their Peace Pursuit role, you will resolve the great majority of relational problems you are likely to encounter between sincere followers of Jesus in the first two Peace Pursuit stages. If you don't reach peace in the early stages, the Peace Pursuit Model will help you identify which person or persons are not seeking appropriate confession and forgiveness.

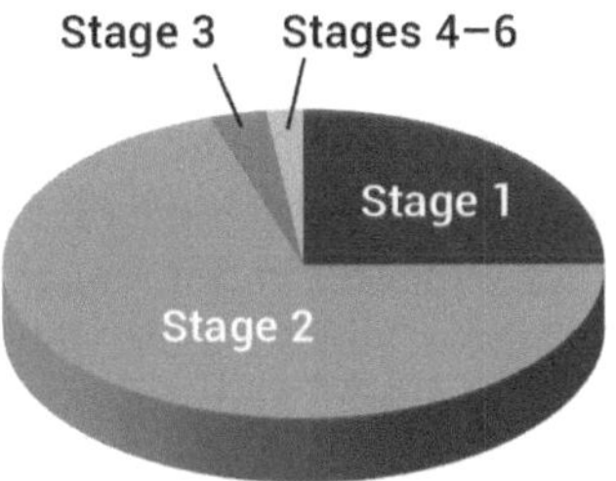

A number of Peace Pursuit principles and practices can also assist you as you resolve relational problems with people who are from other faith traditions or who identify with no faith. However, you should expect more God-honoring results from people who value the Bible and who listen to the Holy Spirit.

Now, let's return to the story of William, Sarah, James, and Deborah.

HOPE FOUND

During the week they met, William, Sarah, James, and Deborah followed the Peace Pursuit Model in this handbook. The mediators coached each one through *Stage One: Meet with God* for their appropriate roles.

To their credit, during that week the four parties each sought God, listened to his voice, and obeyed his word as they processed Peace Pursuit Stage One. They pulled the planks out of their own eyes. They admitted the truth about themselves. They humbled themselves before God. As God promises to the humble, he gave each of them the grace they needed (James 4:6).

On the last day, the mediators brought William, Sarah, James, and Deborah together. It was the first time in weeks that all four had met in the same room.

James asked to start. (Remember, James was the one who would rather tell people about Jesus than make peace with his teammates.) With tears, James confessed his rebellious and judgmental spirit toward his leader, William. James also repented of his initial lack of commitment to pursue peace.

William, the leader, confessed he had not cared for James and Deborah in the pastoral way he should have. William also confessed his prideful belief that he could successfully lead the team without training in biblical peacemaking.

Sarah sobbed as she confessed that she had known that her critical words had hurt Deborah but she had willfully continued to say them. In tears, Deborah confessed that she withheld her love and forgiveness of Sarah and that she consciously withdrew from Sarah. Just days before, these two women did not feel emotionally safe to be in the same room with each other. Now they stood up and released a flood of tears in a lengthy embrace of mutual repentance and forgiveness.

With their spiritual bonds of pride and unforgiveness broken, these four newly-reconciled ambassadors for the Prince of Peace shared a joyous, relaxed meal with each other and their children. Then the two families began the process of rebuilding their mutual love and trust.

The two couples lived for many years among people who had very little knowledge of the Jesus of the Bible. These four testified with their lives—not just their words—that they were true disciples of the Prince of Peace because of the love they had for one another.

Thankfully, the happy ending of their story is not unique. We have seen breakthroughs like this in marriages, families, friendships, churches, and ministry teams when they follow the Peace Pursuit Model.

For William, Sarah, James, and Deborah, hope lost became hope found. Their story can be yours, too, wherever you live.

Welcome to Peace Pursuit.

2. BIBLICAL FOUNDATIONS

THE FIVE PILLARS OF PEACE PURSUIT

A number of Bible verses relate to resolving relational problems between two people. I have synthesized my understanding of those verses into five concepts, which I call the *Five Pillars of Peace Pursuit.*

Pillar 1. God wants you to be at peace with all people.

Pillar 2. Your relationships with people reflect and affect your relationship with God.

Pillar 3. Treat everyone as a unique person created and loved by God.

Pillar 4. Treat everyone alike, without prejudice or partiality.

Pillar 5. Everyone is blessed when you pursue peace biblically.

Pillars 1 and 2 tell us *why* we should make peace.

Pillars 3 and 4 describe *how* we make peace.

Pillar 5 promises that *good fruit will come* from our biblical peacemaking efforts.

Pillar 1: God wants you to be at peace with all people

Here are just a few Bible verses which communicate God's priority for people to be at peace with each other (emphasis mine):

Hebrews 12:14a

"*Pursue* peace with all men" (NASB).

"*Make every effort* to live in peace with everyone" (NIV).

"*Strive for* peace with everyone" (ESV).

Romans 12:18

"*If possible, so far as it depends on you,* live peaceably with all" (ESV).

"*If it is possible, as far as it depends on you,* live at peace with everyone" (NIV).

Romans 14:19

"*Make every effort* to do what leads to peace and to mutual edification" (NIV).

"*Pursue* what makes for peace and for mutual upbuilding" (ESV).

Ephesians 4:3

"*Make every effort* to keep the unity of the Spirit through the bond of peace" (NIV).

"[*Be*] *diligent* to preserve the unity of the Spirit in the bond of peace" (NASB).

"[*Be*] *eager* to maintain the unity of the Spirit in the bond of peace" (ESV).

Colossians 3:15

"*Let the peace of Christ rule in your hearts,* since as members of one body you were called to peace" (NIV).

"*Let the peace of Christ rule in your hearts,* to which indeed you were called in one body" (ESV).

I believe those verses clearly teach these principles:

- God instructs you to be at peace with all people. It is not a suggestion, it's an imperative.
- God holds you personally responsible to actively do your part to pursue peace.

- God does not hold you responsible for the response of other people to your sincere efforts to pursue peace.

Be encouraged. God does not tell you to do something you can't do. Since God instructs you to be at peace with others, you can think of it as his good purpose for you.

You can trust that God will provide you with everything you need to do your part to make peace, whether it is courage, wisdom, counsel, humility, patience, compassion, grace, faith, repentance, or forgiveness. This should give you hope, even in the most challenging conflicts. That has been my experience when resolving my own relational problems and when I have helped others with theirs.

What does the Bible mean by the phrase, "live at peace" or "live peaceably" with everyone?

I describe peace between two people as the point when each party admits whatever they did wrong to the other (if they did anything wrong) and each party forgives the other. You can say it in just four words: appropriate confession and forgiveness. If that's not your definition of peace, maybe you can agree that to reach appropriate confession and forgiveness is at least a good marker on the road to repair a relationship.

Even if the other person chooses not to cooperate, you can do your part toward appropriate confession and forgiveness. To pursue peace from your side means you first meet with God. You make the decision to forgive the person in your heart before the Lord and to keep no account of the biblically-defined wrong they did toward you. Second, if you have committed any biblically-defined wrong to the person, you confess it to them.

What does "live at peace" or "live peaceably" not mean?

The Bible describes a lack of peace with words like jealousy, strife, outbursts of anger, disputes, dissensions, discord, envy, factions, unruliness, rudeness, dishonor, disrespect, bitterness, disobedience, unconfessed sin, and unforgiven sin. Obviously, if you have these in your relationships, you are not at peace, and you must do what you can to make peace.

Of course, God wants you to go beyond simply living in peace with people, especially with others who follow him. Bible concepts like having fellowship and growing in love for one another describe these deeper levels of relationship. You'll know you've gone beyond the minimum level of peace when most of the time your relationship has unity, harmony, grace, blessing, gentleness, honor, respect, submission, confession, and forgiveness.

However, to be at peace with someone does not mean you have to be "best friends" with them. You treat them like you want them to treat you (Matthew 7:12), and make sure there is no unconfessed sin or unforgiven sin between you.

Being at peace also does not mean you have to say, "I totally trust the other person in all circumstances." You can be reconciled with a person over past relational problems, but sometimes you should be careful about placing your future trust in them. Let's be honest. Some people are simply just not trustworthy in some areas of either their character or their competence.

What do I mean by character and competence? To trust in a person's character means you have confidence that their morals, ethics, and motives have integrity and are consistently in line with biblical principles. You can then trust them to be honest and "do the right thing." However, suppose I am a habitual, unreformed thief. You can forgive me for stealing from you, but you should not trust me with your money or valuables until I have proven that I am no longer a thief. Or, let's say I am an unreformed gossip. You can forgive me for gossiping about you, but you should not entrust me with any information you don't want others to hear until it is clear that I can control my tongue.

By trust in a person's competence, I mean confidence in their skill or ability to complete a task. I may be an honest, ethical, trustworthy person of godly character, but you should not trust my competence to do open heart surgery on you or to repair your car's transmission. I don't have competence in those skills.

How can you know when you have fulfilled your biblical role to pursue peace, "so far as it depends on you?"

After a good-faith attempt at reconciliation that seemingly failed, a person with a sensitive conscience asked me, "I know it is God's will for me to be at peace with everyone. I've tried to reconcile with this person—I truly have—but it hasn't worked. So, I am still living in an unresolved relational problem. Does that mean I am sinning against God?"

If you are in a situation like this, remember that since God only requires you to fulfill your responsibility to pursue peace, you can rest with a clear conscience before God if you have done all you can, "so far as it depends on you" (Romans 12:18).

Of course, you should continue to pray in faith that the other person will do their part and you will one day be more fully reconciled.

I believe you can rest with a clear conscience before God that you have done all in your power to make peace when you have tried your best to do things like these:

- You have asked God to search your heart regarding your motives and your attitude about that person.
- You have removed planks from your own eyes.
- You have confessed to the other person with godly sorrow any sin you have committed against them.
- You have forgiven the other person in your heart for any biblical offense they have committed against you.
- You have tried to have more than one respectful attempt at communication with them about the relational problem.
- You have sought wise and appropriate counsel regarding your role in the conflict.

One way to know you have fulfilled your biblical role is to complete in good faith Peace Pursuit *Stage One: Meet with God* and *Stage Two: If appropriate, meet with the other person.*

What about making peace with people who don't follow Jesus?

Many people from different faiths and worldviews have values of peace and reconciliation that are similar to biblical principles. I have found that when I apply Peace Pursuit Stage One and Stage Two in relational problems with people of other faiths (or of no faith), I have more success getting to peace with them than when I haven't done Stage One or Stage Two.

On the other hand, you can't always expect people of other faiths or worldviews to respond in a biblical way to your efforts to pursue peace like you would expect from a Christian who listens to the Holy Spirit. However, God will still honor your attempt to do your part to make peace in obedience to him.

Pillar 2: Your relationships with people reflect and affect your relationship with God

This second pillar focuses on the connection God makes between your interactions with people and your relationship with him.

"Loving God is easy, but loving people is impossible!"

Once I was conversing with a friend from a different faith. He counted on his fingers as he explained to me the essential things you have to do to be an obedient follower in his religion.

Then he asked me how many requirements there are for me to be a faithful and obedient follower of Jesus.

I responded, "Two," and held out my two hands.

Then I paraphrased Mark 12:28–30: "Once a religion expert asked Jesus which was the greatest commandment in all the Law of Moses. Jesus answered, 'Love God with all your heart, soul, mind and strength.' Then Jesus added a second command, 'Love other people like you love yourself.' These are often called the two Great Commands."

My friend smiled and said, "That first command to love God is easy. Loving God is a personal thing inside your heart, just between you and him. But the second command to love other people like you love yourself is impossible!"

You cannot separate loving God from loving people

I thought a lot about what my friend said. Then I realized that he misunderstood the two Great Commands like many Christians misunderstand them. They tend to think the two Great Commands are separate and distinct from each other, as if you can obey one without obeying the other, or you can neglect one without neglecting the other.

Jesus spoke strongly to the Pharisee hypocrites precisely because they thought they could love God by ticking off their lists of religious duties while neglecting to love people (Matthew 23:23, Luke 11:42). I believe Jesus intentionally linked the second command with the first one. He meant to teach them and us that one way we can know how much we love God is to look at how much we love other people.

The New Testament bears this out. I have paraphrased a few examples here:

- Loving other people equals loving Jesus, and not loving people equals not loving Jesus (Matthew 25: 31–46).
- Even if you do all kinds of fantastic spiritual things, if you don't love people the way God defines love, you are "nothing" (1 Corinthians 13:1–7).
- If you really love Jesus, then you will love others selflessly, like he did (Philippians 2:1–8).
- If you don't love others, and yet say you love God, you are a liar and his love is not in you (1 John 4:20–21).

Since the two Great Commands are inseparable, we really can't say with integrity, "Loving God is easy, but loving people is impossible." God doesn't command us to do the impossible.

How the two Great Commands connect

I have found that most Christians will agree that worship and prayer are two essential ways we show our love for God.

Let's start with worship. Jesus clearly taught that we should reconcile with people we have offended before worshiping God. "So if you are offering your gift at the altar and there remember that your brother has something against you, leave your gift there before the altar and go. First be reconciled to your brother, and then come and offer your gift" (Matthew 5:23–24). It's hard to interpret these verses any other way than to say that God simply does not want us to come to him in worship if we haven't reconciled with another one of his children we know we've sinned against.

Now, let's think of prayer as an expression of love for God. In another passage, Jesus made a connection between prayer and making peace: "And whenever you stand praying, forgive, if you have anything against anyone, so that your Father also who is in heaven may forgive you your trespasses" (Mark 11:25). In the center of what is commonly called the Lord's Prayer, he instructs us to pray, "and forgive us our debts, as we also have forgiven our debtors" (Matthew 6:12). Right after the Lord's Prayer, Jesus warns us, "but if you do not forgive others their trespasses, neither will your Father forgive your trespasses" (Matthew 6:15).

You can see from these verses how closely the acts of confessing your sins to the people you have offended and forgiving those who have offended you are tied to worship and prayer.

Matthew 7:12 is often called the Golden Rule: "So whatever you wish that others would do to you, do also to them." I assume you want others to forgive you for your sins against them and you would appreciate it if they acknowledged the offenses they have done to you. In other words, forgiving other people and making right your sins against them are two basic ways of loving others the way you would want to be loved.

If you sin against a person, you sin against God

1 Corinthians 8:12 teaches the principle that when you sin against another believer in Jesus, you sin against Jesus himself: "Thus, sinning against your brothers and wounding their conscience when it is weak, you sin against Christ." Therefore, when you repent to a person for sinning against them, you need to repent to God as well.

Your relationships with people—especially in the context of love, forgiveness, and repentance—reflect and affect your relationship with God.

Pillar 3: Treat everyone as a unique person created and loved by God

God created you as a unique person. No one else is exactly like you. You are a special blend of desires, needs, strengths, weaknesses, feelings, values, expectations, and beliefs about what is right and wrong, good and bad, appropriate and inappropriate. He loves you in your uniqueness, even the parts of you that are not yet transformed into his image (2 Corinthians 3:18).

Every other person is as unique as you are. God created and loves every one of them just as much as he loves you.

When you pursue peace with someone, I assume you want the other person to care enough about you to try to understand how you think and feel about the situation and why it is important to you. Since you want others to treat you uniquely when they pursue peace with you, do the same for them. It's a God-like thing to do. It's the Golden Rule (Matthew 7:12).

Whatever your role in the Peace Pursuit process, the more you can demonstrate to a person that you comprehend and appreciate their unique perspective, the more they are likely to trust you and be willing to pursue peace. The more you try to see the relational problem through their eyes, hear it through their ears, and feel it with their heart, the more understanding and compassion you will have for them, and the more you will see them as Jesus sees them.

If you are in the role of offender, the more you try to understand the pain and cost your offense caused to the other person, the more contrite you will be. If you are in the offended role, the more you understand the offender's situation, the more you will be able to show them the same compassion, grace, and forgiveness that Jesus shows you when you sin against him.

How can you learn to appreciate a person's uniqueness? Try to understand them as much as you want to be understood by them. In practical terms, consider factors like these: age, present and past family life, education, ethnic and cultural background, religious experience, natural personality, spiritual gifting, and so on.

Of course, your uniqueness and my uniqueness do not give us an excuse or license to sin. We just sin against others in our own unique style. However, we are all accountable to the same biblical standards. Which leads us to Peace Pursuit Pillar 4.

Pillar 4: Treat everyone alike, without prejudice or partiality

It may seem that Pillars 3 and 4 contradict each other, but they don't. Pillar 3 focuses on each party's uniqueness, but that does not mean any person should use their uniqueness as an excuse to rationalize away their responsibility for the cause of a conflict or their part in its resolution. Pillar 4 helps keep excuses and rationalizations to a minimum.

I believe you want other people to treat you as a unique person when you are resolving a relational problem (Pillar 3). I also believe you will want every person involved in the problem or its resolution to treat everyone else with equal standards of love and objectivity (Pillar 4). Since you want people to treat you like this, you should treat them the same way, whatever Peace Pursuit role you are in. That's the Matthew 7:12 Golden Rule again.

What does it practically look like to act toward each person without prejudice or partiality? Here is one way. Whatever your Peace Pursuit role, measure each party's words, actions, inactions, and reactions in the light of Bible verses which contain the phrases "one another" or "each other." These teachings apply to every believer in Jesus, without reference to age, gender, ethnicity, culture, or position of leadership in the church.

A main goal of Peace Pursuit is appropriate confession and forgiveness between two people. Whatever your role, do your part to create an environment for mutual truth-speaking, mutual honor, mutual respect, and mutual safety for all parties. At the same time, do what you can to create an atmosphere that will minimize the risk for gossip, slander, fear, shame, wrongful judgment, anger, bitterness, revenge, and factions for all people involved. When you and every other person in the peacemaking process treat everyone else equally, you will very likely reach appropriate confession and forgiveness.

As you treat each other by the same standards, keep in mind that God also looks at both parties through the same eyes. And, remember that if both parties are spiritually regenerate followers of Jesus, the Holy Spirit is inside both of them, and he is the one who comforts, convicts of sin, and leads into all truth (John 14:16–17, 16:8–14).

Pillar 5: Everyone is blessed when you pursue peace biblically

"Blessed are the peacemakers" (Matthew 5:9).

This powerful promise is the basis for the fifth pillar of Peace Pursuit. God assures you and me that we will be blessed if we pursue peace. That is, you and I will be blessed if we have done all we can, as much as it depends on us, to go after peace, no matter what the visible outcome of our efforts look like on the human level (Romans 12:18).

Here's another promise: "Peacemakers who sow in peace reap a harvest of righteousness" (James 3:18, NIV).

I can honestly say that I am blessed every time I fill any legitimate role in the Peace Pursuit process. As I complete Stage One and meet with God in the role of offender, offended, or initiator, my heart and mind are reoriented toward God's love and purposes for me and the other party.

When I am asked to fill the Peace Pursuit role of coach, witness, or mediator, it gives me joy to have had even a small contribution in the holy transaction of two people reconciling with God and with each other. I am also blessed because I have an opportunity to check my heart and integrity before the Lord and depend on him so I can be loving and impartial toward all parties.

Many people have shared with me that they also feel a kind of spiritual renewal when they meet with God at Stage One. And, it goes without saying that reaching appropriate confession and forgiveness at Stage Two is a great spiritual and relational blessing for both parties.

I know that resolving relational problems can require honesty, patience, courage, vulnerability, and large amounts of mental, spiritual, and emotional energy. At some point it may not look like you and others will feel blessed as you pursue peace. Please be encouraged. Trust that God will be glorified by your efforts and that he will keep his promise that you will be blessed when you pursue peace biblically.

THE P.E.A.C.E. PRINCIPLES

People are unique and many relational problems are complicated. However, if you use a God-honoring and people-honoring process to pursue peace, you can navigate the stormy sea of a conflict with confidence that you are sailing in the right direction guided by the wind of the Holy Spirit.

The P.E.A.C.E. Principles below are fundamental values in the Peace Pursuit Model. Whatever peacemaking model you use, I recommend you follow these kinds of principles.

You need two people to have a conflict. I call one the *assumed offended person* and the other the *supposed offender* (I say *supposed* offender because an offended person may wrongly take offense). Depending on the situation, it is possible that both parties can be partially in both the offended and offender roles.

P = Protect all parties

Isaiah 1:17, Isaiah 56:1, 1 Peter 5:2, John 10:11, John 15:13, Numbers 35:25, Matthew 7:12

Do everything you can to protect both of the two main parties, the assumed offended person and the supposed offender.

Protect the **assumed offended person** from:

- Further harm by the supposed offender
- Gossip by others
- Shame
- Their own temptation to gossip
- Their temptation not to forgive the offender
- A harsh, unloving, and unbiblical process

Protect the **supposed offender** from:

- Gossip by others
- Undue shame
- A harsh, unloving, and unbiblical process
- Illegitimate accusations or punishment
- Their own temptation not to be honest, humble, or honoring in admitting their fault

E = Expose truth and error

Zechariah 8:16, Ephesians 4:11–16 and 25, John 3:19–21, Proverbs 12:19, 1 John 1:5–10, Ephesians 5:6–13

- Affirm each party has done what is right and godly in the situation.
- Don't deny the truth about any party's wrong actions, inactions, words, or reactions.
- Bring to light all unconfessed or unforgiven sin relevant to this particular relational problem.

A = Act in love toward all parties

Matthew 7:12, Philippians 2:1–4, 1 Corinthians 13:4–7, Ephesians 4:1–3, John 13:34, Colossians 3:12–14

- Treat each person as you would want to be treated if you were in their role.

- Be humble, honest, gracious, respectful, impartial, and honoring toward all.

C = Complete peace between persons and between persons and God

2 Corinthians 5:17–21, Romans 12:18, James 5:16 and 20, Ephesians 4:3, Hebrews 12:14a, Colossians 3:12–15

As much as possible, pursue peace until each party has:

- Appropriately confessed any sin to God and to the person they offended; and
- Forgiven those who offended them.

E = Exclude inappropriate persons and behavior

Leviticus 19:16; Proverbs 6:16–19, 11:13, 19:5, 20:19, and 24:23; 1 Timothy 5:13; 1 Peter 4:15; James 2:1–4

- Keep gossipers, meddlers, and people who are partial out of the process as much as possible.
- Gently correct anyone who has a legitimate role, but who fails to fulfill their responsibilities.

3. DECIDE WHAT YOU MEAN BY PEACE

I assume you have opened this handbook because you believe you have some role in a relational problem or its resolution. I also assume you want to do your part to pursue peace. (If you are not yet sure you want to do your part to resolve a relational problem, I suggest you read Chapter 2, *Biblical Foundations.*)

The first thing you need to do is decide what you mean by peace. That way you will know when you have achieved it.

Below is a diagram that many people have found helpful. The dashed line in the diagram represents the relationship level between two persons. For the sake of illustration, let's say you are one of the two people in the diagram.

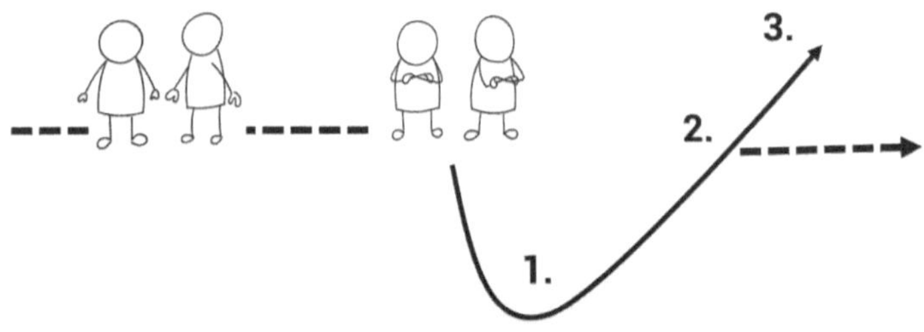

The bounce of peace: appropriate confession and forgiveness

The arrowhead on the dashed line indicates time moving from left to right. Starting from the left of the picture, you and the other person are interacting together at your normal relationship level, however you define normal.

Let's say that sometime later your relationship is damaged by an offense or conflict. To illustrate this, the two figures in the diagram fold their arms and look away from each other. If you don't pursue peace, the warmth, closeness, and trust in your relationship will likely begin to fall below what they have been, as illustrated by the solid curved line.

The warmth, closeness, and trust are likely to continue declining until one or both of you confess and/or forgive the offens(es) that started the problem. That is point 1 at the bottom of the curve in the diagram.

Then, let's say that you rebuild your relationship until it reaches the level it was before the conflict. That is point 2 on the diagram.

Sometimes your relationship could strengthen and grow until it is at a higher level than it was before your conflict. That is point 3 on the diagram.

THE "BOUNCE OF PEACE"

When you and the other person sincerely repent and forgive each other, you and the other person have reached point 1. You have stopped the downward path of your relationship and you can start the climb back up. We call this moment of appropriate confession and forgiveness the "Bounce of Peace."

After you reach point 1 with a person, you can begin to produce appropriate fruit of repentance and rebuild love and trust.

Your relationship might improve right away, or stay at point 1 for a while. To be honest, you might not return to point 2, let alone reach point 3.

In my years of experience, I've observed it's really, really hard for two people to get to point 2 or 3 unless they have confessed and forgiven each other at point 1. That's why I describe peace as when two people have appropriately confessed and forgiven the relational offenses between them.

To be clear, the main purpose of this handbook is to help you fulfill a role to help two people reach appropriate confession and forgiveness. Depending on your role, you may or may not be one of those two people.

Why it is helpful to describe peace as appropriate confession and forgiveness

In the first session of our Peace Pursuit workshops, I ask the attendees to choose which point on the diagram above most closely matches their personal description of peace. In every workshop, some attendees choose point 1, some point 2 and some point 3. Some even choose a point on the curve between two points. There is no shame or embarrassment in choosing one description over another. However, I believe you need to decide at what point you will know you have reached your goal in your pursuit of peace. This is a practical issue more than a philosophical or theological one. If you want to be a peacemaker, you need to know what you are making.

Think of it this way. If you aren't clear about your description of peace, how will you know when you have reached it? And, what if you and the other person in the conflict have different definitions of peace?

Years ago in a workshop, I shared with the group that my description of peace is appropriate confession and forgiveness and I showed them point 1 on the diagram.

One lady raised her hand and enthusiastically agreed with me. However, another woman was not satisfied with my description. "Real peace," she passionately shared, "is when the relationship is completely reconciled and restored to its former level of love and trust. Anything less than that is not peace. With all due respect, I don't agree with your description."

I encouraged the two ladies to explain their different opinions. As they sincerely shared their convictions, their voices grew louder and louder and their cheeks turned redder and redder. I decided to step in before their respectful disagreement over the concept of peace ironically turned into a conflict.

I asked their permission to use their debate as a live case study for the other attendees. After a lively discussion, the group concluded that the two ladies were using the same word peace for two significantly different phases in a relationship. One phase is when no unconfessed sin and no unforgiven sin remain between the two parties. That is point 1 on the diagram. A different phase is when the two parties produce necessary fruit of repentance and build or rebuild mutual trust and increase their love for each other resulting in a thriving, deepening relationship. That is the line between points 1 and 3 on the diagram. We agreed to call the first phase "peace" and to call the second phase "increasing love and trust," which includes appropriate fruit of repentance.

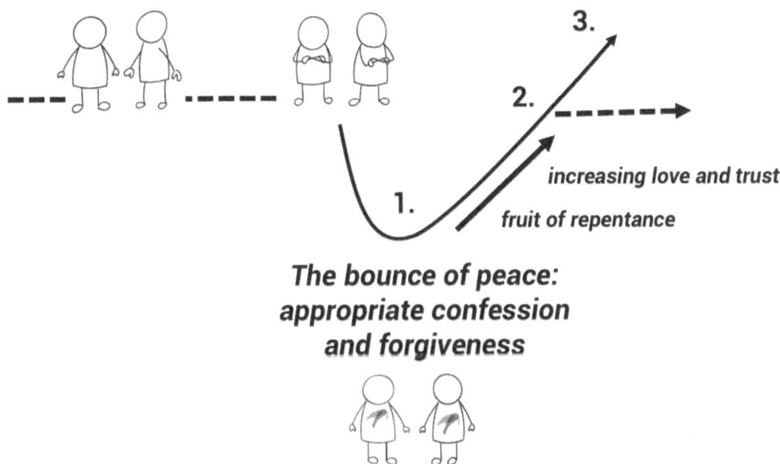

The bounce of peace: appropriate confession and forgiveness

I find it helpful to describe peace as the state of appropriate confession and forgiveness because it is based on actions, not feelings. When someone apologizes to you, you can hear, see, or read what they communicate. It is an act that you can record in a real moment of time. It's the same when you grant forgiveness to someone. You can put a time and date on it. You can record it in your diary. These actions mark a clear reference point in the forgiveness process.

Sometimes, a few weeks or months after two people reach the Bounce of Peace, I ask each person privately where they feel their relationship is on the upward curve beyond point 1. Most often I get two different answers. They each feel a different level of warmth, closeness, or trust. Those are real feelings, but they are hard to define and measure, aren't they? That's why I focus my description of peace on the observable acts of confession and granting forgiveness. I don't include hard-to-define terms like warmth, emotional closeness, or even trust in my definition of peace. Of course, all followers of Jesus should value and work toward those aspects in their relationships to move them beyond point 1. All I am saying is that I don't find it helpful to include those in a definition of peace.

If you and other people you interact with have different descriptions of peace, then I recommend you at least agree on some common words or phrases to describe what you are pursuing when you try to resolve relational problems. That way, you'll know when you've reached your destination.

Q: What is the difference between the concepts of peace, reconciliation, and restoration of relationships?

You have probably already noticed that different Christians have varied definitions of the words peace, reconciliation, and restoration. Those definitions will include varying measures of admission of fault, forgiveness, change of behavior, and rebuilt trust.

Since my goal in this handbook is to help you get to the point of appropriate confession and forgiveness, I'm not going to split hairs about the definitions of peace, reconciliation, and restoration. However, I do believe that if you follow this guide to the Bounce of Peace, you will be well on your way to reconciliation and restoration, however you define those concepts.

I discuss the concepts of confession and repentance in the *Repent of your part* step of Stage One.

Q: If I reach appropriate confession and forgiveness with a person, does that mean I have to trust them?

After you get to the Bounce of Peace, it can naturally take time for one or both of you to rebuild trust in the other.

The offender is responsible to make up for any damage they caused, if possible (Matthew 3:8, Acts 26:20, Hebrews 12:11, Galatians 6:7–8). The offender should also try to regain the trust of the offended person in the area in which they committed the offense. If the offender gossiped about you, the offender needs to prove to you that they can be trusted with your private information. If the offender cheated you, stole from you, or lied to you, they need to prove that from now on they follow rules, they no longer steal from you, and they tell you the truth. You don't have to unwisely trust someone who is simply not yet trustworthy.

If you are the offended person, you are responsible not to be prejudiced or wrongly judge the offender in character areas which are not related to the offense they committed. You should continue to trust them in areas where they are trustworthy.

I say more about the connection between forgiveness and trust in the *Forgive* step of Stage One.

Q: I want to pursue appropriate confession and forgiveness. What if the other person will not confess their part or forgive me? And what if other people ask me about my situation?

If you have done whatever is possible on your part to forgive the other party and confess your sin to them, then you have obeyed God as much as you can (Romans 12:18). Even if the other person doesn't respond, I believe God will be pleased by your humility and obedience to pursue reconciliation.

As for other people asking about your relationship with someone, let's say you have a friend named Arthur who cares about you and knows you had a relational problem with Kevin. You've done all you can to pursue peace with Kevin, but he has not granted you forgiveness, or he has not confessed his fault to you, or both. Let's also say that your relationship with Arthur is such that it is appropriate for Arthur to ask you how it is going between you and Kevin, or even to ask you specifically if you are at peace with him.

In this case, you can respond to Arthur like this: "I have forgiven Kevin in my heart before God, and I have confessed to Kevin my sin toward him as much as I understand it. I am praying that Kevin will do the same." I do not believe this is gossip and you are free to tell this truth to Arthur without sharing details.

If someone who you believe does not need to know the details of your relationship problem with Kevin asks you about it, you can calmly and politely respond by saying something like this: "I appreciate your concern. I believe I am doing everything in my power to be at peace with Kevin, as much as it depends on me."

4. CHOOSE YOUR PRIMARY ROLE

In Peace Pursuit, the description of peace we aim for is appropriate confession and forgiveness between two people. If that is the goal you have decided to go after, the next Peace Pursuit decision you make is to choose your primary role: offended, offender, initiator, or coach.

The Peace Pursuit roles help clarify *what* each person should do, *when* they should do it, and *how* they should do it to resolve a conflict. Knowing these four basic roles will serve you well as you work to resolve the majority of person-to-person problems you will face in life.

Please understand that I am not judging you or anyone when I use names like offender or offended for peacemaking roles. By definition, a relational problem or conflict comes from offenses given and received. Therefore, I call the person who gives the offense the offender. I call the person who receives the offense the offended. Since it is not always clear that the offended person has legitimate reasons to take offense, you will see that sometimes I use the terms "supposed offender" or "assumed offended person" when I refer to the offender and offended roles.

There is not just one "peacemaker" role in the Peace Pursuit Model. I consider any person to be a peacemaker when they fulfill their legitimate Peace Pursuit role in a biblical manner.

Q: What if I think I am in more than one role?

After you read the brief introduction to the roles, you may think, "I feel like I'm partly in the offended role and partly in the offender role." This is very common. Often a person gives an ungodly response or reaction when they are offended, which makes them also an offender. If you are not sure which is your primary role, choose which one you feel best describes you most right now and start

Stage One: Meet with God in that role. Later, you can look at the situation in another role if you need to.

Q: *What if I am part of a relational problem involving more than one other person?*

I have found that the best way to resolve complicated multi-person conflicts is by resolving each person-to-person relational problem one at a time. If there are more than two people involved in your conflict, think about making peace with each person in the group individually. Then, decide which role is your primary one in relation to each person.

For example, let's say you are part of a small group and you have a relational problem with more than one person in the group. There is a married couple named Bob and Marianne, and a woman called Brigitte. I recommend that you consider a situation like this as three separate conflicts. Choose your primary role with Bob, and complete Chapter 6, *Stage One: Meet with God* in relation to Bob. Then, choose your primary role with Marianne, and complete Stage One in relation to her. Then, choose your primary role and complete Stage One in relation to Brigitte.

As you process Stage One in regard to each person individually, you will decide which (if any) of the three people you will have a separate Stage Two conversation with.

Here is a brief introduction to the four primary Peace Pursuit roles, plus one role you want to avoid. After you choose your primary role, you can read about it more in detail in Chapter 5.

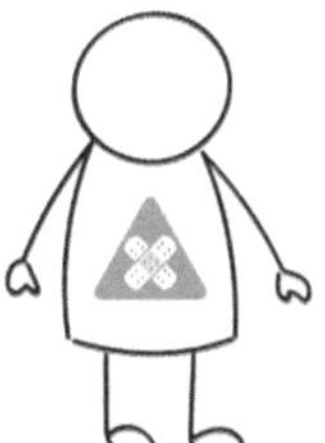

THE OFFENDED ROLE

Choose the offended role as you start the Peace Pursuit process if you feel someone has done something to you that had a negative effect on you. For example, they have:

- Wronged you;
- Hurt you;
- Sinned against you;
- Offended you;

- Frustrated you;
- Disappointed you;
- Made you sad; or
- Anything similar to these.

Maybe you can think of a specific word they said or action they did to hurt or offend you. Maybe it was something you feel they should have done, but they didn't do it. Or, maybe you can't exactly put your feelings into words, but you still feel somehow hurt, frustrated, or angry at this person.

THE OFFENDER ROLE

Consider yourself in the offender role in any of these situations.

- You have noticed that you have hurt, offended, or angered another person. Maybe you can think of a specific word you said or action you did to them and you see by their verbal or non-verbal reaction that they are upset with you. Or, maybe you just have a vague sense that there is a new distance between you and another person and you don't know why.
- Someone has come to you to say that you have personally offended them.
- Someone has told you that they think you have offended a third person.

As I mentioned above, I use the term offender to clarify roles, not to condemn anyone. If it helps, you could say "supposed offender" for this role. If you are in the offender role it doesn't mean you are an evil person. It also doesn't necessarily mean that the other person's feeling of offense is legitimate. It just means that for the sake of clarity, you will begin the Peace Pursuit process in the offender role.

THE INITIATOR ROLE

An initiator appropriately shines light into a relational problem that is not their own. Here are three common situations when you could possibly consider filling the initiator role.

- You observed with your own eyes or ears a relational problem between a supposed offender and another person. The supposed offender does not appear to be taking steps toward making peace.
- You strongly sense there is a relational problem between two people and you do not believe either of them is seeking peace. You may or may not know which is the primary offended or offender.
- You sense that a person has sinned against God, but that person has not yet repented to him. Their sin might not be obvious to others or might not directly harm another person. In this case, you would consider helping that person make peace with God by repenting.

You should only consider the initiator role if you are sure you are not in either the offender role or the offended role in this situation.

If you take on the initiator role, your goal is to encourage one of the parties in the relational problem to begin *Stage One: Meet with God* to fulfill their role toward peace. You are not a go-between person. You are also not in the Peace Pursuit mediator role.

Since you are a third party, it takes careful thought and prayer to fill the initiator role in a godly and appropriate way. Do not rush into this role or take it on lightly.

THE COACH ROLE

Let's say a person wants to talk or pray with you about a relational problem concerning someone other than you. You are not one of the parties involved in the problem. The person who comes to you could be in any one of these roles:

- They think they are the offender.
- They feel they are the offended.
- They are considering the initiator role.

You can consider accepting the coach role in any of those situations. If you accept the coach role, you will help the person who comes to talk with you to fulfill their role at *Stage One: Meet with God* before they talk with another party in the relational problem. You are not a go-between person and you are not in the Peace Pursuit mediator role. In the coach role, you would normally not talk to the other party or parties in the conflict.

THE AGGRAVATOR ROLE

As you have likely guessed from the name, the aggravator is not a positive or helpful role in peacemaking. I use the term aggravator to describe anyone who hinders the Peace Pursuit process either on purpose or unintentionally. The aggravator role is based on these and similar verses: 1 Timothy 5:13, 2 Thessalonians 3:11, 1 Peter 4:15, James 2:1–4, Proverbs 6:16 and 19, Proverbs 19:5, and Proverbs 24:23.

Identifying any person or persons who are behaving in an aggravating way is an application of the second *E* of the P.E.A.C.E. Principles: Exclude inappropriate persons and actions.

Let's say you are not in one of the legitimate Peace Pursuit roles of offended, offender, initiator, or coach in a given conflict. It is possible that you mean well and have good intentions, but you are actually interfering in the peace process from outside by being what the Bible calls a gossip, a busybody, a meddler, or a false witness. If you are behaving in any of these ways and you don't have a legitimate role in the conflict or its resolution, please love the other people involved by removing yourself from the situation.

Or, you may be in a legitimate Peace Pursuit role, but you are not fulfilling your Stage One or Stage Two responsibilities. If so, please love everyone else involved and correct your aggravating behavior.

If you find you have slipped into the aggravator role, examine your behavior and the situation to see if you have also become an offender. If you have, you should work through *Stage One: Meet with God* in the offender role.

5. EMBRACE YOUR ROLE

Now you are ready to explore your options and responsibilities to fulfill your chosen role.

As I describe the various options and responsibilities of each role, you will see this illustration:

It symbolizes a person processing the Peace Pursuit Quick Start Guide at *Stage One: Meet with God*. The Quick Start Guide is available for free at PeacePursuit.org in multiple formats and languages. Of course, you can also complete Stage One in more detail by using this handbook (Chapter 6).

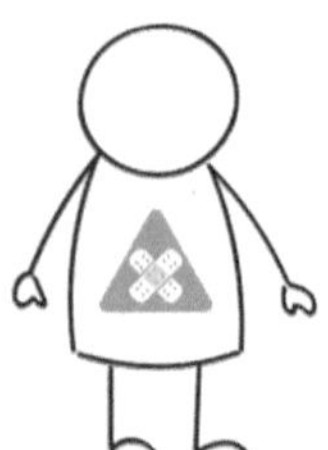

THE OFFENDED ROLE

The icon for the offended role is a triangle with bandages. You feel you have been mentally, spiritually, physically, emotionally, or relationally hurt or injured in some way. In short, think of yourself in the offended role if someone did something to you that had a negative effect on you.

If another person's action or inaction did not affect you personally or directly, but did apparently offend someone else, then you should consider the initiator role instead of the offended role. See the initiator role below.

Your options for the offended role

Humanly speaking, you have four natural options when you are offended by someone.

1. You can choose to forgive the person in your heart before God, but decide not to talk with them.
2. You can choose to forgive the person in your heart before God and then decide to have a peacemaking conversation with them.
3. You can choose not to forgive the person in your heart and also choose not to talk with them.
4. You can choose not to forgive the person in your heart but still talk with them.

Here is a diagram of these four possibilities.

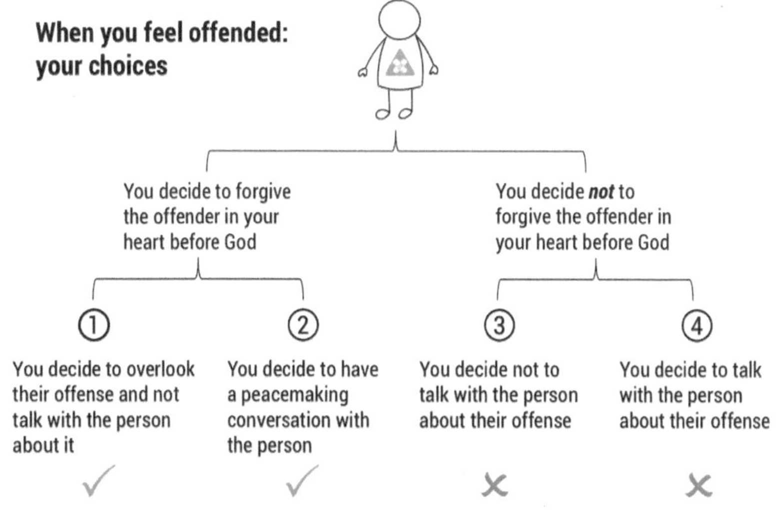

Two biblical options

I believe the only biblical options for a Jesus follower are choices 1 and 2 above.

1. You can decide to forgive the offender in your heart before God, and choose not to have a conversation with them about this problem at this time. This is called "overlooking an offense."
2. You can decide to forgive the offender in your heart before God, then meet with them and explain to them how you feel they offended you. This is called "having a peacemaking conversation."

Look at the diagram below. It uses Peace Pursuit terms and icons to illustrate your two biblical choices in your role as the offended.

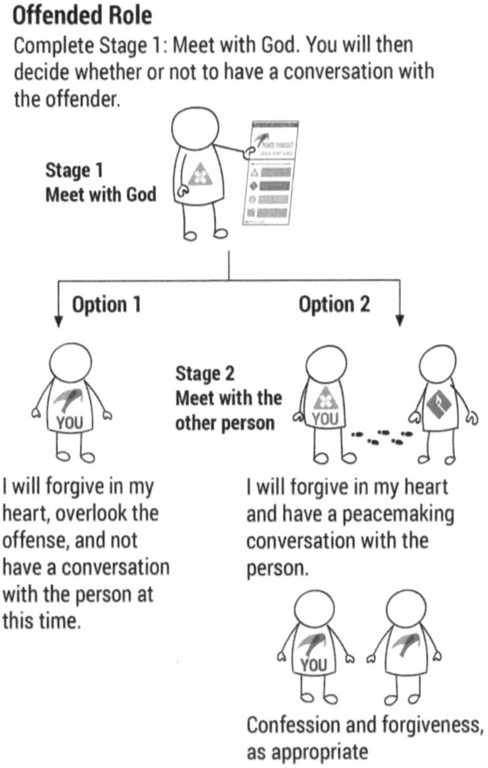

Offended Role

Complete Stage 1: Meet with God. You will then decide whether or not to have a conversation with the offender.

Stage 1
Meet with God

Option 1

Option 2

Stage 2
Meet with the other person

YOU

I will forgive in my heart, overlook the offense, and not have a conversation with the person at this time.

I will forgive in my heart and have a peacemaking conversation with the person.

Confession and forgiveness, as appropriate

Before you decide which of the two valid options you will take, I strongly advise that you meet with God and complete Stage One for your role. As you pray and process the various steps, you will be in a healthy position where you can make the decision to talk with the other person or not. Of course, the *Forgive* step is crucial.

What if you choose option 3 or 4 in the diagram above? In other words, what might be the problem if you don't forgive the offender in your heart before God? During my years of observing conflicts, I've seen two common results.

If you choose option 3 and do not forgive the offender in your heart, you might be tempted to think bad thoughts about the offender. You might avoid them, judge them, gossip about them, or worse. If you continue to nurse a grudge against them, you could even develop unhealthy physical symptoms yourself. None of these are good for your relationship with that person or your relationship with God.

Let's say you decide to choose option 4 and talk with the offender without forgiving them in your heart. It's possible that while you are talking with them, the pain or anger in your heart could come out in strong, emotional words. Jesus said, "For the mouth speaks what the heart is full of" (Matthew 12:34, NIV). This could lead you to commit an offense of word or action against them, which would put you in the offender role and make your relationship even more strained.

Q: How can you say that in the offended role I have the biblical option not to talk with the offender? Matthew 18:15a says, "If your brother or sister sins, go and point out their fault..." (NIV)

It seems Matthew 18:15 is the most quoted Bible verse related to peacemaking. "If your brother or sister sins, go and point out their fault, just between the two of you. If they listen to you, you have won them over" (NIV). Many people will quote this verse to you if they know you are in the offended role. So, it is a good question to ask why you could potentially choose not to talk with the offender.

Obviously, Matthew 18:15 is a clear biblical command. Keeping that in mind, I want to protect you from making your relational difficulties worse by neglecting lots of other clear biblical principles which you should apply before you invoke Matthew 18:15. Here is just one example: "Good sense makes one slow to anger, and it is his glory to overlook an offense" (Proverbs 19:11). The word *offense* in this verse can also be translated as sin, transgression, or trespass. So, it is not a light irritation or frustration.

See the *Evaluate* step of Stage One for a number of biblically-based diagnostic questions that help you decide whether you can, or should, overlook an offense and not talk with the offender about it.

No matter which choice you make, be sure to complete the *Forgive* step of Stage One.

Q: What is my role if I take offense on behalf of another person?

Perhaps you feel a sense of offense when someone mistreats or disrespects your friend or loved one. This is often called taking on the offense of others. If this is your situation, you are actually not in what I call the offended role. However, you could consider filling the initiator role.

For example, let's say you observed someone speaking harshly to your friend at a break during a meeting.

When you observe someone offend another person, you are not in the offended role.

However, you can consider the initiator role.

You were uncomfortable with what you witnessed. The next day, you may feel like saying to the person, "I'm offended by how you treated my friend at the meeting yesterday." However, in this case, I believe your friend would be the person in the offended role, not you. I believe the appropriate role for you to consider is the initiator role, not the role of offended. Why? Because you were not personally mistreated by the other person.

THE OFFENDER ROLE

The icon for the offender role is a flaming match. It appears you have burned someone or started a relational fire, whether you did it on purpose or by accident.

There are three common situations when you could consider yourself in the offender role.

1. You are aware that you are an offender. No one has approached you yet to talk about the situation.

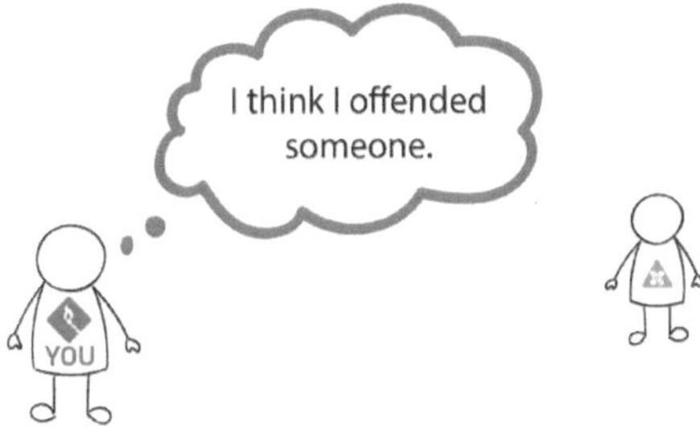

2. You have been approached by someone who feels they have been offended by you. This puts you in the offender role.

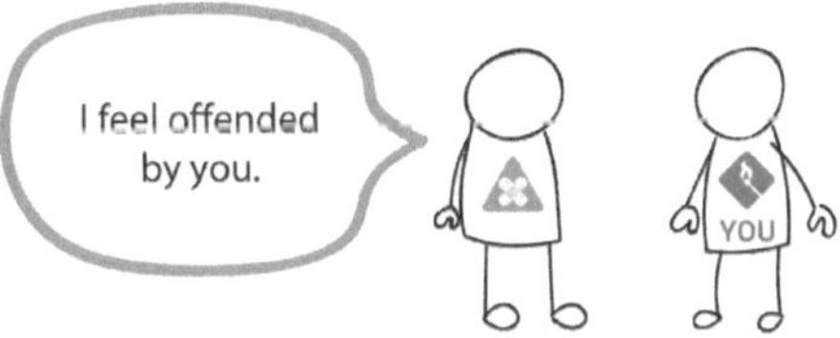

3. You have been approached by someone who is taking the initiator role and who believes you are in the offender role.

Let's look at your options for each situation.

Offender role scenario 1

You are aware that you offended someone. No one has approached you yet to talk about the situation.

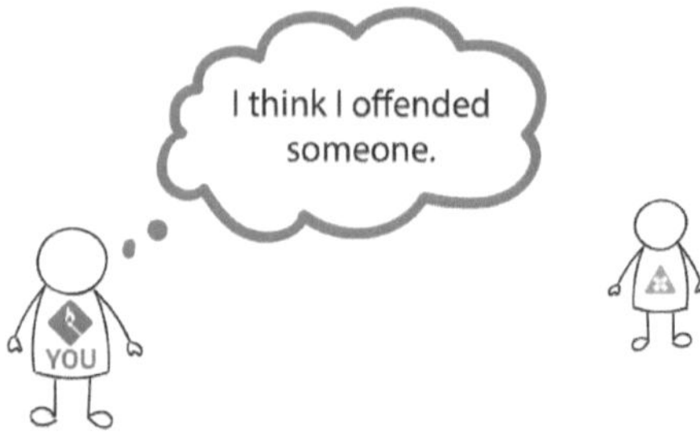

In this scenario, God has brought it to your mind or you have noticed yourself that you have frustrated, hurt, offended, or angered another person. Maybe you can think of a specific word you said or an action you did to them, and you see by their verbal or non-verbal reaction that they are upset with you. Or, maybe you just have a vague sense that there is a new distance between you and another person and you don't know why.

Humanly speaking, you have two options in this situation.

Offender role scenario 1 option A

You can choose to have a Peace Pursuit Stage Two conversation with the offended with the humble and sincere goal to confess your offense and receive their forgiveness. If you make this choice, I urge you to complete *Stage One: Meet with God* before you meet with the offended. Stage One prepares you to approach them in the way you would want to be approached if your roles were reversed. When you talk with them and confirm that you really have offended them, you can confess to them and they can forgive you. If it turns out that they do not feel offended by you, the very process of having a conversation with them will be a blessing to both you and them. Here is what option A looks like. First, you meet with God at Stage One. Then, you arrange a conversation with the other person for appropriate confession and forgiveness.

Offender Role Scenario 1

When you believe you offended someone, complete Stage 1: Meet with God in the offender role. During Stage 1, you will prepare to have a conversation with the offended at Stage 2 to apologize in an appropriate way.

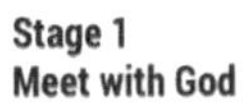

Stage 1
Meet with God

Stage 2
Meet with the other person

Confession and forgiveness, as appropriate

Offender role scenario 1 option B

You could decide not to talk with the person you think you offended. If this is your choice, I strongly recommend that you pursue option A instead. As you process the *Search your heart* step of *Stage One: Meet with God*, ask the Lord to reveal to you why you are not willing to have a conversation with the person you think you offended.

Jesus taught, "So if you are offering your gift at the altar and there remember that your brother has something against you, leave your gift there before the altar and go. First be reconciled to your brother, and then come and offer your gift" (Matthew 5:23–24). That means you should communicate with them before you "offer your gift." I believe today's equivalent to "offering your gift at the altar" would be going to a worship service, Bible study, or similar. I think that it would also include any time of Christian fellowship where that person is present.

I heard about a spiritual leader who was in a conflict with another Christian in his fellowship. He knew the other party felt offended by him, but he said he decided not to approach the offended person. The leader explained, "I decided not to talk with the person out of respect for him, to give him 'space.'" I understand the motive behind this leader's inaction. However, his good intent turned out to be short-sighted and unwise. As the months went by, the offended person's trust in the spiritual leader steadily declined. So much so, the offended person decided to go to a different fellowship. I think a better way for the spiritual leader to show respect for the offended person would have been to process *Stage One: Meet with God* in the offender role and then have a Stage Two conversation with him.

Offender role scenario 2

You have been approached by someone who communicates to you that they feel offended by you. This puts you in the offender role.

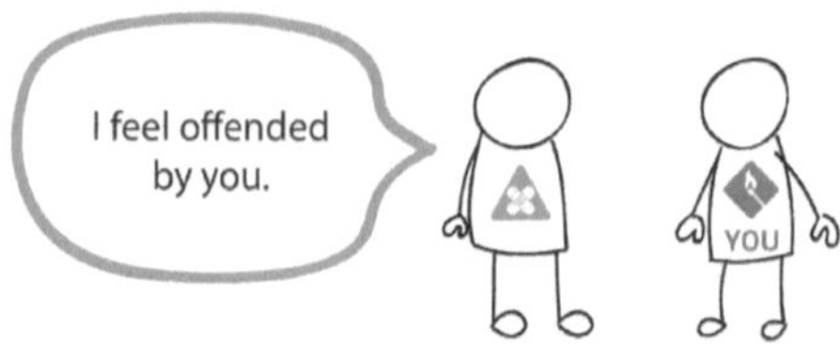

You have two choices in this situation. Option A is a good, biblical choice. I do not recommend option B.

Offender role scenario 2 option A

One option you have is to listen sincerely to what the person has to say and respond with respect. If you make this choice, you create two more valid possibilities, which we will label A1 and A2. In both instances, your motive in the offender role is to make peace in a way that honors God and the person who has come to talk with you.

Offender role scenario 2 option A1

If you accept what the person has to say and you are ready to receive and repent of what they have shared, you can apologize then. In Peace Pursuit terms, this is a Stage Two conversation and looks like this:

Offender Role Scenario 2 Option A1

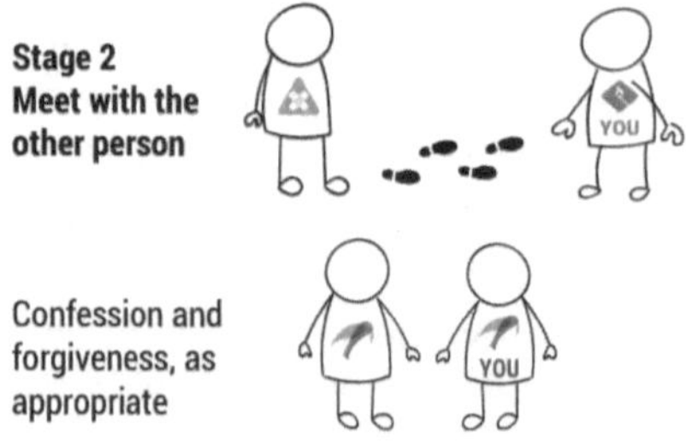

I recommend you visit the *Repent of your part* step of *Stage One: Meet with God* for practical ideas on how to make a biblical apology.

Offender role scenario 2 option A2

If you would like more time to pray and sincerely think about what the person has said to you, you can ask them if you can continue your conversation at another time. You would meet with God at Stage One in the offender role and then you would make an appointment to talk with them.

Here is what this option looks like:

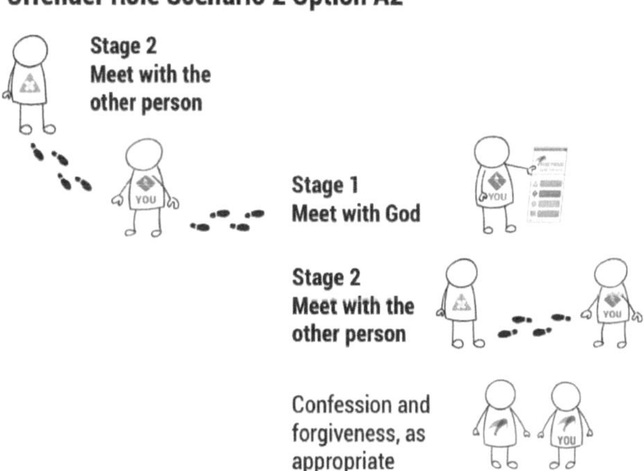

Offender role scenario 2 option B

You can decide not to listen to the person who comes to talk to you. You could outright refuse to talk, or you could just try to ignore the subject, hoping the issue (and maybe the person) will just go away. This choice rarely leads to peace, even if you believe the folk proverb, "Time heals all wounds." Trust me, it doesn't. People who have been deeply offended can remember their hurts and pain for years, even decades.

This is not a valid option for a sincere Jesus follower. I urge you to reconsider option A. You should listen to an offended person at least once.

Offender role scenario 3

You have been approached by someone who is taking the initiator role and who believes you are in the offender role.

A third party has come to you to say that they believe you have offended someone else.

As in offender role scenario 2, you immediately face two options.

Offender role scenario 3 option A

You can decide to listen to the initiator in good faith and have a respectful conversation. You can then process Stage One in the offender role and initiate a conversation with the assumed offended person.

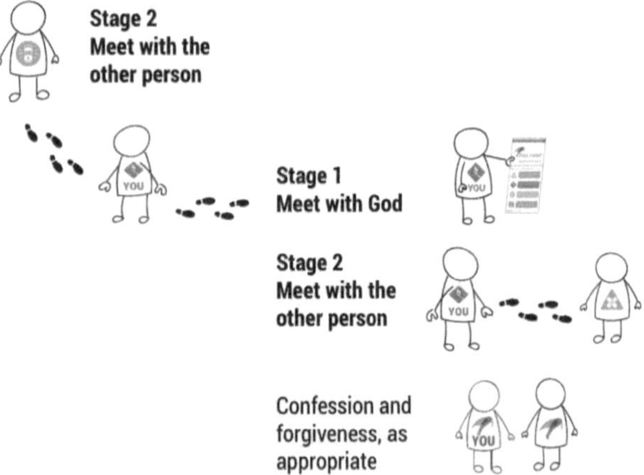

Offender role scenario 3 option B

You can decide not to listen to the person in the initiator role. (Maybe you have heard about people in this situation who have responded to the initiator with statements like these: "This is none of your business, "or "If the so-called offended person has a problem with me, they should come to me.")

If you refuse to listen to someone who has taken time and care to bring up to you a potential offense of yours, you may be missing God's message to you in this situation. If this is your choice, I urge you to pursue offender scenario 3 option A instead.

Q: What if I am not sure a person really was offended by me?

In that case, I think that you should apply what is often called the Golden Rule, "Whatever you wish that others would do to you, do also to them..." (Matthew 7:12). In other words, if you were in their place, would you want someone who thinks he has offended you to care enough for you and your relationship at least to ask you about it?

You really have nothing to lose and everything to gain, if you appropriately approach a person you sense you have offended. If they in fact feel offended by you, then by taking the step to make peace you will please God and you will likely reconcile with the person. If it turns out that they are not offended, by simply asking them about the situation they will likely increase their respect for you and whatever relationship you have could be strengthened. I cover this scenario more in detail in Stage Two.

Q: I am aware a person definitely has something against me, but I feel they have wrongly taken offense. They have not come to me to talk about it. What are my options?

Many biblical principles are involved in this example. It is a situation where you need to take special care and thoroughly process *Stage One: Meet with God.*

Let's consider your potential options. Ask yourself, *What are the implications for me, for them, and for others if I choose one of these?*

For this example, we'll call the other person Anthony.

1. You could decide to approach Anthony to talk about the situation.

   Many people would say that Matthew 5:23–24 applies here. If you know your brother has "something" against you, according to these verses you are supposed to go and "be reconciled" with your brother.

   However, in this example, you don't feel there is a real debt of offense between you, even though Anthony feels there is. Anthony could feel he is right to say that you are not at peace because you haven't repented to him.

   Keeping in mind that God gives grace to the humble (James 4:6), you can still have a conversation with Anthony about the issue after you first meet with God at Stage One in the offender role.

You could begin like this:

> *"Anthony, I understand you feel I have offended you, and I would like to listen as you share your feelings and thoughts about the issue and then respond appropriately. When would be a good time for us to talk?"*

This could open the door for you to have an honest, respectful Stage Two conversation with Anthony.

2. You could wait for Anthony to come to you.

   If you choose this option, it still would be good for you to meet with God at Stage One. While you pray and process the steps of Stage One, God could show you reasons to have a respectful conversation with Anthony. Even if you decide not to talk with Anthony, going through Stage One will help prepare you in case Anthony does come to talk to you at Stage Two.

   However, you have to consider that Anthony might not come to you at all. What might be some consequences if (a) Anthony feels offended by you, (b) you know about his feelings, but (c) he never comes to you, and (d) you don't go to him to talk about the problem? Here are some possible consequences I have observed in cases like these:

   - Anthony could have misunderstood the situation and wrongly taken offense and/or wrongly judged you. He might forgive you in his heart before God. But, do you really want Anthony to think he has forgiven you for something he has actually wrongly judged you for?
   - Or, let's say Anthony doesn't forgive you in his heart. He might nurture a grudge, let bitterness grow in his heart, gossip about you, etc. Do you think it is wise or loving to tempt Anthony into that situation?
   - On the other hand, Anthony could have accurately discerned that you did commit a biblically-defined offense against him. He might forgive you in his heart before God. But, even if he does forgive you in his heart, he would have legitimate reason to be careful in his relationship with you in the future because you did not admit your offense to him. Worse yet, Anthony might not forgive you in his heart before God, which would open him up to bitterness and the temptation to judge and gossip about you. Do you want either of these possibilities?

3. You could choose to see yourself in the offended role because you believe Anthony has become an offender by wrongly accusing you.

   If that's what you want to do, then prayerfully meet with God at Stage One in the offended role. Like any person in the offended role, you'll have the choice to overlook Anthony's offense toward you, or to have a conversation with Anthony at Stage Two. Before you choose this option, I need to say that you should be very careful to be as objective as possible toward yourself and Anthony as you process both Stage One and Stage Two.

THE INITIATOR ROLE

The icon for the initiator role is a lantern. An initiator shines light appropriately into a relational problem that is not their own.

To qualify for the initiator role, you are not personally hurt or angered by the supposed offender. In other words, you are not in the offended role. You are also not in the offender role.

Your goal in the initiator role is to encourage one of the parties in the relational problem to begin *Stage One: Meet with God* to fulfill their role toward peace. You are not a go-between person. You are also not in the Peace Pursuit mediator role.

Since you are a third party, it takes deliberate care, thought, and prayer to fill the initiator role in a godly and appropriate way. Do not rush into this role or take it on lightly.

To consider the role of an initiator, you are a third party in one of these situations:

1. You directly observed someone do or say something to another person which you think offended that person.

2. You strongly sense that there is conflict between two people and you do not believe either of them is seeking peace. You are not sure who is the primary offender or offended.

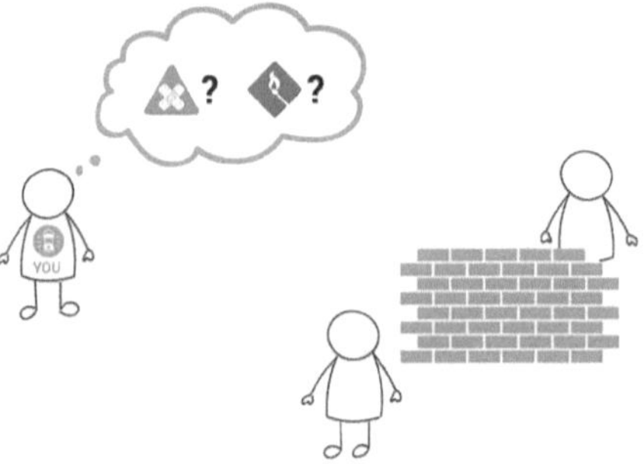

3. You sense that a supposed offender has sinned against God, and the sin is not clearly or directly against another person. In this case, you would prayerfully consider helping that person make peace with God.

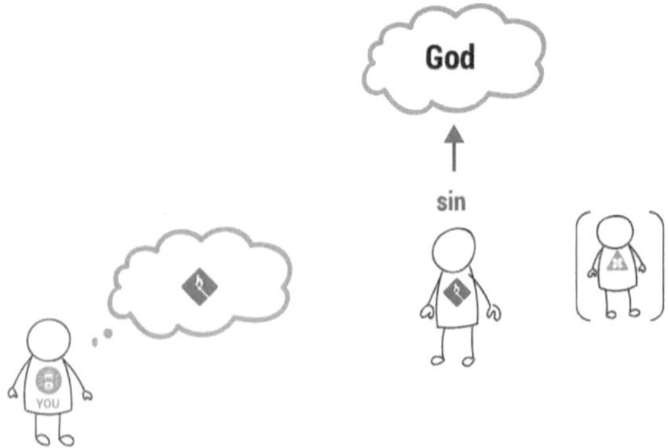

It can be scary to consider the initiator role, but let me encourage you. There is solid biblical basis to initiate the peacemaking process with an offender when you are not the offended person. Mature believers are to gently restore someone who is caught up in sin (Galatians 6:1–2). The book of James closes with this verse: "Whoever brings back a sinner from his wandering will save his soul from death and will cover a multitude of sins" (James 5:20).

And Matthew 7:12, the Golden Rule, teaches us to do to others what we would want them to do for us. As a sincere follower of Jesus who wants to grow in spiritual maturity, if you were caught in a sin or wandering toward death, wouldn't you want someone to rescue you, to hold you back?

At the same time, the Bible also warns us about the dangers of sticking our nose in other people's business. In 1 Peter 4:15 meddlers are mentioned in the same sentence with murderers, thieves, and evildoers. And Proverbs 26:17 paints a vivid picture: "Whoever meddles in a quarrel not his own is like one who takes a passing dog by the ears."

So, if you are considering the initiator role, you need to meet with God by completing Stage One with careful thought and prayer, or you could easily become a meddler, a busybody, or partial to one of the parties.

Stage One will help you decide if you should talk with one of the parties or not. It is possible that at Stage One you will realize you are not an appropriate person to talk with one or either of the parties in this situation. In that case, do not move to Stage Two. However, after you meet with God at Stage One, you might decide to talk with one of them. If so, the steps of Stage One will prepare you for that conversation.

Initiator role scenario 1

You directly observed someone do or say something to another person which you think offended that person.

As far as you know, the supposed offender does not appear to be taking steps toward making peace. You don't believe the offended has talked to the offender about the offense.

There are two possibilities for you to help.

Initiator role scenario 1 option A

In this situation, it is clear to you which person is the primary offender. You meet with God at Stage One in the initiator role.

When you complete Stage One, you might decide that you should not meet with the supposed offender at Stage Two.

On the other hand, if you decide to have a Stage Two conversation with the person who you think is the offender, your ultimate goal is to encourage them to make peace with the person you believe they offended. You accomplish that goal by creating an environment for a relaxed and respectful Stage Two conversation with the supposed offender.

If during your conversation the person accepts that they are the offender, your next goal is to encourage them to complete Stage One in the offender role. Your role as initiator is now finished.

After the offender completes Stage One, they would normally go to the offended alone at Stage Two to apologize. Here is what initiator role scenario 1 option A looks like.

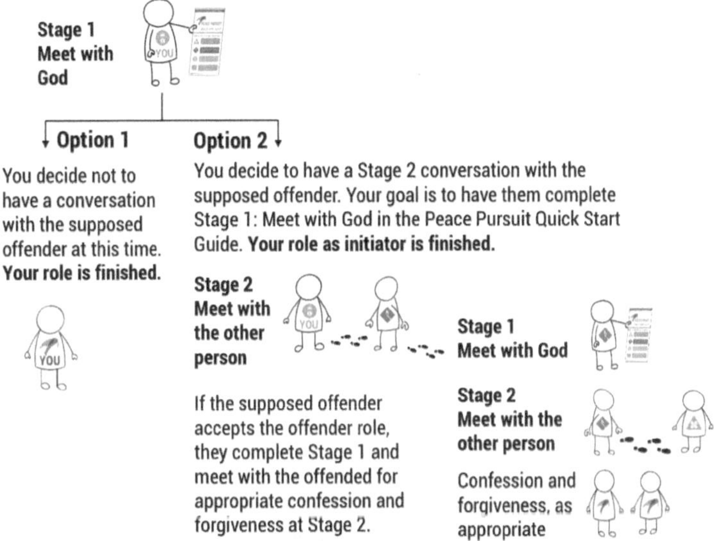

Initiator role scenario 1 option B

In contrast to initiator role scenario 1 option A, after you complete Stage One in the initiator role, you might decide to have a conversation with the person who you think is primarily the offended one. Your goal in that conversation is to encourage that person to meet with God at Stage One in the offended role and for them to consider meeting with the supposed offender at Stage Two. Your role as initiator is then finished. While the assumed offended person processes Stage One on their own, they will decide whether to have a Stage Two conversation with the supposed offender.

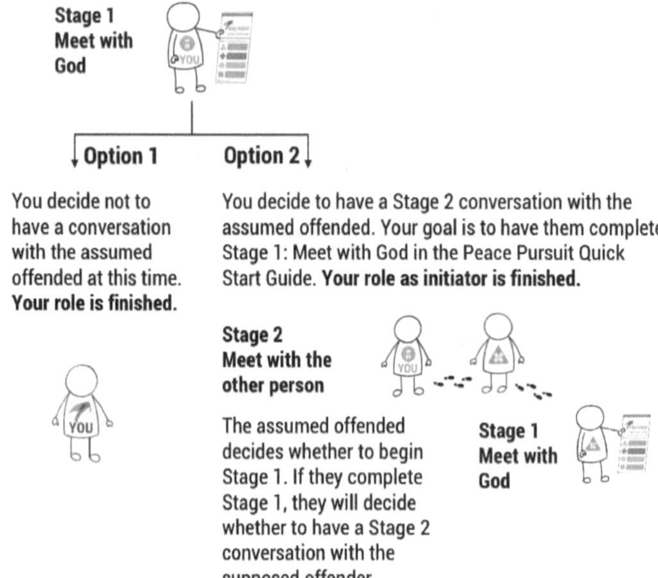

Initiator role scenario 2

You strongly sense there is a relational problem between two people and you do not believe either of them is seeking peace. You are not sure who is the primary offender or offended person. You wonder if you should do something to help them make peace with each other.

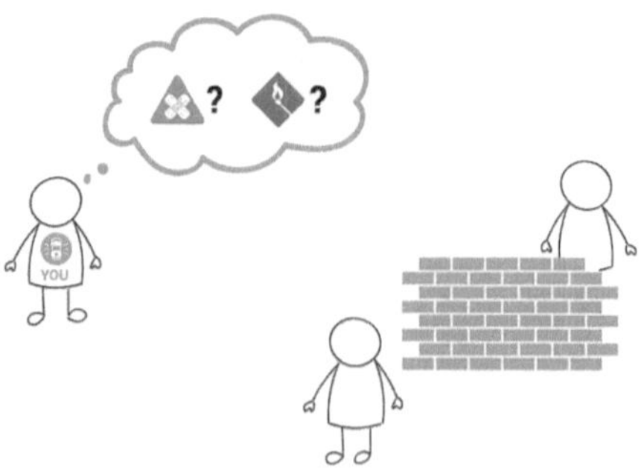

Let's say you are friends with Robert and Sam. You did not witness any visible conflict between Robert and Sam. However, you've recently noticed a change in the relationship between them. For example, you see that Robert has begun to avoid Sam. Or, whenever Sam's name comes up in conversation, Robert displays a negative reaction in his face. Or, Robert may begin to speak critically of Sam when Sam is not around.

You strongly sense something is wrong between them, and you consider helping them in an appropriate role to make peace with each other.

As you process Stage One in the initiator role, separately you will decide to have a conversation with Robert, or Sam, or neither of them. In the Peace Pursuit initiator role, you would not talk with both parties. In other words, if you decided to talk with Robert, you would not talk with Sam, and vice versa. Remember that your role as initiator is to encourage *one* of the parties to choose their role and begin Stage One. Then your role as initiator is finished. You are not a mediator who brings the two together.

Here are some questions for you to weigh while you meet with God at Stage One and decide whether to have a conversation with either Robert or Sam.

- Which of the two parties is most likely to listen to you if you bring up the subject?
- Which of the two parties do you consider to be more mature and therefore more responsible to do their part to make peace?
- What other factors like age, gender, culture, position of authority, and so on affect which one is most appropriate for you to have a conversation with about the situation?

Reminder: In Stage One, you meet with God and decide to have a conversation with either Robert or Sam, or neither one. It is best if you do not have a Stage Two conversation with both. Remember to complete Stage One in the initiator role before you make that decision. If you decide to have a conversation with one of them, it will look similar to initiator role scenario 1 option A or B.

Initiator role scenario 3

You sense that a supposed offender has sinned against God, and the sin is not clearly or directly against another person.

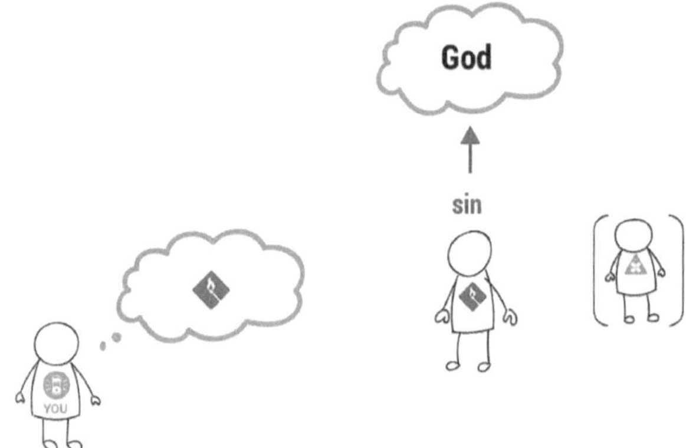

In this case, you would consider helping that person make peace with God.

Almost all of the same principles apply when you want to help someone reconcile with God as when you want to help them make peace with a person.

You can begin the process of reconciling a person to God by completing Stage One in the initiator role yourself. If you decide to meet with the person at Stage Two, you would encourage them to meet with God at Stage One. As they process Stage One themselves, they might realize that they need to make peace with a human being as well as repent to God. Ultimately, just about anything we do that is wrong or sinful in God's eyes negatively affects at least one other person in some way, even if indirectly. Below is an example of this scenario.

Initiator Role Scenario 3

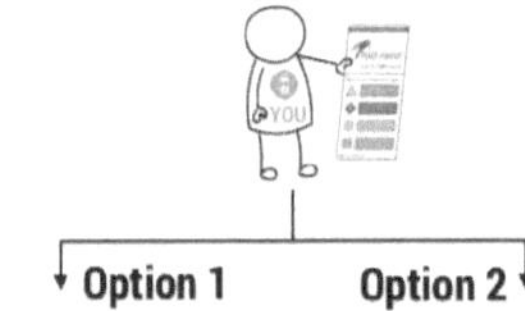

Option 1

You decide not to have a conversation with the supposed offender at this time. **Your role is finished.**

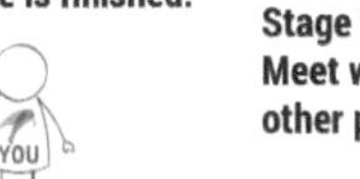

Option 2

You decide to have a Stage 2 conversation with the supposed offender. Your goal is to have them complete Stage 1: Meet with God in the Peace Pursuit Quick Start Guide. **Your role as initiator is finished.**

Stage 2
Meet with the other person

If the supposed offender accepts the offender role, they complete Stage 1 and repent to God.

If they realize they have also offended any person or persons, the offender meets with the offended person(s) for appropriate confession and forgiveness at Stage 2.

Stage 1
Meet with God

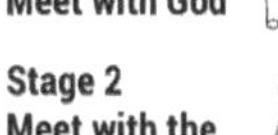

Stage 2
Meet with the other person

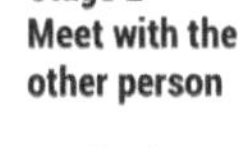

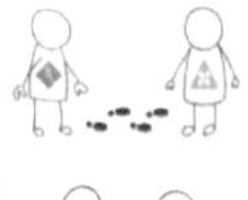

Confession and forgiveness, as appropriate

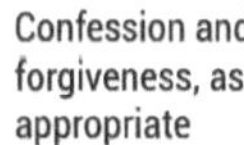

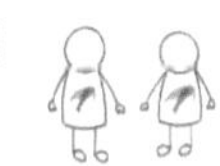

Q: If I complete Stage One and decide to take on the initiator role, is it possible the person I have a conversation with at Stage Two could accuse me of being a meddler or a busybody?

Yes, it is possible. However, if you complete Stage One with thought, care, and prayer, you will reduce the likelihood of being accused of doing something wrong. You will also have much better success connecting the person with God and stimulating them to fulfill their peacemaking role.

Q: Isn't an initiator the same as a Peace Pursuit coach? Don't they both give advice to one of the parties in the conflict?

No, they are not the same role. There are significant differences between the roles of initiator and coach. (I explain the coach role in detail in Chapter 6.)

After completing Stage One, the initiator *starts* a conversation with one of the parties in a conflict they have observed or already know about.

By contrast, the coach *responds* when one of the parties in a conflict comes to them to talk about it. The coach may not have known about the conflict.

There is another big difference in these two roles. As you go through Stage One, you will see that one of the 12 steps gives you the option to seek appropriate counsel from a coach. An initiator may seek wisdom from a coach, but by definition, a coach does not seek help from an initiator.

However, in special circumstances, it is possible you might fill both the role of initiator and coach in the same peacemaking situation, but separately and at different times. Let's say that you consider becoming an initiator. After you carefully complete Stage One, you decide to have a conversation with one of the parties at Stage Two. During your Stage Two conversation, the person might then ask you what to do next. In that case, you introduce them to the Peace Pursuit Quick Start Guide, have them choose which role they are in, and suggest they complete Stage One. When they get to the *Seek appropriate counsel* point, they might then ask you to be their coach. In that case, you would consider transitioning from the role of initiator to the role of coach and follow the guidelines for the coach role.

Q: What should I be careful of in my role as an initiator?

- Do not talk with any of the parties in a conflict unless you have thoughtfully and prayerfully met with God and completed Stage One yourself as much as you can.
- Do not assume a person is an offender if you don't have credible evidence of their offense.
- Except in rare cases, I do not recommend that you gather the supposed offender and the assumed offended to talk with you together as a threesome before they have had an opportunity to meet with each other one-on-one. Meet with one of them first, encourage that person to complete Stage One in their role and then encourage them to talk alone one-on-one with the other party at Stage Two.

THE COACH ROLE

The icon for the coach role is a map with a starting point, a path, and a destination. When a person has come to you to talk about a relationship problem that does not involve you, as a coach you can help the person travel the path from where they are now to their destination of peace.

Let's say a person wants to pray or talk with you about a relational problem or conflict that does not involve you.

Here are some common scenarios:

They are sure they are the offender, or they think they might be.

They are considering the initiator role.

They feel they are the offended.

They are an aggravator: a gossip, busybody, or meddler (though they may not be aware of that yet).

Your options for the coach role

If a person wants to talk to you about a relational problem or conflict in which you are not the offender or the offended, you have two good biblical options to choose from. You also have an option you should avoid.

Two biblical options

- You could decide to fill the coach role as I describe here.
- You could respectfully decline to take on the role of coach. You are not biblically obligated to accept this role.

The option to avoid

You have the potential to fill a role that is not helpful for the two parties to reach peace, the aggravator. Do not be what the Bible calls a gossip, meddler, busybody, or whoever may be partial to one side in a conflict. Obviously, you don't want to choose this role. You also don't want to be drawn into it by someone else's words or behavior.

Q: What qualities or traits do I need to be effective in the Peace Pursuit coach role?

You don't want to accept the coach role lightly, nor do you want to automatically assume you are not qualified to assist a sincere person meet with God at Stage One. You do not need professional training as a counselor. You don't have to be perfectly wise and all-knowing like Jesus, either. Below are skills and qualities that make an effective Peace Pursuit coach. The more of these you have for a given situation, the more likely you can be an appropriate coach.

- Skill in active listening
- Skill in asking helpful and relevant questions that lead the person to discover for themselves what they should do next
- Self-control to avoid talking too much
- Maturity to not gossip
- Maturity to be objective and not become partial to any party involved
- Courage to speak the truth in love

Q: What are my commitments as a coach?

As a coach, you promise to:

- **Avoid gossip yourself.** You won't speak to anyone inappropriately about anyone in the conflict. (Proverbs 16:28, 25:8–10, 26:20)
- **Be objective and impartial toward all parties in the conflict.** You'll help the one coming to you try to see the perspective of the other person in the conflict as well as their own. You'll coach them to treat the other party like they would want to be treated if their roles were reversed. You will also speak the truth in love as needed. (Proverbs 18:17, Proverbs 27:6 and 9, Ephesians 4:15, 1 Timothy 5:21, Philippians 2:2–4, Matthew 7:12.)
- **Give wise counsel.** You'll listen to their story with empathy and understanding. You will also wisely guide them to make their own wise and God-honoring decisions as they fulfill their role on the road to peace (James 3:17).

Q: What do I do specifically as a Peace Pursuit coach?

If you accept the coach role, you agree to help the person coming to you to meet with God and fulfill the responsibilities of their role at Stage One. You are not a go-between for the parties and you are not in the Peace Pursuit mediator role. Your role is to prayerfully coach and counsel the person so they do what God leads them to do to get to peace. If they do decide to have a conversation with the other party, you can help them prepare to talk in a godly, loving way.

As a coach, you do four things:

- Listen
- Coach
- Counsel
- Pray

To listen means you will hear the person's story and hear how they process *Stage One: Meet with God* before you offer advice.

Often a person will tell you their story and then ask, "What do you think I should do?" To coach the person means that you do not give them your answers first. You should first point them to the Stage One questions for them to answer for themselves while they meet with God. If they get stuck, you coach them further by asking additional relevant questions. Give them plenty of time and space to discover the answers themselves through prayer, listening to the Holy Spirit, and interacting on their own with the Bible passages in Stage One.

You may need to give them counsel if they are still unsure what to do after they work through the questions of Stage One, or if you believe they misunderstood one or more points. To counsel means you give wise advice to affirm or correct their understanding of what the Bible says for them to do at this stage.

What does wise advice look like? Here's a description of wisdom from the Bible: "Wisdom from above is first pure, then peaceable, gentle, open to reason, full of mercy and good fruits, impartial and sincere" (James 3:17).

To give wise counsel also includes having to speak the truth if you discern that the person you are coaching has any of these hindrances to peace:

- A plank in their eye they haven't seen
- A wrong motive toward the other party
- A desire to take what appears to be the easy way out because they are either not humble or they are unreasonably fearful

Pray before they share their story with you, pray as they tell their story, and pray as they meet with God and work through Stage One for their role. If they decide to have a conversation with the other person at Stage Two, pray for them during that time. You can also make yourself available to pray and debrief with them afterwards.

It's your choice

You may choose to either accept or decline someone's request to be their Peace Pursuit coach.

If for some reason you feel you should not be a person's coach, respectfully thank them for asking you and decline their request.

If you have the characteristics of a coach and you want to accept a person's request, I suggest you read the questions about the coach role below. After you read the questions and answers, go to the *Seek appropriate counsel* step of Stage One for more detail on the coach role as seen from the perspective of the other roles.

Q: How do I introduce the Peace Pursuit role of coach to someone who comes to me to talk about their relational problem?

Let's say Theresa comes to you to talk about a conflict that involves another person. Let's assume Theresa has come to you to sincerely seek your counsel, and let's assume you will accept if she asks you to fill the role of coach for her.

Your conversation could look something like this:

> THERESA: Do you mind if I ask you some advice about my situation with another person?
>
> *YOU: I don't mind at all. I'd be happy to try to help you.*
>
> *How about if we pray and then you start sharing with me a bit of your story? You can choose to tell me who the person is or not. I'll then ask questions to help you make decisions for going forward.*
>
> THERESA: That would be great. Thanks!

After you pray with Theresa and hear part of her story, you can introduce her to the Peace Pursuit Quick Start Guide. It is a condensed version of Peace Pursuit Stages One and Two in this handbook. If you don't have a printed or digital copy of the Quick Start Guide, you can access it at PeacePursuit.org. Many people keep a digital or printed copy of the Quick Start Guide handy for unexpected times like this.

> *YOU: When I have a question or problem about relationships, I've found it helpful to figure out what biblical role I am in and then proceed from there. The Peace Pursuit Quick Start Guide helps me make those*

decisions. It begins with the question in the band across the top: "Do you want to resolve a relational problem?" I understand that is what you want to do. Am I correct?

THERESA: Yes, I want to do my part to resolve this problem.

YOU: Great. Now, choose your role. As you read these roles, which one describes you most in regards to your present situation?

When Theresa has chosen her role from the Peace Pursuit Quick Start Guide, you could say something like this:

YOU: OK. Now that you have chosen your role, you can follow your icon through the steps of Stage One: Meet with God. You can take the Quick Start Guide home to pray and begin to work through Stage One alone when you have time. I'll pray for you as you process Stage One and meet with God on your own. As you work through each step, it's best if you write down notes so you can easily remember your insights and reflections as you make your next decision. You can also note places wherc you might want help.

You can see here that one of the Stage One steps for your role is an optional one called Seek appropriate counsel. *The icon for the coach role is a map with a starting and ending point. A coach comes alongside you while you meet with God in Stage One to assist you on your journey from where you are now to the destination of peace in your situation.*

If you want—and this is your choice—you could ask someone to fill the coach role. If you want me to be your coach and you have some time now, we could get started on a few steps of Stage One. Then you could finish processing Stage One at home by yourself. After you complete Stage One, we could meet again, if you want.

Let me point out that in just a few minutes, you have already helped Theresa resolve her relational problem by providing her with the Quick Start Guide and showing her the choices she has to move forward.

To continue this example, let's say that Theresa wants you to be her Peace Pursuit coach and to start processing the Quick Start Guide with you in the time you have together now.

THERESA: Thank you much for this. I've not used the Quick Start Guide before and I think I'd like some help. I do have some time now. If you also have time, would you be my coach?

YOU: I'd love to. To clarify expectations, let me share with you what I promise to do as a coach. Like it says here in the Quick Start Guide, as a coach

I promise to be an unbiased listener and to help you complete the Stage One points for your role. I promise to love both you and the other person in the sense that I will look at you both with the same eyes and view you both as I would want to be viewed if I were in either of your roles. I promise to be a true friend to you, which means I will listen to you with understanding and empathy. It also means I will be honest as we look at the motives of your heart and potential planks in your eyes.

How does that all sound? Do you still want me to be your coach?

THERESA: Yes, I do.

YOU: OK. In that case, let's pray and ask the Lord to speak to you as we meet together and process your role at Stage One.

Let's say that Theresa was not able to complete all the steps of Stage One in the time she had with you. This is not unusual. Most often, a person who is not familiar with the Quick Start Guide will need more than one session to thoughtfully and prayerfully meet with God through Stage One. You could continue to help her by saying this:

YOU: Theresa, this has been a good start. I suggest that you continue to meet with God at home and finish the rest of the Stage One steps for your role. As you go along, you might feel you don't need any more help. Or, you might find there are topics you might want to process with me. If so, I would be happy to meet with you again.

THERESA: OK. I will let you know. Thanks.

Let's say Theresa completes all the points of Stage One and you meet with her again. If she decides to have a Stage Two conversation with the other person, you could finish your coaching time like this:

YOU: Theresa, let me know when you are going to have your Stage Two conversation with the other person. I will pray for you before you meet with them and while you are meeting. If you want, you can contact me after your meeting so we can pray together and you can share with me how your time with them went.

THERESA: That sounds wonderful. Thanks!

Q: What if I feel I should not be a person's coach, even if they ask me?

You have the option to politely decline to be a coach. Maybe you just practically don't have the time.

Or, maybe you are concerned you might be partial toward one party or prejudiced against another.

In the example above, here's how you might politely decline Theresa's request that you be her coach:

> *YOU: Theresa, thank you for asking me to be your coach. I would like to be able to say I will do it, but for certain reasons not related to you, I'm sorry I can't this time. I hope you'll understand. However, I can recommend that you go through the Peace Pursuit Quick Start Guide either by yourself, or with another appropriate person who could fill the coach role.*

Assuming Theresa does understand, you can feel good that you have actually helped her by at least introducing her to the Peace Pursuit Quick Start Guide. Now she has the choice to continue pursuing peace by meeting with God at Stage One alone. Or, she can find another coach to help her with the Quick Start Guide.

Q: What if I sense from the person's story that they have not come with good motives and just want to gossip or grumble about the other party?

You have a couple of options here. One is better than the other.

One not-so-good option is to say this:

> *YOU: Herbert, I sense you are gossiping about that person and I don't want to hear it. Please stop it right now.*

Herbert will likely stop talking to you about that person. However, you will have missed a chance to gently help Herbert transition from the aggravator role to his legitimate role, if he has one. And you will not have equipped or encouraged Herbert in a biblical pursuit of peace.

Here's a better way you could respond to Herbert's gossiping or grumbling about someone:

> *YOU: Herbert, I see you have some concerns about this person. Would you like me to help you consider your potential biblical role to move this situation toward peace?*

Now, Herbert has a chance to stop himself from gossiping or grumbling against that person. Let's say he responds positively to your offer.

> HERBERT: Umm. Sure, that would be fine.

> *YOU: Great. How about if you have a look at the Peace Pursuit Quick Start Guide and choose which role best fits your situation with that person? You can then go through Stage One and meet with God to see what he might guide you to do next.*

If you respond to Herbert's gossip or grumbling like that, he just might transform from an aggravator to a legitimate Peace Pursuit role. And he just might ask you to be his coach.

Keep in mind that whenever a person like Herbert comes to you with either good or bad motives, you have several biblical options to help him be a legitimate peacemaker in an appropriate role.

Q: If someone asks me to be a coach, is it OK for me to hear details about the other person in the conflict?

Yes, but only as much as is necessary, and only if you have the required qualities of a Peace Pursuit coach (you are skilled at listening and asking appropriate questions, self-controlled, mature, courageous, etc.). Your role is to help the person who comes to you to fulfill their role in moving toward peace. You should focus more on what they should do next rather than the entire history of what happened. Your role is not about you hearing all the details so you can dispense wisdom and guidance. Before you give them counsel, give them the chance to discover the answers to the questions in the 12 steps of Stage One for themselves through prayer, thought, and listening to God.

Q: Can I be a coach for someone without knowing who the other party is?

It's possible. One idea is for the person who you coach to use substitute names as they tell their story.

Q: What about confidentiality?

You should promise not to gossip or talk to anyone inappropriately. However, it is not wise to make an oath that will bind you to silence in case the person shares something illegal or that is dangerous to them or others.

Q: What cautions should I keep in mind as a Peace Pursuit coach?

- Don't pre-judge what you think is the person's role when you hear their story. Let them decide for themselves. You might be surprised by what role they choose! And, if they do choose the opposite of what you think, control your tongue. You could ruin your coaching relationship right away if you blurt out, *"You seriously think you are in the offended role? Are you kidding?"*
- Don't get so caught up in just listening to their story that you forget to have them choose their role and process the steps of Stage One. You want them to make a forward-looking decision for how they will resolve their conflict. Just listening to them share their heart or blow off steam has limited value. Coach them to take practical steps forward. Ask them what they are going to do next to go after peace.

Ask them the very first question at the top of the Quick Start Guide: Do you want to resolve a relational problem?

- Don't talk much. Remember, this situation is not about you and your story, even if it seems similar to a situation you experienced yourself. Your primary role is to actively listen to them, then introduce them to Stage One so they can meet with God. Pray with them and for them, so that they can discover what God wants them to do. Ask them questions from the steps of Stage One first. Only tell them what you think they could do or should do if necessary.
- Don't accept their request if the person you are coaching asks you, "Will you go talk with the other person for me?" If you are in the coach role, you are not a mediator, a go-between, or an initiator.
- Don't volunteer to talk with the other party in the conflict.
- Be sure to follow the Quick Start Guide as closely as possible and ask enough self-discovery questions before offering counsel.
- Don't hesitate to offer counsel or advice to the person you are coaching if they need it after they have completed all of the steps of Stage One.

Q: What if both parties in a conflict come to me separately for advice?

You are free to accept the role of coach for each individual, under the same conditions you would if just one came to you. That means you help them individually and privately meet with God and complete Stage One for their role. In this case, you will need to be extra careful not to be partial or to share inappropriate information with either party. I normally don't tell either party I am coaching the other one. If they want to share that information with each other, I leave it to them to decide.

When both individuals complete Stage One, they would normally meet together at Stage Two alone, without you or anyone else ("just between the two of you," Matthew 18:15). This gives the two parties a chance to reconcile just between themselves, and raises the probability that they could do it alone the next time they have a relational problem. However, there are some legitimate exceptions to this norm which I explain in Chapter 7 (*Stage Two: If appropriate, meet with the other person*).

This diagram shows how you would coach each person alone, separately.

How you could coach both people in a conflict separately at Stage One

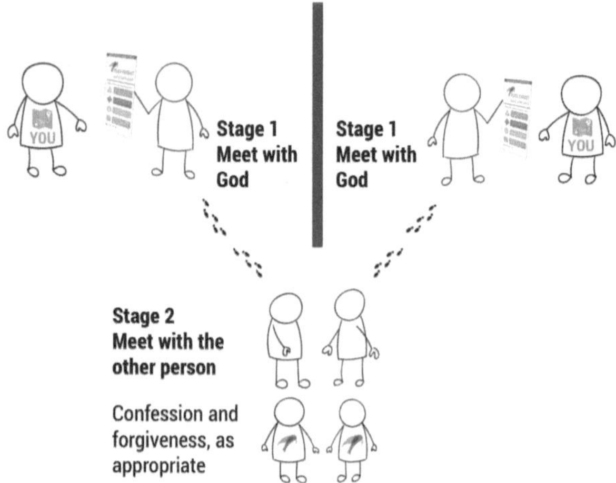

However, if they have tried to reconcile at Stage Two multiple times and have not been successful, they might ask you to meet with them together with you in the witness role as they try Stage Two again. Or, if they ask you to meet with them at Stage Three, you could transition from the role of coach into the role of mediator, if they both consent.

Q: What's the difference between a Peace Pursuit coach and initiator?

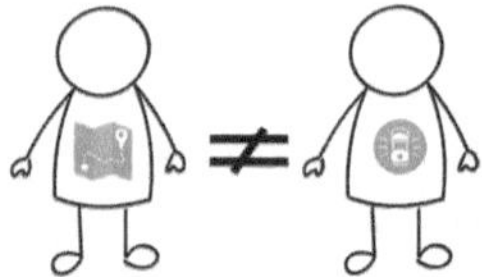

The coach role is responsive. Someone comes to you for help about a conflict you may not even know exists.

The initiator role is proactive. You are aware of a conflict between two other people. You pray and consider helping them get to peace. You complete Stage One yourself. After you meet with God alone you might decide to initiate a conversation with one of the two parties.

Q: *I know someone who is struggling with a conflict, but they haven't come to me to talk about it. I care for this person. Is it OK for me to volunteer to be their coach?*

In this situation, the initiator role is more appropriate for you to consider than the coach role. I suggest you process Stage One as a potential initiator and then decide to talk with them or not.

Later, if they go through Stage One, they might decide to seek appropriate counsel and ask you or someone else to be their coach. I advise that you wait for them to come to that decision.

Q: *What is my role as a coach at Stage Two?*

Your role as a Peace Pursuit coach is limited to Stage One. However, you can certainly pray for the person you coached as they have their Stage Two conversation in another location.

When I coach someone, I offer to debrief and pray with them after they have their Stage Two conversation with the other party.

This gives them a chance to celebrate their successful reconciliation and/or review what went well or could have gone better. As a coach, my agreement to debrief with a person creates an added incentive for them to fulfill their Peace Pursuit role at Stage Two and have a conversation with the other party.

Q: I coached someone at Stage One, but their Stage Two conversation didn't go like we expected. The two parties did not reach appropriate confession and forgiveness. What are their options?

Their options depend on their role and the type of response the other party made. Here's how you can help them.

Debrief with them about what went well and what didn't go so well during their conversation. Ask them where they think things could have gone better to get to appropriate confession and forgiveness.

Take them to Chapter 7 in this handbook. Locate the graphic for their role (offended, p. 174; offender, p. 183; initiator, p. 194) that outlines possible responses by the other party. Ask them to identify which of those responses most closely describes what happened during their Stage Two conversation. Then ask them which of the options they want to do next.

Of course, they can ask you to coach them as they decide which option to take. This will likely involve reviewing Stage One, possibly from the viewpoint of a different role. If you are not able or available to coach them, they can ask another person to coach them, if that person has the qualities of a Peace Pursuit coach.

How to Introduce the Peace Pursuit Coach Role

1. Do you mind if I ask you some advice about my situation with another person?

2. I don't mind at all. I'd be happy to. When I have a relational problem, I've found it helpful to use the Peace Pursuit ***QUICK START GUIDE***. Would you like me to share it with you?

3. Sure, I would like that. Thanks!

4. As you can see, the first question in the purple band is "Do you want to resolve a relational problem?" Just to clarify, is that what you want to talk about?

5. Yes, I want to do my part to resolve this problem.

6. Great! Now, as you read the blue triangle, dark pink diamond and orange circle roles in the ***QUICK START GUIDE***, which one describes you most in regards to your present situation?

7. I think I am mostly in the _____ role.

8. OK. Now you have a couple of options. One is for you to pray and work alone through Stage One: Meet with God for your role. I'll pray for you as you meet with God. After going through Stage One, you might like some help. You could call me and we could meet. That's the optional step of Stage One called Seek appropriate counsel.

Or, if you'd like, I have time now and I would be happy to help walk you through Stage One.

9. I have time now. I would like you to help me with Stage One.

10. Great. To clarify expectations, let me share with you what I aspire to do in the Peace Pursuit Coach role. It's the green map icon in the ***QUICK START GUIDE***. I aspire to give you wise counsel. I aspire to be objective and impartial as I help you complete the Stage One steps for your role. I aspire to love both you and the other person in the sense that I will look at you both with the same eyes and view you both as I would want to be viewed if I were in either of your roles. I aspire to be a true friend to you, which means I will listen to you with understanding and empathy. It also means I will be honest as we look at potential planks in your eyes. And, I promise not to gossip or share about your situation with anyone inappropriately.

How does that all sound? Do you still want me to be your coach?

11. Yes, please let's continue.

12. Perfect. Let's pray and follow your icon through Stage One.

6. STAGE ONE: MEET WITH GOD

After you decide what you mean by peace and choose your primary Peace Pursuit role, meet with God in Stage One.

The Peace Pursuit Stage One steps are biblical and practical points I've brought together over the years after reviewing a number of peacemaking situations. Depending on your role, you will complete 10, 11, or all 12 of them as you meet with God at Stage One. I list them all here so you can become familiar with their names. I will explain them later.

THE HUB

Airlines publish route maps with curved lines connecting the destinations where they fly. Most of those lines are connected to one city or a handful of cities. The airlines call these hubs. If you fly with that airline often, sooner or later you will go through their hub to get to your final destination, even if it appears to be an indirect route on a map.

Stage One: Meet with God is the hub of the Peace Pursuit Model. Whatever your role and present level of conflict, I urge you to go through Stage One sooner rather than later if you want to arrive at your destination of peace. Even if you have to backtrack to get to Stage One, it is actually the most direct route toward peace.

Sometimes I am asked to be a mediator in a complicated conflict that has already gone past Stage Two. In almost every case, I discover that the reason the conflict escalated to a higher stage was because one or more of the parties did not meet with God and fully complete Stage One. So, I guide the parties back to the hub of Stage One. This gets them on the right route toward peace.

Normally, you won't go to Stage Two before you complete Stage One. However, if you find that you have already been in Stage Two, don't worry. Simply go back to the hub. Meet with God back at Stage One, then repeat Stage Two if necessary.

Q: What are the benefits of Stage One: Meet with God*?*

Stage One is an encounter with God. That is always beneficial for you. Through prayer and reflection on his word, you engage your mind, emotions, and spirit alone with him before you talk with another party in the conflict. Stage One helps you see yourself, the other party, and the problem objectively in the light of biblical principles. Many people call Stage One an exercise in personal spiritual renewal. One person has even used Stage One in her devotional times.

Stage One creates an environment for the Holy Spirit to speak to you and for you to hear him clearly, whatever your role. As you prayerfully and thoughtfully process the 12 steps, the Holy Spirit will comfort, help and encourage you (John 14:16–17). He will guide you into all truth (John 16:13).

Stage One helps you approach the relational problem objectively, whatever your personality, temperament, or spiritual gifting. If you are the type of person who tends to rush in to correct wrong situations, Stage One gives God the opportunity to slow you down. It lets you take a breath and look at the conflict from all sides before you act out of well-meaning, but impatient, haste.

If you are the type of person who tends to "give the benefit of the doubt" and is cautious or fearful about addressing relational problems, Stage One gives God an opportunity to gently nudge you toward an appropriate Peace Pursuit role.

Q: Which roles need to do Stage One?

The offended, the offender, and the initiator. I recommend that each one meet with God before talking with another person in the relational problem. Depending on your role, you will process the Stage One steps from a somewhat different perspective.

Q: Stage One looks like a lot of work. Do I really have to complete every step every time?

A close friend of mine has earned his living for more than 35 years as a pilot of multi-engine jet airplanes. His job includes training other pilots and inspecting their competence. He tells me that he still manually goes through a check list before every take-off. Why does such an experienced and skilled pilot still manually complete a check list he could recite from memory? He does it just to make sure he does not miss even the simplest step out of pride, laziness, impatience, or neglect.

Each of the 12 steps of Peace Pursuit Stage One is meant to protect you from crashing on take-off as you pursue peace. Stage One will protect you from moving too fast, delaying too long, or forgetting an important principle as you begin. The 12 steps protect you from turning a simple relational problem into a disastrous explosion.

Practically speaking, and based on experience, you will more likely reach peace if you meet with God at Stage One before you talk with the other person than if you don't complete Stage One. If you don't invest the time and effort to process Stage One, you could create much more work and heartache than is necessary for you and others later. The more you practice going through Stage

One, the more you will know which steps you can go through quickly and which ones you need to spend more time on in a given situation. Still, make sure you have a look at each one for your role before you go to Stage Two.

Q: Where do I begin Stage One?

You can begin Stage One in many places. You can also move back and forth between steps you have already completed if you get new insight from processing one or more of the other steps. Some steps will take longer to pray and work through than others. The important thing is that you meet with God and complete all of the steps for your role before you go to Stage Two, if that is what you decide to do.

Most people start with the steps highlighted above before going on to the other points of Stage One. But don't stop with these. Pray and process all the steps of Stage One for your role before you make your final decision to move to Stage Two or not.

THE 12 STEPS OF STAGE ONE

Avoid gossip

ROLES INVOLVED

PURPOSE

To remind yourself not to involve others inappropriately in your relational problem. If you have already talked with others inappropriately, even in a seemingly innocent prayer request, this point will show you options for what to do next.

KEY QUESTION

Have you talked to anyone inappropriately about any of the parties in this conflict?

The Bible describes gossip and slander as divisive and destructive to families, friendships, churches, and work relationships. They are serious sins. They are the opposite of the biblical values of unity, building up each other, and doing to others what you would want them to do to you.

Here are some Bible verses that refer to gossip and/or slander.

- "Whoever goes about slandering reveals secrets, but he who is trustworthy in spirit keeps a thing covered" (Proverbs 11:13).

- "A dishonest man spreads strife, and a whisperer separates close friends" (Proverbs 16:28).
- "Whoever goes about slandering reveals secrets; therefore do not associate with a simple babbler" (Proverbs 20:19).
- "What your eyes have seen do not hastily bring into court, for what will you do in the end, when your neighbor puts you to shame? Argue your case with your neighbor himself, and do not reveal another's secret, lest he who hears you bring shame upon you, and your ill repute have no end" (Proverbs 25:7–10).
- "For lack of wood the fire goes out, and where there is no whisperer, quarreling ceases.... The words of a whisperer are like delicious morsels; they go down into the inner parts of the body" (Proverbs 26:20, 22).
- "I fear that there may be discord, jealousy, fits of rage, selfish ambition, slander, gossip, arrogance and disorder" (2 Corinthians 12:20, NIV).

Q: How do you define gossip?

I've found that what is considered gossip can vary from person to person. My definition of gossip is probably different from yours, and yours is probably different from the person who sits next to you at work or at church.

Even announcing news or sharing a prayer request about someone can become gossip when it crosses a line. How do you know when you are about to cross that line?

Let's say you are thinking about sharing true information about Adrian with Kim, but you want to know if it is appropriate.

Here are some questions to ask yourself to see if what you want to share with Kim could be considered gossip about Adrian.

- *What is my motive for telling Kim this information about Adrian?*
- *How will Adrian be honored and loved if I tell Kim this information?*
- *If those same facts were true about me, and Adrian shared them with Kim, would I feel honored and loved?*
- *How will Adrian be blessed, encouraged, or given grace as a result of my words to Kim?*
- *What opinion about Adrian will I leave in Kim's mind?*
- *What will Kim think of me after I talk about Adrian?*
- *What might Kim do with this new information about Adrian?*

Q: How do you define slander and libel?

Definitions of slander vary, but they generally contain three components:

- Saying something false about someone
- With malice or intent to harm
- Which harms their reputation

Libel is spreading false information about someone in print or visual media. Both slander and libel fall into the category of defamation, which is harming someone's reputation or making them look bad in another person's eyes.

Even if you say you did not have a motive of malice when spreading false information harmful to someone else's reputation, this is still a grave offense and is the opposite of speaking the truth in love (Ephesians 4:15).

Q: What does it mean to talk "appropriately" or "inappropriately" with others about a relational problem?

If you are in a Peace Pursuit role, it is appropriate for you to talk with a person who is part of the conflict or with a person who has another legitimate role.

For example, you have the biblical option of talking with a coach, as I describe in this handbook. I believe you are not gossiping or slandering if both of these statements are true:

- Your motive truly is to seek impartial help going through the various points of Stage One as they pertain to you in your role; and
- The person you ask to coach you meets the defined characteristics for a Peace Pursuit coach.

If your motive is wrong, or if you choose a person who does not have the qualities of a coach, you risk committing gossip or slander.

Timing is also important. You should only talk to people who fill legitimate roles in the peacemaking process during the appropriate stage. For example, if you are at Stage One, you would normally not go and talk with the offender's leader or person they are accountable to. This could look like you are escalating the process to a higher stage prematurely.

Q: What if I may have already committed gossip about a present situation?

If you have knowingly committed gossip, you first need to confess and repent to God.

Then, in prayer, ask God and yourself these kinds of questions that may reveal why you gossiped:

- *Did I somehow want to impress the one I gossiped to with my special or secret knowledge?*
- *Did I want their sympathy?*
- *Did I want to draw them to my side?*
- *Did I want to tear down or punish the one I gossiped about?*

If you answer yes to any of these, you may have to repent to God of deeper-rooted sins in your heart that produced the destructive fruit of gossip.

Q: Should I repent to the person I gossiped about?

If the one you gossiped about knows that you gossiped about them, then normally you should go and repent to them. See the *Repent of your part* step for ideas on how to make a good confession.

Q: What if the person I gossiped about is not aware that I have gossiped about them?

If they don't know you gossiped, and you know your gossip has not negatively affected them, then you could treat this like a private sin or sin of the heart (see the *Repent of your part* step for an explanation of private sins and sins of the heart). The three purposes of a confession are to be honest about the offense, to humble yourself, and to honor the one you offended. Going to the one you gossiped about and honestly admitting to them what you did would certainly be a humbling experience for you. However, you should ask yourself, would it honor them? Usually, it would not.

Here's a true story to illustrate what I mean. Ashley's church youth group was doing a project to raise money for a relief organization. The youth group planned to fast from food for a weekend to have a temporary experience of hunger to empathize with people who don't have enough to eat. Each member of the youth group found sponsors who would give a donation to the relief organization if the young person completed the fast.

When Ashley's youth pastor heard from another teenager that Ashley was joining the fasting event, he joked, "Yeah, the fast will be good for her. She needs to lose weight."

Later, the youth pastor felt bad about this remark. Even though Ashley had no idea the youth pastor had said anything about her to the other teenager, the youth pastor went to Ashley to apologize for what he said. Ashley was shocked and embarrassed, and cried. But she granted the youth pastor her forgiveness.

Years later, Ashley reflected on her experience. She said, "I think the youth pastor apologized to me just because he felt guilty and wanted to clear his conscience. It seemed that he was thinking more of himself than of me. Sure, his confession was honest and humble, but it certainly did not honor me."

Q: Should I confess to the person I gossiped to?

Usually yes, with special caution and care. You need to communicate clearly what you are confessing and to do it without making it seem that the person you gossiped to is somehow at fault.

For example, let's say that I said some things to Kim about Adrian. Later, I feel conviction from the Holy Spirit that I was wrong to do so for one or more reasons. Depending on what I said to Kim, I could confess to Kim like in one or a combination of these examples:

> *"Kim, after our conversation the other day when I talked to you about Adrian, I realized I said those things about Adrian with unloving motives. If I had been in Adrian's place I would not have wanted me to share them with anyone. I have repented to God for this and I want to confess to you because I sinned against Adrian in your presence."*
>
> *"Kim, I believe that what I told you about Adrian did not honor Adrian. There was also no need for you to hear the things I said about Adrian. It was unloving for me to put you in a difficult situation to hear my words about Adrian which could affect how you now view Adrian. In this way, I not only sinned against Adrian, but I sinned against you."*

Notice that the word gossip is not in these confessions. Why? Maybe Kim's personal definition of gossip is different than mine and what I said about Adrian does not fit in to Kim's definition. I don't want to tempt myself to let my time of confession of serious sin slip into a theoretical debate with Kim about what gossip is and what it isn't.

See the *Repent of your part* step for more on how to make a biblical confession.

Q: What should I do if I have knowingly and willingly listened to someone else's gossip about a conflict?

Let's say your conscience or the Holy Spirit showed you after the fact that you *willingly and knowingly* listened to Vivian gossip about Briana. (Note my emphasis on the words *willingly* and *knowingly*.) Before you talk to anyone else, first meet with God. Ask him to search your heart as to why you wanted to dine on those "delicious morsels" that "go down into the inner parts of the body" (Proverbs 26:22). Ask yourself and God questions like these.

- *Do I have jealousy, envy, or unforgiveness toward Briana?*
- *Did I want to be seen as supporting Vivian?*
- *Was I somehow afraid to say to Vivian that it appeared she might be gossiping about Briana?*

If you answer yes to any of these, you should confess and repent to God.

Should you apologize to Briana for listening to Vivian's gossip about her? Before you answer that question, consider these questions first:

- Would it really honor Briana if you say something to her like, "I am sorry that I listened to Vivian's gossip about you"?
- If you were in Briana's place, would you want someone to apologize to you for listening to gossip about you that you did not know about?

However, if Briana is somehow aware that you knowingly and willingly listened to Vivian's gossip about her, you should complete Stage One in the offender role and you should repent to Briana at Stage Two.

This example brings up an awkward question. Should you bring up to Vivian your belief that you were wrong to willingly and knowingly listen to her talk about Briana? If you believe you should, what could you say to her without directly or indirectly accusing her of the sin of gossip in the same sentence? Before you say anything to Vivian, process *Stage One: Meet with God* in both the offender and initiator roles. You might decide that it is most wise and loving to all parties not to bring up Vivian's sin of gossip to her this time. However, you should prepare your heart and mind for what to say the next time Vivian or someone else begins to gossip to you (see the question below).

Q: What do I do if I sense someone is starting to gossip to me about a third person?

Let's say Paul is talking to you about Dave and you sense Paul is crossing the line into gossip. You could say something like the following, depending on what Paul is saying to you about Dave.

- *"Paul, with all due respect, I don't feel I need to know any more about Dave's situation."*
- *"Paul, I'm not sure I am an appropriate person to hear about this."*
- *"Paul, I can see you are concerned about your relationship with Dave. May I suggest that you have a look at the Peace Pursuit Quick Start Guide and choose which role best fits your situation with Dave? You can then go through Stage One and meet with God to see what he might guide you to do next."*
- *"Paul, I can see you are concerned about Dave's relationship with ____. May I suggest that you have a look at the Peace Pursuit Quick Start Guide and choose which role, if any, might be most appropriate for you to help in Dave's situation? You can then go through Stage One and meet with God to see what he might guide you to do next."*

Analyze

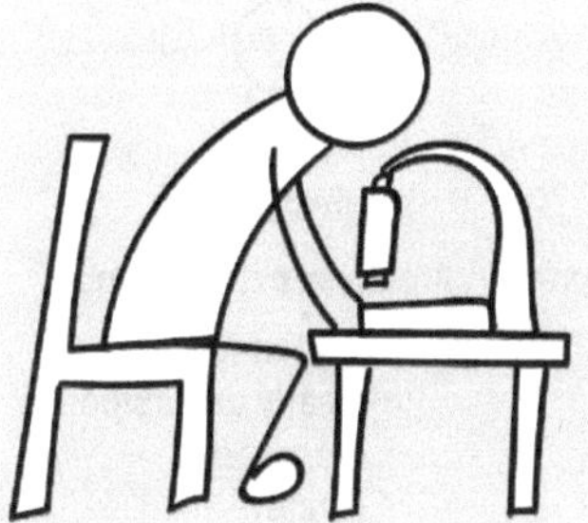

ROLES INVOLVED

PURPOSE
To identify the nature of the relational problem and analyze what source or sources caused it.

KEY QUESTIONS

What happened?

What expectations did each party have?

What expectations were not met?

Were those expectations legitimate, clearly understood, reasonable, and loving?

I will dive into detail in this step because it is essential for reaching appropriate confession and forgiveness. To say it simply, the offender needs to understand clearly what words and/or actions they will repent of, and the offended needs to understand clearly what words and/or actions they will forgive.

The *Analyze* step has three parts.

① **Describe the problem objectively**	② **Identify expectations**	③ **Question expectations**
What happened? • words • actions • inactions • reactions	What did I expect them: • to do? • to say? • not to do? • not to say?	Are these expectations: • legitimate? • clearly understood? • reasonable? • loving?

Analyze part 1: Describe the problem objectively

First, ask yourself, *What happened?*

Look back at the specific incident or series of incidents in this relational problem as if they are audio or video clips. Be as specific and detailed as you can about who did and said what.

Things don't "just happen" to cause a relational problem; a human being who has a name does them. Words don't just come out of the air; a person with a name speaks them. When you describe the problem, connect a supposed offender's name with a specific behavior.

Here are some examples of helpful and not-so-helpful descriptions:

Not helpful	*Helpful*
Some people at work aren't pulling their share of the load.	Tom did not complete his monthly report.
Disturbing things seem to be happening in the church.	At the last elder board meeting, the pastor proposed the idea of changing the time of the worship service.
The people in management don't know what they are doing.	Carl announced the termination of Joe's and Kathy's positions.
Words were said that hurt people.	Michael told Paul, "Your idea is stupid!"

Describe each person's behavior based on facts, not feelings. Try not to use words that contain your own emotions or judgment about the situation. Again, think of describing the situation as if it were an audio or video clip.

Look at the facts in terms of these categories:

- Words: Who said what words, when did they say them, how did they say them, and to whom did they say them?
- Actions: Who did what action, when did they do it, and how did they do it?
- Inactions: Who did not do something or did not say something?
- Reactions: How did each person react to another person's words, actions, or inactions?

Reminder: Be careful not to add your own interpretation or judgment of motives in this step.

Words

What did each person say (or not say)?

Jesus taught, "I tell you, on the day of judgment people will give account for every careless word they speak, for by your words you will be justified, and by your words you will be condemned." (Matthew 12:36–37). The book of James has much to say about how the tongue causes relational problems (James 1:26, 3:1–12). So, it is important for you to try to remember each person's exact words as you analyze a situation. You are not trying to "trap" anyone. Your purpose is simply to find where the problem started.

When you analyze the situation, don't assume sin is involved. First ask if it is simply a matter of miscommunication. It is possible you could have a relational problem with someone simply because your personal definitions for words are different than their definitions of those same words.

Take special care as you analyze words when the two parties do not speak the same mother tongue or dialect.

In real-life situations, we have traced the source of intense conflicts between people in churches and ministry teams to individuals simply having different definitions of common words like worship, fellowship, evangelism, discipleship, authority, leadership, accountability, and mentoring. We've also seen conflicts in groups caused by people's different definitions of simple, practical values like what it means for a meeting to start "on time" or to dress modestly.

Christians sometimes even have relational problems over definitions of biblical terms. Think of the words kindness, patience, respect, honor, hospitality, and generosity. These are biblical values Jesus followers agree we should practice with each other. But what you mean by these may be very different than what I mean by them, or what they mean to a person in your church. These definitions vary greatly from person to person, friendship to friendship, family to family, church to church, and culture to culture. People's different definitions create different expectations, and when people's expectations are not the same, you have a recipe for potential conflict.

How did the person say their words?

The majority of what you communicate comes from your tone of voice, facial expressions, posture, and gestures as you speak words. The combination of these is called body language. So when you analyze a relational problem caused by what someone said, also describe the *way* the person said them. Here are some examples of things to look for.

- The volume and inflection of their voice. Was it soft, normal, loud? Did their sentence tone trail up or down?
- Their eyes. Were they normal, bulging, squinting, or tearful? Where were they looking?
- Their facial expression. Were they smiling or frowning? Were the corners of their mouth turned down? Were their eyebrows raised? Was their chin trembling? Did their face show no expression at all?
- Their body position and gestures. Were they standing close, or standing far away? Were their arms at their sides, waving, or folded across their chest? What direction was their head facing? Was it toward you or away from you?
- Timing. Did they interrupt someone or talk over a person who was speaking? Did they give a delayed response (or no response) to a question?
- Place. Where did they speak these words? In private or in public? At home, work, church, or an informal gathering?
- Who else heard these words? Family, friends, strangers, co-workers?
- What did each person *not* say? Sometimes a person becomes an offender by not saying what another person

expected them to say, or when they expected the person to say it.

Actions

- What exactly did each person do?
- How did they do the action? Was it quickly, slowly, softly, roughly, gently, loudly, silently? (Keep in mind that your definition of quickly, slowly, etc. could be different from the other party's definition.)
- When did they act? Too early, too late? Too quickly, too slowly? (Be aware that your definition of too early, too late, etc. might be different from the other person's definition.)

Inactions

- What did the person *not* do? Frequently, the offense is because a person did not do what they were expected to.

Reactions

- What did each person either do (or not do) or say (or not say) in response to the other person's words, actions, or inactions?

Try to carefully reconstruct the full sequence of events of a relational problem. This will help you objectively establish which person is responsible for what offense, if any.

Why it is important to describe the problem in such detail

From what I have written, it may seem like I am asking you to be a police investigator or a courtroom prosecutor. I'm not. The most direct way to the source of the problem is to discover and accurately analyze the exact facts of the situation. This can save your precious resources of time and emotional energy as you try to resolve a conflict.

Sometimes an offender is not aware that they have offended anyone. They may not see what might be obvious to you and others. It's usually not helpful to say to an offender, "You know what you did was offensive, don't you?"

The loving way to help them see what they have done to hurt someone is to accurately explain to them exactly what they did, when they did it, and how they did it. Once they understand exactly what they did (or didn't do), you can show them how their behavior did not fit with others' legitimate expectations. This loving process can potentially help them grow and become less offensive to others in the future.

Sometimes an offended person is so caught up with emotion that they cannot see planks in their own eyes until someone helps them look at all the facts of the situation objectively. This loving process can help protect innocent people from being wrongly accused by an overly-emotional person who is easily offended. If it's a challenge for you to explain your story with a minimum of feeling words, perhaps a coach can listen and then use words based on fact to paraphrase your narrative for you.

Sometimes a potential initiator has difficulty seeing the problem from both sides. Sticking to the facts can help them stay objective and impartial.

Sometimes a coach can be overly empathetic and slip into partiality when listening to an offended person's story. If you focus on the facts when you coach, you can protect yourself from becoming partial to the offended. Remember that as a coach of one of the parties, you are only hearing the facts that one party remembers and/or chooses to share with you. There is another side to the story.

Whatever your role, after you describe the facts of the situation like a video or audio clip, you can look for the likely source of the conflict: expectations.

Analyze part 2: Identify expectations

I am convinced that the source of virtually every relational problem is the unmet expectations of one or more persons. I know that I just used strong and nearly absolute words, but my experience in helping resolve conflicts validates my belief.

The % of conflicts caused by unmet or unequal expectations:

99.9999999999999999999999999...

I'll try to explain the connection between expectations, conflicts, and peace with a variety of statements. I am consciously going to use some absolute words.

- The only time you are hurt or offended or frustrated or irritated by a person is when they don't do or say what you think or feel they should, when they should, or how they should.
- You have no conflict with someone who does what you think they are supposed to do, at the right time and in the correct manner in which you think they should.
- You are at peace with someone who treats you like you feel you ought to be treated.
- You have no relational problem with a person who meets your expectations for how they should speak and behave toward you.
- The only time you offend someone is when your words or behavior do not match their expectations of you.

Now, I'll explain what I mean by an expectation.

What is an expectation?

I describe an expectation as a value, principle, rule, standard, or behavior norm you believe another person should share, meet, obey, comply with, agree with, or uphold.

Sometimes you can identify your expectations when you use the words expect or expected to describe the problem. For example:

- *I expected Joe to pay me my money by Thursday, like he agreed. He did not pay me on Thursday.*
- *I did not expect Felicity to tell anyone what I shared with her in confidence. She told three other people.*
- *I expected Billy to clean up his room this afternoon. He played football instead.*
- *I did not expect Robert to make fun of my new hairstyle. He laughed and pointed to my head when he saw me.*
- *I expected Martha to give me more appreciation for the work I did. She did not even acknowledge I completed it.*

At other times, it may be a challenge to use the word *expectation* in a sentence when you are trying to explain why you were offended by someone. In cases like that, here is some help. Try to use one or more words like the ones in this list when you describe what the offender did or did not do:

ought	enough	good
should	much	bad
right	need	hope
wrong	more	deserve
fair	supposed to	normal
proper	less	better
appropriate	want	

Here are a few examples of what I mean.

Facts	*The offended person's possible expectations*
I think my employer pays Bob more than he pays me.	I deserve at least as high a salary as Bob. My employer should be fair.
The meeting normally ends at 9:00. Ralph was in charge of the meeting. He ended the meeting at 9:22.	Ralph needs to respect our time. He should manage meetings better.
A teenager did not give up his seat to me on the bus today. That seat is clearly labeled as reserved for the elderly. I am 75 years old.	The teenager ought to follow rules. Showing respect for the elderly is the proper thing to do.
We had a one-hour prayer meeting last night for our eight-person small group. Kathleen talked for 24 minutes. This was the fourth week in a row she talked for more than 20 minutes.	All eight of us should be given equal time to share. Kathleen needs to learn more self-control. Our group leader should have told Kathleen not to talk so much.
For the third time, Brad did not offer to pay his share of the lunch bill.	Brad ought to be more generous. He should be more aware of what it means to be polite.

Q: What if I can't explain the problem in terms of what I think the offender did wrong?

If you can't clearly describe the offense, look at the situation the other way around. Rather than trying to describe what the person did wrong, ask yourself what you would have expected the person to do that would have been right or appropriate in that situation. You might find that their offense was actually inaction on their part. James 4:17 is clear: "Whoever knows the right thing to do and fails to do it, for him it is sin." Some people call this the sin of omission.

Ask this: How did the person's words, actions, inactions, or reactions fit with Bible passages such as Ephesians 4:29–32, Philippians 2:1–5, and 1 Corinthians 13:4–7? How did they fit with God's expectations for all Jesus followers and God's expectations for specific people (see *Analyze part 3*)?

Analyze part 3: Question expectations

After you identify the unmet expectations of each offended party, question those expectations by four criteria.

Are the expectations placed on the offender:

- Legitimate?
- Clearly understood by them?
- Reasonable?
- Loving toward them?

Expectations question 1: Are the expectations placed on the offender legitimate?

After you have successfully put your expectations into words, you need to see if they are legitimate. If your expectations of a person are legitimate, and that person does not meet them, you could say you are correct to consider that person to be in the offender role. However, if your expectations are not legitimate, you could wrongly take offense when a person does not meet them.

What makes an expectation legitimate? I believe you can consider your expectation of a person to be legitimate if it aligns with an objective standard or code apart from or beyond your own personal preference or desire. For example, if you say, "It's just not right!" or "That's not fair!" or "How shameful!" you need to refer to some measure, principle, or value shared by people other than yourself which defines what is right, fair, or shameful.

Romans 12:17 and 2 Corinthians 8:21 indicate that we should take care to do what is right and honorable according to other godly believers. As Jesus followers, you and I don't have the right to establish our own personal standards of right and wrong which conflict with clear and informed biblical teaching which is affirmed by mature and godly leaders in a biblical community.

Legitimate expectations from society in general

Naturally, you and I have legitimate expectations for others to abide by in the societies we live in. These include:

- Civil and criminal laws;
- Rules, ethics, and codes of conduct of a workplace, school, volunteer organization, etc.; and
- Unwritten norms for members of a family, an organization, a business, etc.

If a person does not follow accepted laws, rules, ethics, or codes of conduct, you should respond accordingly in the role of an offended person or as an initiator. That may mean talking with the person yourself or reporting that person to an authority. However, before you talk with the person, I recommend you meet with God and complete Stage One, even if the person is not a follower of Jesus.

When you are hired by a company or join a church or voluntary organization, don't assume you automatically understand that group's unwritten norms or shared expectations. You can make relational mistakes if you bring in your own assumptions and expectations which don't match theirs.

Keep in mind that if you are part of the same society, group, culture, company, or organization, other people have the same set of legitimate expectations for you, too.

God's expectations of all Jesus followers

If you are a follower of Jesus, you have another set of expectations in your life beyond those of the general society you live in. In the Bible, God has given us clear statements of his expectations for how we should treat each other. Many are easy to spot because they are in the form of commands ("do this," "don't do that") and contain the phrases "one another" or "each other" or "everyone." There are many of these "one anothers" and "each others" in the Bible.

A foundational one is John 13:34. "A new commandment I give to you, that you love one another: just as I have loved you, you also are to love one another." Below are some specific examples that show us how to apply God's love to one another. (All quotes are from the ESV, except as noted.)

- "Be at peace with one another" (Mark 9:50b).
- "Be devoted to one another in love" (Romans 12:10a, NIV).

- "Outdo one another in showing honor" (Romans 12:10b).
- "Live in harmony with one another" (Romans 12:16).
- "[Do] not pass judgment on one another" (Romans 14:13a).
- "Accept one another" (Romans 15:7, NIV).
- "[Do not envy] one another" (Galatians 5:26).
- "Instruct one another" (Romans 15:14b).
- "Stir up one another to love and good works" (Hebrews 10:24).
- "Serve one another" (Galatians 5:13).
- "Bear one another's burdens" (Galatians 6:2).
- "Bear with [or *put up with*] one another" (Ephesians 4:2).
- "Be kind and compassionate to one another" (Ephesians 4:32, NIV).
- "Confess your sins to one another" (James 5:16).
- "Clothe yourselves, all of you, with humility toward one another" (1 Peter 5:5).
- "[Forgive] each other as the Lord has forgiven you" (Colossians 3:13).
- "[Submit] to one another out of reverence for Christ" (Ephesians 5:21).
- "Do not lie to one another" (Colossians 3:9).
- "Comfort one another" (1 Thessalonians 4:18).
- "Build each other up" (1 Thessalonians 5:11).
- "Do not speak evil against one another" (James 4:11).
- "Do not grumble against one another" (James 5:9).
- "Encourage one another" (1 Thessalonians 4:18).
- "[Do not provoke] one another" (Galatians 5:26).
- "Regard one another as more important than yourselves; do not merely look out for your own personal interests, but also for the interests of others" (Philippians 2:3b–4, NASB).

Since God has commanded us believers to apply these "one anothers" in community, God has a legitimate expectation that we will actually put them into practice. Therefore, you can legitimately expect other Jesus followers to treat you according to these verses. And, if they don't, you might say you have a "right" to be offended. However, don't forget that they have the same "right" to expect you to treat them according to these same verses. So, before you go and show a person their fault because they did not do a "one another" verse to you, make sure you examine yourself to see if there are any "one another" verses you have neglected to apply to them.

God's expectations of specific people

In addition to the "one another" commands applicable to all believers, God has special expectations for people in certain roles in life. For example, God gives specific, direct commands to fathers, husbands, wives, children, young men, young women, older women, older men, employers, employees, the rich, church leaders, church members, and so on.

Here are some examples:

- Children, honor and obey your parents (Ephesians 6:1–2).
- Fathers, do not provoke or embitter your children (Colossians 3:21).
- Husbands, live with your wives in an understanding way (1 Peter 3:7), love them and do not be harsh with them (Colossians 3:19), love them as you love yourselves (Ephesians 5:33), nourish and cherish them, and give yourselves up for them as Christ gave himself up for the church (Ephesians 5:25–29, 33).
- Wives, respect and submit to your husbands as the church submits to Christ (Ephesians 5:22–24, 33).
- Spiritual leaders, shepherd [feed, guide, protect] your flock, be an example, serve willingly, and do not lord it over them (1 Peter 5:1–4, NIV).
- Church members, obey and submit to your leaders so as to make it a joy and not a burden for them to lead you (Hebrews 13:17).

If you are in any of these life positions that are addressed in these verses, it is fair to say that God expects you to treat the persons mentioned in those verses as he instructs you to. That means other people can legitimately expect these things from you, whatever life position you hold in relation to them.

To illustrate what I mean, I have interpreted and paraphrased the verses above in terms of legitimate expectations:

- Parents, you can legitimately expect your children to honor and obey you (Ephesians 6:1–2).

- Children, you can legitimately expect your fathers not to provoke or embitter you (Colossians 3:21).
- Wife, you can legitimately expect your husband to live with you in an understanding way (1 Peter 3:7), to love you and not be harsh with you (Colossians 3:19), to love you as he loves himself (Ephesians 5:33), to nourish and cherish you, and to give himself up for you like Christ gave himself up for the church (Ephesians 5:25–29).
- Husband, you can legitimately expect your wife to respect you and submit to you as the church submits to Christ (Ephesians 5:22–24, 33).
- Church members and members of other spiritual communities, you can legitimately expect leaders to shepherd you [guide, protect], to be an example, to serve willingly, and not to lord it over you (1 Peter 5:1–4, NIV).
- Church leaders and other spiritual leaders, you can legitimately expect church members to obey and submit to you and to make it a joy, not a burden for you to lead them (Hebrews 13:17).

As you analyze the source of a relational problem, consider which party (or parties) met or did not meet God's "one another" and specific life role expectations for them.

What behavior can be considered sin?

When you analyze the nature of a relational problem, I believe it is important to address a problem caused by sin differently than one caused by personality or cultural differences. Why? Because our sins are so serious that they separated us from God and Jesus had to die for them to reconcile us to God (Romans 3:23–24, 5:1–11).

Jesus did not suffer and die on the cross for our personality differences. God intentionally created us with a unique mix of personality traits, and he expects us to bear with one another, be patient with one another, and so on as we relate to each other's differences (see the "one another" verses above).

If what we do to someone is sin, we need to confess and repent of that sin to God and to that person. If what someone does to us is sin, we need to forgive them for that sin. Since our working definition of peace is appropriate confession and forgiveness, we need to know what sin we are confessing and forgiving in order to reach peace.

I know that Christians disagree with each other about the definition of sin. This handbook is not a theological treatise, and I am not going to try to persuade you of a particular definition of sin. However, I will share with you principles that I have found to have a fairly broad acceptance among those who base their faith primarily on the teachings of the Bible. I use these principles to help myself and others understand if a person's word, action, inaction, or reaction can be considered a sin. I offer these for your consideration.

- If the Bible clearly forbids me from doing something, and I do it, that is sin.
- If the Bible clearly instructs or commands me to do something, but I don't do it, that is sin.
- If the Bible describes a thought or behavior with terms like evil, defiling, foolish, ungodly, or unrighteous, that thought or behavior is sin.
- If the Bible contrasts something with obviously good behavior, or uses phrases like "those who do these things will not inherit the kingdom of God," those things are sin.

Here are a few lists in the Bible of these kinds of things:

- Things God "hates" (Proverbs 6:16–19)
- "Defiling" words and actions that come from the heart (Matthew 15:10–20)
- "The ungodliness and unrighteousness of mankind" (Romans 1:18–32)
- Things "unrighteous" people do (1 Corinthians 6:9–10)
- "Works of the flesh" (ESV) or "deeds of the flesh" (NASB; Galatians 5:19–21)

I also consider something to be sin if it is the opposite of the good and godly traits listed in these sample verses:

- *Agape* love (1 Corinthians 13:4–7)
- The fruit of the Spirit (Galatians 5:22–23)
- Wisdom from above (James 3:17)
- The "one another" verses and God's commands to specific people (see the lists I mentioned earlier).

Expectations question 2: Are the expectations placed on the offender clearly understood by them?

Let's say you have decided that your expectations of the offender were legitimate. Next, ask yourself if your expectations were clearly understood by them.

I believe that an offender's degree of responsibility for not meeting your expectation is directly related to how well they understood that expectation. Maybe they didn't meet your expectation because they simply didn't know you had that expectation on them. In other words, they could be innocently ignorant of your expectation. Perhaps you mistakenly thought they should know the "unwritten" procedures at work or the "assumed" code of conduct of your business, church, or organization. Maybe you simply did not clearly communicate your expectation. You can't legitimately expect a person to read your mind.

If a person is a new follower of Jesus, they may not yet be familiar with the "one another" and role-specific Bible verses. Or, they might be from a family, generation, or cultural background in which biblical concepts like respect, honor, politeness, and generosity are defined and applied differently.

If you realize that your expectations on the offender were not clearly understood by them, don't approach them with an attitude of correction. Have a calm conversation with them to clarify expectations. "Instruct one another" (Romans 15:14).

Expectations question 3: Are the expectations placed on the offender reasonable?

Even if your expectations of someone are (1) legitimate and (2) clearly understood by them, your expectations may not necessarily be reasonable all the time. Before you take offense or want to correct a person, ask yourself these kinds of questions:

- Did you expect them to do too much in too little time?
- Did you expect them to act beyond their level of natural or spiritual maturity?
- Did you consider any emotional or physical hindrances that might have prevented them from meeting your expectation at that time?
- Was your expectation reasonable in the context of other legitimate expectations on them from you and/or others?

- Might there have been special circumstances that contributed to their not meeting your expectations?
- How reasonable was your expectation of the offender? To answer that question, put yourself in their place. Try to understand their context.

Expectations question 4: Are the expectations placed on the offender loving toward them?

I assume that when you hurt, disappoint, or irritate another person, you want them to give you some grace and give you the "benefit of the doubt" before they show you your fault. You want them to be sure their expectations are legitimate, clearly understood, and reasonable before they come to talk to you.

I also assume you want their expectations of you to be loving. Therefore, your expectations of them should be loving, too.

Here are three biblical examples of loving expectations.

- You would want them to have the same expectations of you if your positions were reversed. Treat other people like you want to be treated. This is the Golden Rule in Matthew 7:12.
- Your expectations of them would not include insisting on your own way (1 Corinthians 13:5).
- Your expectations of them would consider them more significant than yourself, and you would have in mind their interests over yours (Philippians 2:3–4).

So, when you are analyzing an offense someone has done to you, the loving thing to do is to ask yourself questions like these:

- *Even if my expectation of them is legitimate, clearly understood, and reasonable, would I want them to have that expectation of me, if our roles were reversed?*
- *Am I insisting on my own way?*
- *Am I considering them more significant than myself and thinking of their interests over mine?*

Q: What if my expectations of the offender do not pass the test of all four of these questions?

You can rejoice that you showed love to the offender and yourself by prayerfully and thoughtfully looking at the problem with biblical light. You can be encouraged that by taking the time to analyze and question the expectations you placed on them, you avoided these possible situations:

- Having an awkward conversation with the person
- The temptation of wrongly judging them
- The temptation to develop a bitter spirit toward them

If you are in the offended role and you realize your expectations of the offender do not meet all four criteria, you have two options. Whichever of these two options you choose, you will have completed the Peace Pursuit *Analyze* step in your role as offended for this particular relational problem.

When your expectations do not meet the four criteria

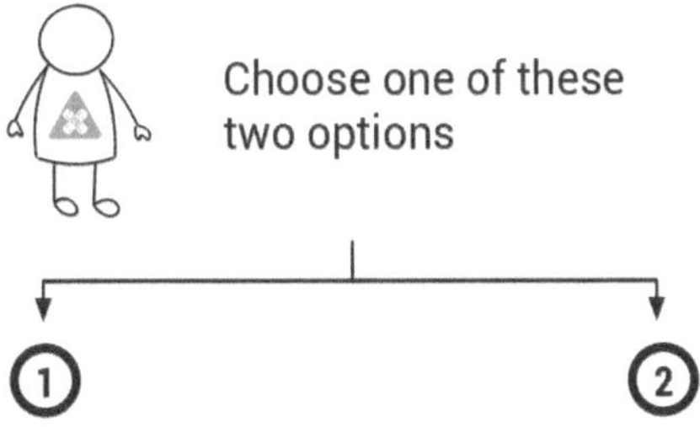

In your mind and heart, you can adjust your expectations of the person so those expectations fit these four criteria:

- Legitimate
- Clearly understood by them
- Reasonable
- Loving toward them

You can carry on your relationship with the person without talking to them about your sense of offense at this time.

You can have a calm conversation with the person about clarifying your expectations for your relationship with them.

This would not be a "peacemaking" conversation. You would simply have a talk with them for the purpose of making your relationship grow and work more smoothly.

If you choose option 2, you could introduce that conversation by saying something like this:

> *"Patrick, I've been thinking about our relationship [or 'how we work together']. Could we meet and talk about some things that have come to my mind? I just want us to clarify*

that we have the same understanding of expectations for each other."

If you consider yourself in the initiator role and at Stage One you realize your expectations of the supposed offender do not meet the four criteria, you need to be careful what you decide to do next. Normally, you would not talk with the offender about the situation. Your role is probably finished in this case.

Q: What if I believe my expectations are legitimate, clearly understood, reasonable, and loving?

If you have just one or two offenses you want to have a conversation about, go to the *Evaluate* step or the *Take the plank out of your eye* step of Stage One.

However, if you have let offenses build up over time and you have more than a few in mind, take time to organize your thoughts. You don't want to overwhelm the offender with an unnecessary number of offenses or too much detail. You also don't want the offender to be able to say to you, "It looks like you have been like the 'sin police' keeping a long list of my offenses. The Bible says, 'Love keeps no record of wrongs'!"

- List the offenses under the categories of words, actions, inactions, and reactions.
- Try to combine the offenses into subjects or themes. For example, "Ways I feel disrespected by you in public" or "Things you do and don't do that show you aren't keeping your commitment to our partnership (or work agreement, etc.)."
- If you have a number of examples of the same theme, choose which two or three examples might be clearest and easiest for the other person to understand when you bring them up.
- After you have grouped the offenses into topics or themes, ask yourself, "Which of these are the most important for me to talk about?" Then list them in order of priority. This will help you focus and prepare you for the next step of Stage One.

Here is what these two choices look like:

When your expectations meet the four criteria

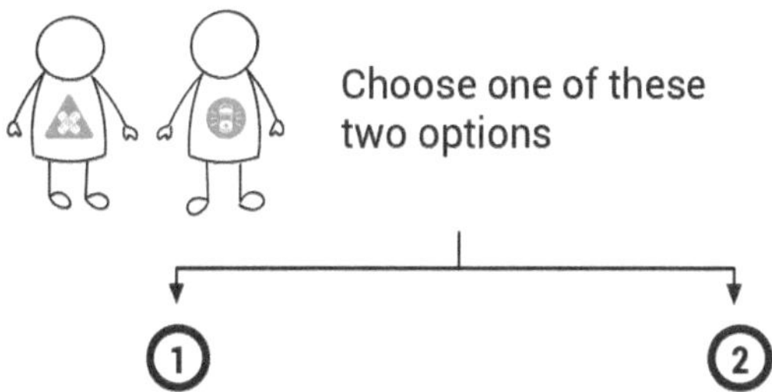

1. You only have one or two offenses you want to talk about.

Move on to another step of Stage One, such as *Evaluate* or *Take the plank out of your eye*.

2. You have a fairly long list of offenses you want to bring up with the offender.

- List the offenses under the headings of words, actions, inactions, and reactions.
- Combine the offenses into subjects or themes.
- Choose two or three clear examples.
- Prioritize these examples in the order you want to talk about them.

Q: I know that a person took offense at something I did. But I've analyzed the issue, and I don't think what I did was "sin." Now what?

Let's say you and Maria were in a meeting yesterday. During the meeting, you expressed your opinion about something. You later noticed that Maria started treating you differently than normal. You went through the *Analyze* point of Stage One in the offender role and you decided that neither what you said nor how you said it could be considered a sin according to the Bible. Since it is clear to you that Maria has "something against you" (Matthew 5:23), you should meet with God and complete the rest of the steps of Stage One. I advise you to consider having a Stage Two conversation with her.

You could start a Stage Two conversation with Maria like this:

> *YOU: Maria, I noticed that yesterday morning we seemed to be communicating normally. Then, during our meeting I expressed my opinion about what I thought should be done. For the rest of the day, it seemed like you were not smiling at me and you seemed to be avoiding eye contact with me. I'm just wondering, is there something you would like to talk about regarding what I said in the meeting?*

If you approach Maria like this, you could open the door for her to explain why her demeanor changed during your meeting. She might say that yes, she was offended or upset and you can discuss the issue calmly and rationally.

Or, she may say, "No, nothing's wrong." This may be true. Or, she may really be offended but for some reason, she does not want to admit that to you. In either case, I believe you will have done what you could to make peace with her (Romans 12:18). At this point, you could be proactive and affirm your relationship with her by saying something like, "Maria, I value our relationship and hope that we can talk together when we perceive that we aren't both understanding a situation in the same way."

Q: What if I am convinced my offense was actually my reaction to what the other person did to me first?

You have two choices here. Let's say your relational problem is with Jacob.

1. After you complete the other steps of Stage One, your first option is simply to confess your part in the relational problem and not refer to the offenses you feel Jacob has done to you. Here's an example of how you could start that Stage Two conversation:

    > *"Jacob, I'd like for us to talk about our relationship. I want to confess that when we interacted the other day, I demonstrated impatience, I spoke inappropriately, and I acted disrespectfully towards you. I take full responsibility for my words and actions."*

    If Jacob doesn't want to talk with you, you can rest in the fact that you put yourself in the offender role and tried to make peace with him.

    If Jacob does consent to talk with you, he might forgive you and conclude that part of your conversation. Or, he might forgive you and then voluntarily admit some or all of his part in the relational problem. In my experience, this is what normally happens among sincere Jesus followers.

2. Your second option after you complete Stage One is to have a talk with Jacob when you plan to confess your fault to him and bring up his offenses toward you in the same conversation. This option takes much careful thought and choice of words.

Let's say you apologized to Jacob like the example above:

> *"Jacob, I'd like for us to talk about our relationship. I want to confess that when we interacted the other day, I demonstrated impatience, I spoke inappropriately, and I acted disrespectfully towards you. I take full responsibility for my words and actions."*

If Jacob doesn't volunteer to apologize for his part, you could say:

> *"May I talk with you about the situation we were in at the time I offended you?"*

Jacob could answer yes or no to your question. If he says yes, then you could explain your perspective of the problem in the offended role, and give Jacob an opportunity to respond. This could lead you to appropriate confession and forgiveness with Jacob.

However, you need to be aware that if you choose this option, Jacob could feel that you have apologized in order to manipulate him into confessing something, even if that was not your motive.

See *The offender role at Stage Two* in Chapter 7 for more about this type of conversation.

Evaluate

ROLES INVOLVED

PURPOSE
To weigh the seriousness of the offense or offenses as you decide whether to have a conversation with the supposed offender.

KEY QUESTIONS
Is the offense serious enough to talk about with the offender?
Should you, or can you, overlook it this time?

The biblical qualities of love, patience, and discernment are essential when you evaluate a relational problem. You don't want to be fussy about every little offense. You also don't want to miss a chance to rescue a person who is caught up in a serious sin.

How to decide whether to have a conversation with the offender

Here are some practical questions you can ask to decide if the offense is serious enough to bring up to the offender. The more serious the offense, the less likely you should overlook it.

- How might the person's words or behavior negatively affect themselves physically or spiritually?
- Might this behavior lead them into further temptation?

- How might other people be negatively affected by the offender's words or behavior?
- Are there people you could protect from being hurt by the offender in the future if you address the offender's fault now?
- How might this offense hurt the offender's reputation or their relationships with others? For example, are other people avoiding them because of this offense?
- If the offender claims to be a follower of Jesus, what would people who don't follow Jesus think of his or her behavior?
- Is their behavior a bad example that might lead other Jesus followers to stumble?
- Is this offense a one-time event they committed under stress or extraordinary circumstances, or can you see a habitual, repeated pattern in the offender's life?
- Can you use biblical terms to describe the offense as sin?

Q. What does it mean to overlook an offense?

To overlook someone's offense toward you means that you will forgive them in your heart before God for that offense and then decide that you will not converse with them about it.

Overlooking does not mean that you deny that the person committed the offense. On the contrary, before you can overlook the offense, you need to analyze it to identify if it is biblically defined sin, or a simple communication problem, or a personality difference. If you determine that the offense is sin, you forgive it and then process the decision to either overlook it or have a conversation with the offender about it.

Q: If the offense is clearly a sin, shouldn't I always have a conversation with the offender about it?

All sin is serious, and if the offense is clearly defined as a sin in the Bible, then you need to take it seriously. You also should evaluate it in the light of a number of scriptural principles.

Bible verses that encourage you to overlook an offense

The Bible connects the principles of love, honor, and wisdom with your choice not to react or respond when you are offended. These verses point you toward overlooking when you are insulted or provoked or offended.

- The famous "love chapter" of 1 Corinthians 13 teaches that love is not easily angered (NIV), irritated (ESV), or provoked (NASB), and does not keep account of wrongdoing (1 Corinthians 13:5b).

- Proverbs 12:16 says, "Fools show their annoyance at once, but the prudent overlook an insult" (NIV).
- Proverbs 19:11 equates glory with overlooking an offense.
- The Apostle Peter reminds you that deep love covers a multitude of sins (1 Peter 4:8).

Bible verses that encourage you to have a conversation with the offender

A number of Bible verses prompt you to talk with the one who has offended or sinned against you or another person.

- Galatians 6:1–2 tells you to gently restore those caught in a sin, which assumes you would need to have one or more conversations that would lead to their restoration.
- Leviticus 19:17 exhorts you to rebuke / reprove / reason frankly with your neighbor so that you will not share in his guilt.
- The last verses of the book of James (5:19–20) promise that if you turn a sinner from the error of his way, you will save him from death—and cover a multitude of sins.
- Luke 17:3 says to rebuke someone if they sin.
- Probably the most quoted verse when Christians offend each other is Matthew 18:15: "If your brother sins [some translations add 'against you'], go and show him his fault..." (NASB).

If you believe you should have a conversation with the offender, keep in mind that your attitude and the way you talk with them are as important as your decision to go or not. That's why you should meet with God and complete all the steps of Stage One for your role.

Bible verses that encourage you to proceed with caution

You could say that the two sets of verses above are the "go" and "don't go" verses. Here are a couple of "proceed with caution" verses.

- A key caution verse is Matthew 7:12: "Do to others what you would would have them to do to you" (NIV). If you were caught up in a serious sin or were stumbling toward a cliff, of course you would want someone to hold you back and gently restore you, wouldn't you? But, if one time you let slip a stray word that hurts someone, or if you neglect to do something expected of you one time because of busyness, you don't want someone to nit-pick at you about it. So, treat others in the same way.
- Another relevant passage is Philippians 2:2–4. Quite simply, consider others' interests more important than your own. If having a

conversation with the offender is in their best interest, out of love for them you can proceed with caution and arrange a time to talk with them. Don't forget to complete the other points of Stage One first.

Q: Isn't it easier for everyone if I just overlook the offense?

The easiest thing isn't always the right thing or the most loving thing. Remember, you want to treat the offender as you would want to be treated if you were in their shoes. Of course, you would want someone to overlook a small, infrequent fault of yours. On the other hand, if you were caught up in a habitual and serious sin, you would want someone to help you out of it and restore you. Or, if you hurt someone but didn't know it, you would like to hear about it so you could work to restore your relationship with that person.

Besides, overlooking isn't always easy. As one of our workshop attendees pointed out, if you choose to overlook a sin, you are still committed to forgive that person in your heart. You can't hold it against them, and you commit not to bring it up to them later in a moment of frustration or anger. That may be more of a challenge for you than to have a calm, respectful Stage Two conversation with them about the problem now.

Q: What if I decide not to talk with the offender, but later I feel that was the wrong decision?

If you decide not to approach someone even though you answered yes to many of the questions in the *Evaluate* step, just be patient. If it is a habit, they will most likely commit a similar offense again, and you will have another opportunity to love the offender by having a conversation with them about it.

On the other hand, if you find that you begin to distance yourself from the person, you should process Stage One again.

In the offended role, after you process the *Evaluate* step, you will lean toward either having a Stage Two conversation with the offender, or toward overlooking the offense this time. In either case, you need to forgive the offender in your heart before God.

Now, go to the *Forgive* step if you haven't been there already. If you have forgiven the offender, I recommend you keep meeting with God and choose which step of Stage One you want to work on next.

In the initiator role, you will lean one of two ways after you have evaluated the problem.

- You could lean toward preparing to have a conversation with the offender. In that case, you should continue to meet with God before you talk with the offender. Choose which step of Stage One you think would be most helpful for you to process next and go there.
- Or, you will decide not to talk with the offender about this offense at this time. In that case, go to the *Consider your responsibility* step before you finally decide not to have a Stage Two conversation with the offender. After that, entrust the situation to the Lord and do not dwell on it.

Take the plank out of your eye

ROLES INVOLVED

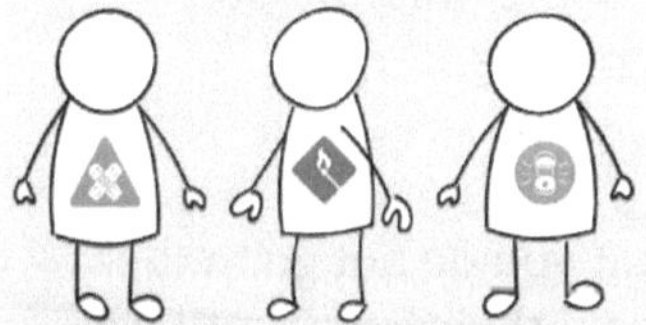

PURPOSE

To uncover anything in you that might hinder you from seeing the relational problem accurately.

KEY QUESTIONS

How might you have contributed to the problem?

What might be in your heart or mind that could hinder you from seeing yourself or the other person objectively and from God's perspective?

How might the other party interpret the facts of the situation?

The familiar phrase "Take the plank out of your own eye" (NIV) comes from Matthew 7:3–5, where Jesus warns his disciples against wrongly judging others. He creates the picture of a hypocrite with a large plank in his eye trying to pick the speck out of another person's eye. You've probably heard similar sayings like "When you point your finger at someone, you've got three fingers pointing to yourself" and "The pot shouldn't call the kettle black."

A "plank" (or "log" or "beam") in your own eye can be anything that keeps you from seeing the other person or the conflict from their side or from God's perspective. Here are some common planks people can have in their eyes. Pray and think if any of these describe you in this situation.

- Prejudice
- Envy or jealousy
- Unnecessary fear
- Unjustified or irrational anger
- Being overly sensitive
- A feeling of injury greater than the offense would normally give to others
- Wrongly taking offense
- Having unrealistic expectations of the other person
- Calling something a sin that the Bible doesn't
- Taking offense for another person

I strongly suggest that you do not go to the offender to "show them their fault" until you have removed from your own eyes any wrong belief about God, yourself, or the offender. You will likely make the relational problem worse. Or, you might start a new conflict. A coach may be able to help you see that your reaction to an offender's behavior might reveal a need for you to grow in grace, truth, and forgiveness, and that you should not have a Stage Two conversation with the offender.

Some say that when Jesus speaks of the plank in your eye, he is referring to the same type of offense you believe the offender committed. For example, some say that if you lie more frequently or more seriously than the lie you want to point out in the offender, you've got a plank in your eye. This implies that you have little moral ground to stand on and you would be a hypocrite to show your brother his fault (the "speck" in his eye).

You may say to yourself, "I'm not perfect. Who am I to show him his fault?" But Jesus says to get the plank out of your own eye *so that* you can help get the speck out of your brother's eye. Both of you remain visually impaired if you leave either the plank in your eye or the speck in your sibling's eye. Thank God and rejoice that this relational problem has provided the opportunity for both of you to clear out your eyes so you can both see better.

If you are in the role of offended or initiator and have started Stage One with the *Analyze* and *Evaluate* points, you've been focused on what you think the offender did wrong. Maybe your list of the offender's faults and sins has gotten longer the more you think about the conflict. Getting the plank out of your own eye brings you back to looking at yourself.

Here's a true story to illustrate what I mean. Franklin had been in a painful conflict with George for some years. Franklin asked me to be his Peace Pursuit coach. Franklin identified himself in the offended role. The hurts and offenses Franklin felt were deep and many. As Franklin processed the *Analyze* step, he wrote a list of sins and offenses he felt George had done to him, complete with Bible references. It was three pages long.

Then Franklin moved to the *Take the plank out of your eye* step. When he finished this step, he came to our coaching time and humbly confessed, "When I asked God to show me my own planks, I started writing them down. My own list of planks turned out to be longer than my list of George's faults!" This was a huge breakthrough in the Peace Pursuit process, and resulted in a beautiful reconciliation.

To see if you have planks in your eye, go back to the *Analyze* step, this time looking at yourself. Review your words, actions, inactions, and reactions in the light of the "one-another" verses and God's expectations for you in your life roles (husband, wife, child, employer, employee, leader, and so on).

Here's another clue to uncovering planks in your own eyes: sometimes what you are offended by might have been the other person's reaction to something you did or failed to do first. I do not mean that in every relational problem you should automatically say, "I must have done something wrong to them." I am simply recommending that you ask yourself, "Is it possible that I have done (or not done) something that sparked that response in them?"

Even if you are in the offender role, you should complete this step as well. You might have planks in your eye that either keep you from clearly seeing the extent or seriousness of your offense, or that hinder your ability to see the problem from the other person's perspective.

Judge rightly

ROLES INVOLVED

PURPOSE

To make sure you treat yourself and the all other parties without prejudice or partiality.

KEY QUESTIONS

Have you pre-judged or made conclusions about any of the parties without the facts?

Are you partial toward any of the parties?

Have you either denied or exaggerated the truth about any legitimate offenses?

Have you applied equal amounts of grace and truth to all parties?

Certain Bible passages warn you not to judge others, such as Matthew 7:1–2, Romans 2:1–3, and Romans 14:1–12. I understand these passages to mean you should not judge in these circumstances:

- If you judge with wrong motives.
- If you judge without hearing all relevant facts.

- If you judge someone for the same thing that you do but you don't confess or repent of it.
- If you judge a person's whole character in general based on one or two small offenses.
- If you do not have some legitimate authority that gives you responsibility to judge that person's behavior in an appropriate context.

When I named this step *Judge rightly*, I had those same warnings in mind, and more.

At the same time, every person in any Peace Pursuit role needs to strive to be spiritually mature as described in Hebrews 5:14: "Those who have their powers of discernment trained by constant practice to distinguish good from evil." To judge rightly means to discern between good and evil, neither denying nor exaggerating the truth about any legitimate offenses by any party.

Beware of prejudice or partiality toward yourself or any other party

To be prejudiced literally means you "judge before" you have the facts. Being partial means you are biased toward one party or you treat that party better than another. Here are some examples of prejudicial statements you might hear from people.

- "You are probably right about him. After all, he's a man isn't he?"
- "She acted just like women do in that situation."
- "If you say he used abusive speech, he probably did. All leaders do that kind of thing."
- "What else would you expect from a teenager?"
- "Everybody from his country acts like that."
- "You should never trust what any person in that profession says."
- "People from that generation are all the same."

These statements are biased and prejudiced. They put millions of innocent men, women, leaders, and teenagers in the same baskets, as if all men, women, leaders, and teenagers are the same.

To help yourself avoid prejudice, you should measure the actual words, actions, inactions, and reactions of an individual person according to biblical and other legitimate expectations. When you judge rightly, you won't automatically look at that person in a negative light, even if they happen to be a man, a woman, a leader, a teenager, or a citizen of any given country.

How can you avoid the sin of partiality? Envision yourself in the place of the other person or persons in the relational problem. How would you want to be viewed and treated if you were in their shoes? Then, keep in mind the wise saying, "There's always another side to the story." The Bible also reminds you, "The one who states his case first seems right, until the other comes and examines him" (Proverbs 18:17).

Understand how personality, culture, and spiritual gifting can affect the creation and resolution of relational problems

The *Five Pillars of Peace Pursuit* in Chapter 2 of this handbook explain our fundamental approach to resolving relational problems among Jesus followers. Here is Pillar 3: "Treat everyone as a unique person created and loved by God." God has created each person with a unique blend of personality, culture, and spiritual gifting.

Let me caution you that there are two mistakes you can make when you consider the influence of personality and culture on the causes of conflict. The first is to give them too much weight. The second is to ignore them.

A ministry leader with decades of experience once said to me, "I believe that all conflicts come from personality differences." I am fully aware how different personality traits and cultural values can both create conflict and hinder its resolution, but I don't agree with the absolute nature of this statement. I briefly explain the connection between expectations and culture in the *Analyze* step of Stage One.

When you pursue peace, learn as much as you can about the other party's personality, temperament, and culture. However, here is another caution. Some offenders hinder the Peace Pursuit process by rejecting the light that an offended person, or initiator, or coach is trying to shine into their lives. They use their individual personality or culture as a "trump card" to end the process. They say things like these:

- "I just acted according to the personality type God gave me. You have no right to judge me."
- "You don't understand. We do things differently than you do in your culture."
- "You can't say that I sinned simply because your personality is different from mine. What about Peace Pursuit Pillar 3: Treat everyone as a unique person created and loved by God"?

Situations like these are the reason we also have Peace Pursuit Pillar 4: "Treat everyone alike, without prejudice or partiality." This means we analyze and measure every unique individual's own words, actions, inactions, and reactions by the same biblical standards that are expected of every other unique individual in a similar situation. I recommend that you review the *Analyze* step of Stage One when personality and/or culture become hindrances to peacemaking. I also address the topic of culture in Chapter 7.

As for spiritual gifting, you can see examples of the variety of spiritual gifts in these Bible passages: Romans 12:3–8, Ephesians 4:11–12, 1 Corinthians 12:4–31, and 1 Peter 4:10–11.

Ironically, your spiritual gifts can make a relational problem worse, if you expect every other person to see an issue exactly as you do. People with the gift of exhorting or teaching can tend to focus on correcting thoughts and behavior that are wrong, but they might be short on compassion. Those with the gift of mercy can tend to overlook thoughts and behavior that really should be brought to light and addressed.

If your situation involves some aspect of personality or cultural difference, you could look for a coach who has a similar personality or culture to the other party, helping you view the other party with objective, impartial eyes.

Remember your own personal tendency toward truth or grace as you pursue peace

Jesus was full of both grace and truth (John 1:14), but few of us are full of both. When it comes to pursuing peace, each of us can tend to lean toward one or the other. Which of these describes you best?

You Lean Toward Grace	You Lean Toward Truth
Maybe you are cautious about rushing in to resolve relational problems. You might have gifts in mercy or compassion.	Maybe you are quick to resolve relational problems. You might have gifts in prophecy, teaching, or exhortation.
You emphasize that we are to be patient, to forgive one another, and to bear with one another.	Jesus said the truth will set you free and you know that people in a conflict are not free. You want to release them.
You know that love covers a multitude of sins. You practice love that is not easily provoked or angered and does not keep a record of wrongs.	You see that unforgiveness and unconfessed sin destroy the unity of the body of Christ. You want to protect that unity.
You believe the best about all of the parties involved.	You know that even mature Jesus followers can sin.
You are careful not to judge wrongly.	You know you have authority to judge right from wrong.
As a result of all of the above, sometimes you may be tempted not to judge at all, even when you should.	As a result of all of the above, sometimes you can judge too quickly in your haste to expose the truth.

Try to be full of both grace and truth toward all parties, all the time. I'm not saying this is easy. To be honest, I've noticed that when I am in the offended role, I tend to want 100 percent truth applied to the offender, and when I am in the offender role, I tend to want 100 percent grace applied to me. That's why I aspire to meet with God and process Stage One myself when I have any role in a relational problem. Stage One helps me look at myself and the other party with equal amounts of grace and truth.

Consider your own personal tendency to admonish, encourage, or help

I wrote this in the Introduction (Chapter 1): "There's a folk proverb that says, 'If your only tool is a hammer, you see everything as a nail.' For some Christians, Matthew 18:15 ['go and tell him his fault'] is their hammer, and the offender is the nail.... Peace Pursuit is...a craftsman's case full of biblical tools you choose to use according to the need of each person at any given moment." 1 Thessalonians 5:14 is one of those tools: "We urge you, brethren, admonish the unruly, encourage the fainthearted, help the weak, be patient with everyone" (NASB).

Here the Bible describes three types of people, and gives three ways to react to them. What you should do appears to be simple. If they are unruly, you admonish them. If they are fainthearted, you encourage them. If they are weak, you help them by strengthening them in the area in which they are weak. In every case, you are to be patient with the other person.

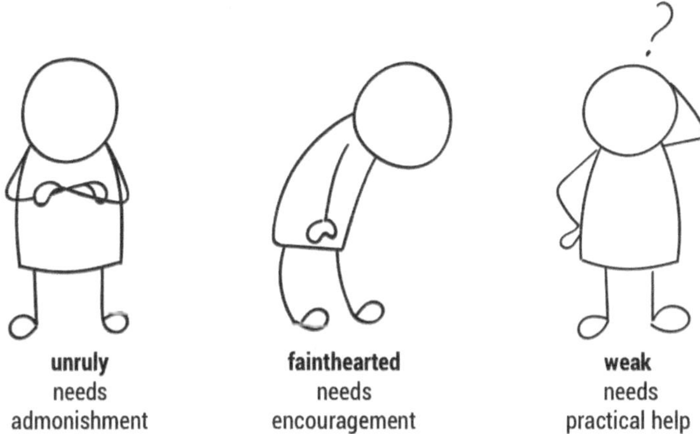

unruly
needs
admonishment

fainthearted
needs
encouragement

weak
needs
practical help

Earlier I suggested that your natural temperament, personality, culture, and spiritual gifting can affect how you pursue peace. This combination of your traits has also possibly given you a default tendency to admonish, or encourage, or help an offender. Think about your natural or default approach to offenders. Are you primarily an admonisher, an encourager, or a helper?

It's important to know that on any given day, a person can be a combination of unruly, fainthearted, or weak. One or more of those conditions can lead to their failing to meet your expectations of them. In other words, their unruliness, their discouragement, or their weakness (or some combination of the three) can put them in the offender role. If you want to judge rightly, you will need to be patient and loving enough to discern what the offender needs most at the moment. Right now, do they mostly need admonishment, encouragement, or help?

This illustration shows how an individual can have differing amounts of unruliness, discouragement, and weakness.

I have found that an offender is often not just purely and willfully unruly. Take me for example. Sometimes I sin against others out of pride or stubborn will. But, sometimes I commit sins of omission (inactions) because I am timid, or fainthearted, or discouraged in that time and context. Or, there are occasions when I don't do what I am supposed to do because I am weak; I'm not equipped or skilled or strong enough to meet others' legitimate expectations of me at that time. Or, I am just not sure what I am supposed to do. Thankfully, my wife and others in my community patiently discern with me whether I need correction, encouragement, or help in a given situation.

Let's say your default tendency is to admonish. By definition, a person who has been unruly, disorderly, or out of line is an offender to some extent and 1 Thessalonians 5:14 instructs you to warn or admonish him. However, let's say he has not acted appropriately because he is primarily discouraged. If you only admonish him, you will possibly discourage him even more. You might even crush his spirit. Or, if an offender has fallen out of line because of weakness, and you only admonish him, he will likely repeat the offense unless you or someone else actually gives him practical help.

On the other hand, let's say your natural default tendency is to encourage. If an offender is willfully unruly, and you only encourage him, he will likely continue to be undisciplined. (A word of caution: I've noticed that unruly and undisciplined people are attracted to leaders or counselors who they know tend to be generous in giving empathy, compassion, and encouragement, but who rarely admonish.)

Or, maybe your tendency is to say, "Offenders just need some practical help and training to overcome their weakness." That may be true. But, if you only offer practical help to an offender who is willfully unruly, and you don't admonish that person when needed, that practical help is not likely to be effective.

Whether you are in the offended role or the initiator role, the point here is for you to be patient with the offender long enough to understand what they need most at this time. Are they mostly unruly, mostly discouraged, or mostly weak? Don't just default to your natural tendency to admonish, encourage, or help. Be patient and love the offender enough to give them what is needed at the moment.

Repent of your part

ROLES INVOLVED

PURPOSE

To confess and show contrition to God for any sin of yours that is part of the relational problem before you have a conversation with the other person. This step also prepares you to confess your part to the other person appropriately.

KEY QUESTIONS

How might you have contributed to the problem?

Are you prepared to repent to God for any offense that might be yours in this situation?

Are you ready to confess appropriately to the other party all offenses you know you have done or might have done to them?

Christians aren't the only people in the world who see the value of confessing faults. If you do an internet search for topics like "how to apologize at work," you'll see that secular professors and consultants advise business people and politicians to be sincere, truthful, and prompt in making confessions. It turns out to be good for public relations.

Of course, as followers of Jesus, we have even more significant reasons to apologize with thought and care. Confession is such a fundamental part of the peace process that I will go into some detail in this step.

Q: *Do you make a distinction between confession and repentance? You call this step of Stage One* Repent of your part*, yet you define peace at Stage Two as appropriate confession and forgiveness.*

The Bible word translated as confess means to agree, admit, and/or acknowledge fault. So, when I confess to the person I offended, I agree, admit, and acknowledge as much as I understand that I have hurt them or sinned against them.

Repentance includes more than words of confession. The Bible word translated as "repent" means to change my mind and heart so that my outer behavior will become the opposite of the offense I am repenting of. When I repent to God at Stage One, I admit to him what I did wrong and I show genuine remorse for my sin against him and the person I offended. In 2 Corinthians 7:8–11, godly sorrow is described as a sorrow that leads to deep repentance, which in turn produces godly thoughts, motivations, and behavior.

At Stage One, I communicate to God my intention to change my mind, heart and behavior, and to make amends for what I did. I sincerely ask God to help me change. If necessary, I will even make a plan and have someone hold me accountable to carry out my amends.

Ephesians 4:22–32 describes this process of change as putting off our old self and putting on our new self as we are "renewed in the spirit of [our] minds" (v. 23). If I have been a liar, I will become a truth teller. If I have been a thief, I will become a worker who contributes to others. If I have been a person who tears others down with my words, I will become one who encourages others with timely, grace-filled speech (vs. 25–29).

So, you could say that repentance is "confession plus deeds." Confessing, saying sorry, or apologizing are verbal acknowledgments of my offense. Those are good steps toward repairing the relational damage I have done. However, if I am truly remorseful for what I did, I will continue the renewal process so that my sorrow for sin won't just remain words.

I see the concept of "confession plus deeds" in the scene from Matthew 3:6–8. People from Jerusalem and surrounding areas came to John the Baptist "and they were baptized by him in the river Jordan, confessing their sins." John discerned that some people verbally confessed their sins without the intention in their heart to follow their words with appropriate action. He exhorted them to "bear fruit in keeping with repentance."

As you'll see below, I suggest that a well-rounded confession to the other person at Stage Two will go beyond simply admitting fault and will include elements to show you are sorry and contrite. You will also see that I think that it is appropriate to verbalize your intention to change and make amends for your offense, if that is possible. When you combine all of these concepts into an apology to the offended person at Stage Two, you could call it "agreeing about my offense and expressing intent to change."

Here's what this looks like on the "Bounce of Peace" diagram you saw earlier. The downward trajectory of the relationship stops with the exchange of confession and forgiveness. Then begins the process of repairing the relationship through bearing fruit of repentance and increasing love and trust.

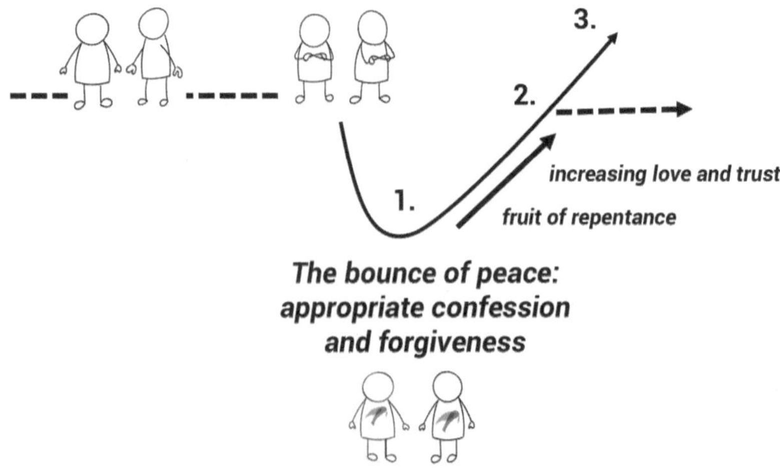

The bounce of peace: appropriate confession and forgiveness

Q: What about terms like apologize, say sorry, and ask for forgiveness? Are they the same as making a confession?

I have heard Christians use the terms *apologize*, *say sorry*, and *ask forgiveness* as synonyms for making a confession. There is so much overlap in the popular understanding of these terms I decided to use them interchangeably in this handbook. Maybe you are like me and choose to use one term or another depending on whether the context is legal, religious, formal, or informal and whether the person you are admitting your fault to is a follower of Jesus or not.

Your macro culture might even influence which word you use. I've noticed that Americans tend to apologize while the British tend to say sorry.

Honesty, humility, and honor: the motives that produce a good confession

A good apology is not just a collection of carefully crafted words. Let's say you create a perfectly worded confession complete with every element I describe below, but your motives are not right. The offended person will probably notice your wrong attitude from your timing, your tone of voice, or your body language. That won't lead you to peace.

On the other hand, if your motives and heart attitudes are right, the offended person will sense how sorry you are, even if you don't include all the basic elements or say just the right words in your apology.

As you prepare your confession, ask yourself the three questions below. They are like the three legs of a stool. You need them all for your apology to stand strong. You will see these same principles of honesty, humility and honor from a different perspective in the *Forgive* step of Stage One.

How can I show honesty about what I did (or didn't do)?

This is about the offense, whether it is something you committed or omitted. Be truthful about it. "...let each one of you speak the truth with his neighbor, for we are members one of another" (Ephesians 4:25b). Call it what it really is, no more, no less. If what you did can be described with Bible terms as sin, call it sin. Don't say it was just a mistake or slip-up.

How can I humble myself?

This is about you, as the offender. Do you want grace from God and from the one you offended? God promises he will give you grace when you humble yourself: "Clothe yourselves, all of you, with humility toward one another, for 'God opposes the proud, but gives grace to the humble'" (1 Peter 5:5b). God will give you grace, even if the offended person doesn't.

Humility is different than humiliation. When you confess, I do not mean for you to humiliate yourself, or to put yourself in a situation where you could be cruelly humiliated by the offended person or anyone else.

How can I honor the person I offended?

This is about the person you hurt or offended. Think hard about the emotional and practical effect your offense had on them. Ask God for wisdom how to acknowledge those effects to the one you offended and how you could repair the damage you caused them. "Outdo one another in showing honor" (Romans 12:10b).

Q: How long should my apology be?

There is no perfect length that makes one apology better than another. It depends on the nature of your offense, how serious the offended person has taken it, and so on. When you bump into someone in a busy market, you automatically say, "Sorry," or "Excuse me" and usually that's enough. On the other hand, some famous people have felt the need to publish their autobiographies which amount to book-length confessions.

Q: Why should I carefully prepare my apology?

Think of a time when someone apologized to you, but their confession just didn't seem right, or even made you feel more hurt or offended. Was it the words they said (or didn't say)? Was it their tone of voice or facial expressions? Was it too quick or too slow? Was it the wrong time or wrong place? Did you feel it was it so poorly done that it would have been better if they hadn't apologized at all?

It's better to wait to apologize until you have prepared your heart. If you have godly sorrow that leads to repentance (2 Corinthians 7:10), you'll take the time, thought, and effort to prepare so that your words of apology will give grace to the one who hears them.

Here are some situations that indicate you are probably not yet ready to apologize. If your heart attitude is like any of these, you probably need to work on your motives of honesty, humility, and honor before you go to Stage Two.

- When you don't truly mean it. Even if you are trying to make the offended feel better, don't add the sin of lying or deception to whatever your original offense was.
- When you are just trying to relieve your conscience.
- When you are simply doing it out of duty, or because you "have to," or to "tick a box."

- When you just want to be done with the subject and move on. A confession should open the door for more discussion between you and the offended, not shut it down.
- When you just want to impress someone else that you are a spiritually mature person.
- When your intention is to manipulate the other party to make an apology to you.
- When you want to shift attention from your offense to the offended person's obligation to forgive you.
- When you want to use a so-called confession to show the person you think they wrongly took offense.

If you have any of these or similar questionable motives, I don't recommend apologizing until your motives are as pure as you can make them. See the *Search Your Heart* step of Stage One.

Some basic ingredients of a well-rounded confession

When you apologize or when you say sorry, you want to be honest about the offense, to humble yourself, and to honor the offended. The *way* you communicate these principles can vary according to the situation and the individual you have offended.

Without being rigid or legalistic, below are some ingredients I've found helpful to include in a confession to apply the principles of honesty, humility, and honor. Think of these as ingredients in a recipe that can vary depending on the situation. You might know of others you could add to the recipe. Or, think of them as individual flowers in a bouquet. The vase may still look beautiful even if one or two flowers are missing. Below, I'll expand on each element of the list.

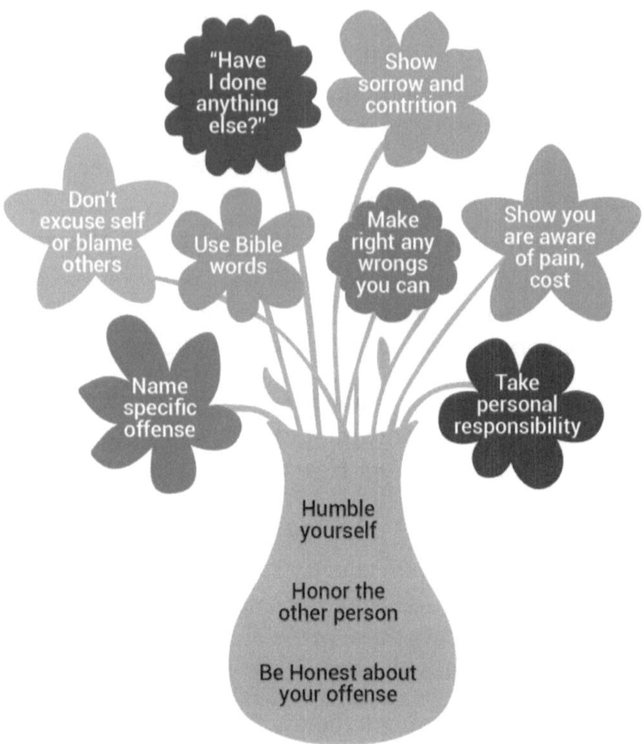

- Use Bible words, not euphemisms, when you confess sin.
- Take personal responsibility.
- Don't excuse yourself or blame others or circumstances.
- Name the specific offense(s).
- Communicate that you have a contrite spirit.
- Demonstrate that you feel, or that you are at least aware of the pain your offense caused the offended and what it cost them.
- Ask the offended, "Is there something else I did or didn't do that you want to explain to me?"
- Make right any wrongs you can.

Use Bible words, not euphemisms, when you confess sin

A euphemism is a mild, indirect, or vague term used in place of words that seem harsh, blunt, or offensive. When confessing your sins, don't use euphemisms. Jesus died for our harsh, blunt, and offensive sins, not for our mild, indirect, or vague euphemisms.

Why use Bible words? Biblical language unifies Jesus followers all across the world. I am re-convinced of this every time we are invited to train Christians in countries where we don't speak the local language. When we confine our teaching as much as possible to Bible words, our trainees know we are simply reminding them of the universal truth of God's word. They are confident that we are not imposing a "Western" cultural norm on them.

The discipline of learning to use Bible words keeps your focus on the unchanging Word of God and constantly renews your faith in its transforming power (2 Timothy 3:15–16, Hebrews 4:12, Isaiah 55:11).

Using Bible words helps protect you from the temptation to soften or hide the truth in your confession. For example, let's say you want to confess that you included untrue information in a report. Instead of saying, "I'm sorry I exaggerated," you should use Bible words like "I was dishonest," "I lied to you," or "I tried to deceive you."

When you use Bible words for sin in your confessions, others are less likely to brush off or minimize your repentance and say, "That's OK," or "No worries." The person you offended can then use Bible words when they forgive you for your sin. They can respond, "I forgive you for deceiving me." Or, "I forgive you for failing to honor me." And so on.

Confessing with Bible words can also prevent you from inappropriately seeking forgiveness. Some Christians are so sensitive that they ask forgiveness for things that even God does not consider sin. Of course, you should say you are sorry for a mistake or for unwittingly hurting someone, but if the Bible doesn't call what you did sin, you shouldn't call it sin either. You can no more repent of a word or action that is not described as a sin in the Bible than you can repent of having brown hair or blue eyes or of being born a citizen of any given country.

Here's an example of why using Bible words is important. Pete was an American man worshipping with an international fellowship overseas. To his credit, he wanted to apologize for things he regretted he did during a previous worship meeting. He confessed, "I'm sorry I acted like a jerk." There was just one problem. The word jerk is American slang and the Africans, Europeans, and Asians in the fellowship didn't fully understand its meaning. From his facial expressions and tone of voice they sensed he was sorry for something, but they had no idea what that was. Therefore, they didn't know what to forgive him for.

If Pete wanted to convince non-Americans that he was sorry for being a jerk, he could have said he was rude, unkind, thought too highly of himself, and didn't consider others more important than himself. If he had used Bible words like these, they would have understood him perfectly. (See 1 Corinthians 13:4–5, Romans 12:16, Philippians 2:2–3.)

You may not be able to relate to the cross-cultural aspect of this example, but even if everyone in your Christian community is from the same culture and speaks the same mother tongue, you may need a reminder to use Bible words when you confess your sins to each other.

Take personal responsibility

Have you heard these so-called confessions?

> "I'm sorry that happened."
>
> "Forgive me that words were said."
>
> "I'm sorry our conversation didn't go well."

It's as if the person apologizing doesn't know who did what or said what, when in fact they were the one who committed that particular offense.

You don't want your confession to sound like these. So, when you apologize, use words like "I" and "my" connected to your specific actions, words, inactions, or reactions. Identify yourself as the one who committed the offense. This will show the offended that you personally own the fact that you were at fault.

Don't excuse yourself or blame others or circumstances

Do you remember when our forefather Adam tried to hide his responsibility for eating the forbidden fruit in Genesis 3:8–13? Adam spoke to God as if it was indirectly Eve's fault and ultimately God's fault that he sinned. At the same time, Eve blamed the serpent for her sin.

Don't add words like "but" or "however" to your confession or tell the offended why you think your offense really wasn't your fault.

Name your specific offense(s)

If you only say, "I confess I was wrong last week," the offended person may not know what you are talking about. Or, the offended person may remember you committed an offense last week, but they may be thinking of a different offense than the one you have in mind!

Quote the words you used and clearly describe your actions, including the time and the place you committed your sin. That way, the offended will have no doubt about what you are confessing.

Specifically confess everything you can think of that is your responsibility related to the offense. However, you don't have to be wordy or long-winded.

Communicate that you have a contrite spirit

Be so sincere and transparent that the other person can see that you have a contrite heart. Try to demonstrate that you are sincerely sorry and repentant for what you did in whatever way the offended person will understand. Your definition of sincere sorrow may not be the same in the offended person's culture or personal dictionary. For some people, careful and thoughtful words are enough. Others might expect to see tears or practical actions instead of words. Some look for all three. So, it is important for you to try to demonstrate honesty, humility, and honor in ways the offended person can understand.

Demonstrate that you feel, or that you are at least aware of, the pain your offense caused the offended and what it cost them

Show the offended by your words and body language that you know your offense had a negative effect or caused consequences for them. Those consequences could include emotional pain, embarrassment, loss of respect, loss of time, loss of money, and so on. Don't assume too little or too much. It may be obvious to you what your offense cost the offended. Or, you may not realize the full consequences of the pain and trouble your offense was to them. It can be a good sign of humility for you to ask them how your offense hurt them or what it cost them.

Ask the offended, "Is there something else I did or didn't do that you want to explain to me?"

Even if you meet with God, complete all the steps of Stage One for your role, and consult a coach, there is no guarantee you have discerned everything you need to about your offense. When you ask the offended this question, you honor them and you demonstrate humility. You also give the offended the opportunity to share with you their feelings about the offense you are confessing, and perhaps other offenses you have not yet seen.

Make right any wrongs you can

After your confession, do what you can to repair or correct the damage your offense caused to the offended. This is part of honoring them (Romans 12:10b), bringing forth fruits in keeping with repentance (Matthew 3:8, Acts 26:20), yielding the peaceful fruit of righteousness (Hebrews 12:11), and reaping what you have sown (Galatians 6:7–8).

Q: Do I have to include all the basic ingredients in a confession?

I do not recommend you follow a stale formula or legalistic ritual when you apologize. You can decide which ingredients to include in your confession based on factors like these:

- How serious your sin or fault was
- How deeply offended the other person was
- The nature of your relationship with the person (family, friend, co-worker, leader?)
- Your shared cultural values and communication style
- The personality and spiritual gifting of the offended

Think of the basic ingredients of a confession like a recipe for a salad or soup. Which ingredients will the offended person appreciate most? For example, some people appreciate it when you describe your offense specifically and with Bible words, while others may care more that you simply showed contrition and that you are trying to sympathize with the hurt or pain you caused them. However, the more of the ingredients you leave out, the more you risk leaving the recipe with a bland taste.

At the end of the day, do whatever it takes to communicate you are truly humble, sincerely sorry, completely honest about your offense, and want to honor the offended person.

Here is an example of a scripture-soaked gourmet meal of biblical repentance. It's an excerpt from a real-life confession written by a ministry team member to a fellow team member after the offender met with God and fully processed Stage One. I have edited out the specific details, but you will recognize the other ingredients.

> *"I have sinned in the way I have habitually spoken with you. I have been harsh. I have lacked gentleness and have not been tenderhearted towards you. My words have been hurtful and I know that the way I have spoken them added greatly to the pain they caused you. Please forgive me for not being wise and self-controlled, not speaking with kindness, honor and love.*
>
> *"My general attitude has been prideful and haughty and dishonoring. I can see how this must have constantly made you feel rejected. Please forgive me for this continual hurt that I have caused you.*
>
> *"When I put myself in your shoes, I don't imagine that I could have remained kind and gentle like you did while experiencing such pain. Thank you for not treating me in the same way I treated you.*
>
> *"Thank you for listening to me and if there is anything else that I need to repent of, please tell me whenever you feel comfortable."*

As you can imagine, as this person confessed the details and the other party forgave them, this full-course confession helped transform a deep and hurtful conflict into a delicious banquet of peace. You can use this as a kind of template, adding your own details as appropriate.

Make your confession like the offended person would want to receive it

This point is an application of the principle to honor the person you offended. It takes into account the offended person's personality, temperament, spiritual gifting, and so on.

Patricia and Christine's friendship was once deep and full of trust. But over several years, their friendship had become strained because of offenses Patricia had done to Christine but had not apologized for. Eventually, Patricia wanted to make peace with Christine. Patricia went through Stage One and prepared a good, thorough confession. Patricia wrote a confession full of biblical words, complete with references. She named specific offenses, including dates and locations. She took personal responsibility for each and every offense. She didn't blame anyone else. It was a beautiful confession. Patricia arranged a Stage Two conversation with Christine and shared her confession.

Later Patricia debriefed her experience with a coach. She said, "I didn't get through the second paragraph of my confession before Christine burst into tears and cried out, 'I actually don't care about all of those details! I just want you to empathize with me and show me you understand how much you hurt me!'"

What went wrong with Patricia's beautiful confession? It was only beautiful to someone like Patricia who emphasizes truth when resolving conflicts, whose spiritual gifts are teaching and exhortation, and whose personality type emphasizes reason and logic. It was beautiful to Patricia, but not to Christine.

Patricia failed to think about Christine's unique personhood in preparing an apology to her. She didn't consider that Christine's personality type is very strong in feeling and expressing empathy. She forgot that Christine is grace-oriented in resolving conflicts and has the spiritual gifts of mercy and compassion.

If Patricia had truly put herself in Christine's place, Patricia would have begun her confession acknowledging the hurt and pain she caused Christine. Then, Patricia would likely have received Christine's forgiveness in that first Stage Two conversation. Later, Patricia and Christine had a wonderful reconciliation. However, they could have reached that point sooner if Patricia had prepared her confession with more careful consideration of Christine's personality.

Here's another example, from a different angle. Joshua was head of a teaching team of seven people responsible for a week-long leadership training course. All of the trainers were busy with lots of other responsibilities. It was a challenge to gather them all together in one place for planning meetings. Knowing this, Joshua carefully prepared goals, materials, and an agenda to make the planning meeting effective and efficient.

During the meeting, Danny often brought up subjects that were off the topic Joshua was presently addressing. Danny also initiated off-topic personal interactions with other members of the team that distracted the course of the meeting.

Joshua didn't say anything to Danny, but his body language apparently communicated something.

Afterwards, Danny came to Joshua and said, "You didn't say anything about this in the meeting, but I could tell from your non-verbal behavior that my talking about things other than your agenda hurt your feelings. I want to say I am sorry for that."

Joshua replied, "Thank you, Danny. I appreciate your coming to me. To be honest, what you interpreted as my frustration had nothing to do with my feelings. I was trying to honor everyone on the team by preparing an efficient meeting so we could be good stewards of our limited and valuable time together. Your behavior didn't hurt my feelings. It dishonored my role and the careful planning I invested in the meeting."

Danny apologized for the subjects Joshua mentioned, and Joshua forgave Danny for them.

In both of these examples, Patricia's and Danny's confessions were honest and humble. The problem was that Patricia and Danny did not consider what would honor Christine and Joshua with their respective apologies.

See the *Judge rightly* point of Stage One for more on how spiritual gifting and temperament can affect a person's approach toward resolving a conflict.

Q: What's the difference between making excuses for what I did and honestly explaining the context of my offense?

It is appropriate to explain the context or circumstances you were in when you committed the offense. The key is to explain the context in a way that does not take away any deserved blame or responsibility from you. For example, you may be late for a meeting because there was a traffic accident blocking your route. That is a valid explanation. However, it is not a valid excuse if you got caught in traffic because you didn't plan ahead enough to avoid normal rush hour, if you could have.

Maybe you were short-tempered or impatient today because you didn't get enough sleep last night. That leads to other questions, such as, did you not sleep enough because you were up late watching television (a poor excuse) or was it a baby's crying that kept you awake (a valid explanation)? In either case, you are still responsible for your words and actions.

If you blame someone else for your offense, your "confession" will only communicate that you are not truly and sincerely sorry. For example, you're almost better off saying nothing than making half-confessions like, "I sinned against you, but it was because you..." or "I admit I said that to him; however, if he hadn't done such-and-such to me first...."

I need to say one more thing. The moment you apologize is usually not the time to explain that what you did to offend the other person came out of pain or unhealed memories from your past. There may be another appropriate time for you to share these things with the offended, but not while you are confessing an offense you did to them.

Q: Should I promise I will make up for my offense?

It is a biblical principle when you repent to make appropriate restitution for any cost your offense caused a person (Matthew 3:8, Acts 26:20, Hebrews 12:11, Galatians 6:7–8). Do everything you can to repair the physical, emotional, and relational damage.

However, take care that you only promise to make up the damage you've caused if you are sincere about it, and if it is actually possible. Some things you can't replace or repair. If you have wasted a person's time, you can't put those minutes or hours back into their day. If you have broken a one-of-a-kind vase that their grandmother gave them, you can't replace it. If you have gossiped or dishonored them through email or on social media, you may not be able to stop it from spreading.

If it is possible to right the wrong you did, don't just promise to make up for it. Actually do it, even if it humbles you more or costs you money or time.

Q: Should I promise I will never commit the offense again?

It is important for you to be both sincere and realistic. Your confession needs to be honest, humble, and honoring. If you promise something you can't really guarantee, you may intend to be humble, but it's neither honest nor honoring to the offended. Rather than saying, "I promise I will never do it again," you can say something like, "I aspire not to repeat this offense," or "I will try my best to break this habit."

If you can show the offended that you have taken concrete steps to get help, training, or mentoring in this area, you will go a long way toward making it less difficult for the offended to forgive you and easier to rebuild their trust in you.

Q: Should I "ask forgiveness" when I apologize?

Asking the person you have offended to forgive you is a good way to demonstrate humility and contrition.

However, let me add a word of caution. Your confession is meant to communicate to the offended what you did wrong, how sorry you are, and that you understand you injured them. It's about you being honest, you being humble, and you honoring the offended. But when you ask the offended for forgiveness, there is a subtle change in the focus of your conversation. You take the focus off of you and put it on them.

Let's say you make a good confession and add, "Will you forgive me?" If the offended is a follower of Jesus and is aware of biblical teaching, they will know that they are required by God to grant you forgiveness and will likely be happy to do so.

This is normally fine if your offense is small. But, if your offense is severe, or prolonged, or both, they may feel pressure to immediately grant you forgiveness without having had a chance to pray and process your confession in their heart and with God. In some circumstances, it might be more loving for you make your confession and then say something like this:

> *"I know that it could be very difficult to forgive me. I am not demanding that you do, and I am certainly not expecting you to grant me forgiveness right now. However, if you could forgive me sometime, I would be sincerely grateful."*

Confess to God before you apologize to the offended

Before you move on to another point of Stage One, stop and make a prayer of confession and repent to God for the offense you committed against the offended person. If you have consulted a coach, I recommend that you make this prayer to God when the coach can witness your confession. As a witness to your prayer to God, your coach can affirm to you the truth of 1 John 1:9: "If we confess our sins, he is faithful and just to forgive us our sins and to cleanse us from all unrighteousness." This affirmation by a coach is helpful for you to remember in case your conscience, or the devil, or the offended person ever accuses you of not repenting to God for this offense.

Q: What thoughts of mine might hinder my motivation to confess?

The Bible makes a connection between what we believe in our hearts with what we say and do. Here are just a few references: Jeremiah 17:5–8, Psalm 1, Matthew 12:33–35, and Luke 6:43–45. You can think of your beliefs about God, yourself, and others in your heart as "roots" that produce the "fruit" of your words, actions, inactions, and reactions. Here is a simple diagram to illustrate this analogy.

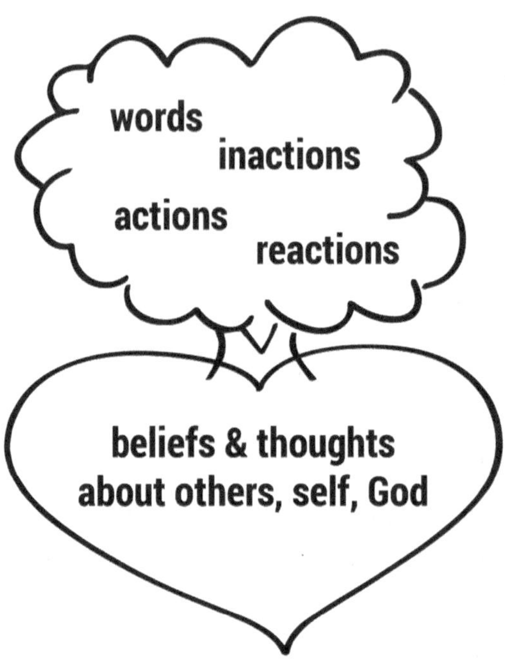

Some people have shared with me root thoughts and beliefs in their hearts that have made it difficult for them to confess their offenses to the person they offended. These kinds of root thoughts often come from what they have heard and experienced in their family and culture. Here are some common ones:

- *Why should I repent to that person? They are more at fault than I am!*
- *What if they don't forgive me? I don't want to risk that.*
- *If I don't confess, maybe time will heal all wounds and they'll eventually forget about it.*
- *If I apologize, I will give them an advantage over me.*
- *Confession means weakness. I am strong!*
- *Love means never having to say you are sorry.*
- *If I apologize, they will gossip about me. I need to protect my reputation.*
- *If I confess, they will throw it back in my face.*
- *They should apologize first.*
- *They won't forgive me anyway, so why should I bother?*

Any of these thoughts might hinder you from repenting of your fault in a relational problem. These thoughts could also lead you to other inactions, words, and actions which will not help you reach peace with a person.

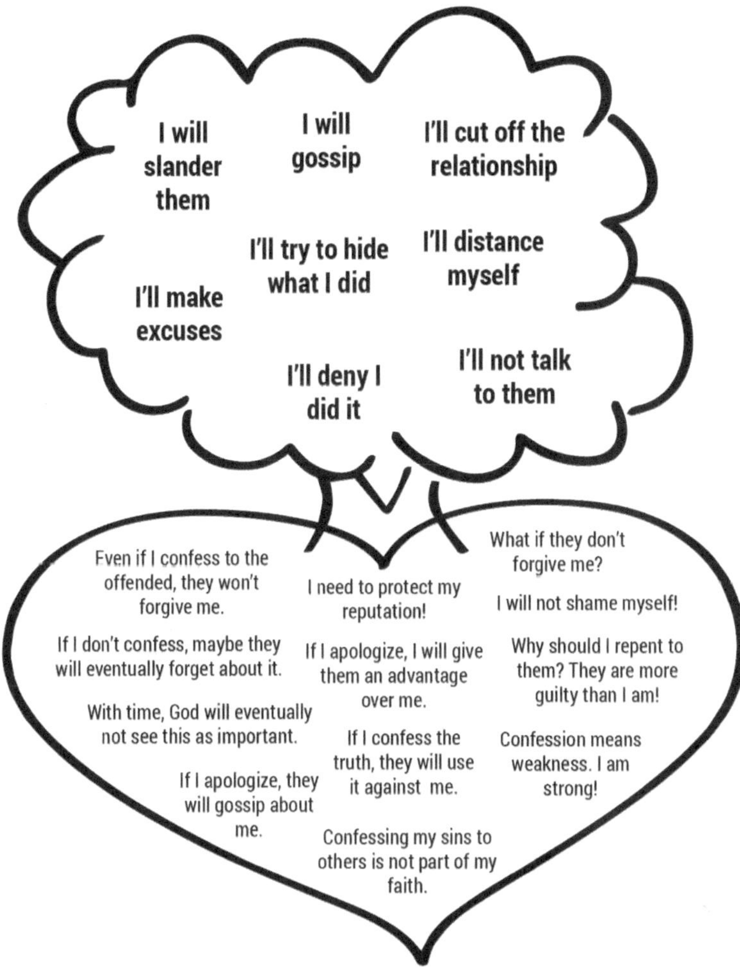

If you or someone you coach has any of those thoughts which make them reluctant to confess, consider replacing those thoughts with these paraphrased Bible truths:

- *I should reconcile before I worship* (Matthew 5:23–24).
- *Pride brings a person down, but humility brings them honor* (Proverbs 29:23, NASB).
- *If I were the offended person, I would want the offending person to apologize to me. Therefore, I should apologize* (Matthew 7:12).
- *Fearing man is a snare, but the one who trusts in the Lord is safe* (Proverbs 29:25).
- *God will give me strength to honestly confess* (1 Corinthians 10:13).

- *If I say I have no sin, I deceive myself and God's word is not in me* (1 John 1:8, 10).
- *God is opposed to the proud, but gives grace to the humble* (James 4:6).
- *God knows my heart and my motivation. I can't hide from him, so I should be honest with the person I offended* (Hebrews 4:12, 1 Corinthians 4:5).
- *If I confess my sins, God will forgive me and cleanse me* (1 John 1:9).

The diagram below shows how a heart full of biblical roots leads to "a harvest of righteousness...sown in peace by those who make peace" (James 3:18).

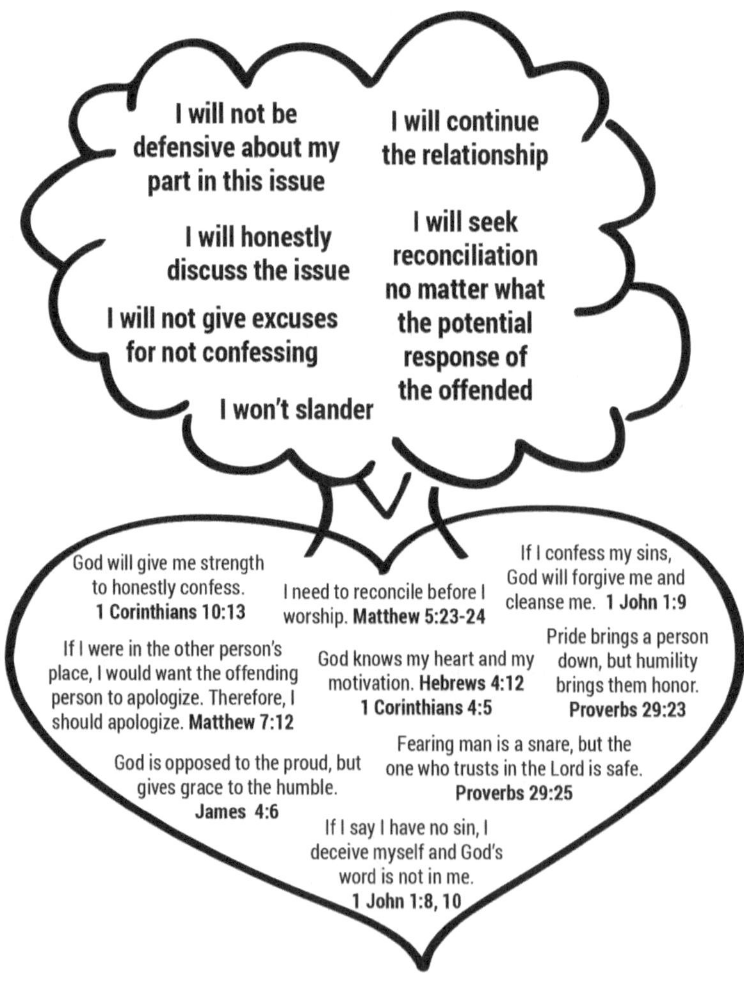

Q: What about confessing "private" or "secret" sins?

Some people have especially sensitive consciences and want to confess every sin that comes into their mind. It's true that you should always confess your sins to God. However, there are some sins you should not normally confess to the one you sinned against.

Take the example of lust. What if a man went up to a woman and said, "I confess I have lusted after you and committed adultery with you in my heart"? In our workshops we have asked women how they would feel if a man did this. Not one woman has said that she would be blessed to hear these words. In fact, some have said they would feel violated by the man. A man who wants to make a confession like this might have the motive to be honest and to be humble, but he would not be honoring the woman.

Or, take the sin of jealousy. How would you respond if you had no prior indication that a person was jealous of you and they said to you, "I confess I have been jealous of your [wealth, success, beauty, family]. Do you forgive me?" Would you be honored if someone made that confession to you? Of course, it is different if they have acted on their jealousy resulting in some harm to you. But that would no longer be a private sin or sin of the heart.

"Confess your sins to one another" (James 5:16) can apply to secret sins like this. Let's say you sinned against a person in your heart only. Instead of confessing to that person, you could confess to God in the presence of another believer who will pray for you and affirm to you the truth of 1 John 1:9: "If we confess our sins, he is faithful and just to forgive us our sins and to cleanse us from all unrighteousness." However, be extremely careful to verbalize only appropriate detail. God knows the details.

A Peace Pursuit coach, as I describe in this handbook, can be a good person to help you decide what to do about confessing secret sins, private sins, and sins of the heart. As I mentioned earlier, a coach could also be a witness for your confession to God for those kinds of sins.

Q: How should I present my confession to the offended? In person? In a voice call? In writing? By email? By social media?

Remember, you want to communicate honesty, humility, and honor to the person you offended. The actual words you say are a small percentage of what communicates to another person. The majority of what the offended will receive from your confession will come through your choice of timing, location, your tone of voice, facial expressions, hand gestures, and posture.

The more the offended person can see your body language and hear your tone of voice, the more likely you are to communicate honesty, humility, and honor, and therefore the more likely they will receive your apology and forgive you. Do all you can to make your apology in person unless there is some major reason you should not. If confessing to them in person is not an option, then see if you can meet with them by video over the internet. If that's not possible, then connect by voice somehow. If a voice call is not possible, you can write a hand-written letter or card to communicate your care and sincerity as you apologize. Email or texting should be among your last choices. Please do not even think about using social media.

If your offense is deep or prolonged, or when you have offended a person in more than one way, consider writing out your confession. This will help you clarify your thoughts and feelings and will help you make sure your confession is honest, humble, and honoring. You then have the option of reading it to the offended. Of course, only read it if it helps you focus, and if your tone of voice and facial expressions when you read it communicate honesty, humility, and honor to them.

Q: What if I'm not totally certain I offended a person?

I addressed this question earlier in the detailed explanation of the offender role, but I believe it is good to review it here.

There are four possibilities in this situation. Two of your options involve having a conversation with the person, two do not. What are the implications of each choice you could make?

Possibility 1

They really were offended and you go to them to apologize. You will likely reach peace. That's a good outcome.

Possibility 2

They really were offended, but you don't go to apologize. You will not be at peace, and you risk harming your relationship with them further. This is not good.

Possibility 3

They actually were not offended, but you approach them with honesty, humility, and honor to confirm with them if they were offended. They will probably appreciate your care for the relationship and the mutual respect between you will probably increase.

Possibility 4

They actually were not offended and you decide not to go to them to find out. In this case, you will have guessed right. But, ask yourself, "Is it worth the risk of being wrong?"

If you ever wonder if you have offended someone, I suggest that you assume that you did offend them. I've found that it never hurts to go and appropriately ask whether I have offended someone, especially after I've met with God and worked through the related points of Stage One.

Here's an example of how you could approach a person you are not sure you have offended:

> *"Sam, I've been thinking about what I said in our meeting on Wednesday. I'm wondering how I came across to you when we discussed the third point on the agenda. I feel like I might have said something to offend you. If I did offend you with what I said or how I said it, I'd like to hear your perspective."*

Q: In my culture, we don't apologize like you have described. We have different ways to demonstrate we want to make peace.

Honesty, humility, and honor are biblical principles included in the Peace Pursuit definitions of confession and repentance. I know that the definitions of the words honesty, humility, and honor may vary from person to person and from culture to culture.

For example, an offender from one society may show that they are humble, that they are honest about their offense, and that they honor the person they offended through direct, verbal, or written communication. However, an offended person from another culture may expect to receive different, less direct expressions of those principles.

Whatever culture you are from, make sure that your confession communicates your honesty, your humility, and your honor of the person you offended, according to their personal culture. You could ask a coach from that culture to help you prepare your apology.

Q: Who needs to hear my apology, in addition to the person I offended?

Some teach that your apology should spread to all who know of your offense. This can be appropriate in some cases. However, it is important to be wise and cautious here. Keep in mind the same principles of honesty, humility, and the honor of the offended when you make a confession to people other than the individual you offended.

Think and pray about the questions below when you consider whether someone else should hear your apology in addition to the offended. You might not be able to answer these questions on your own. A coach might be able to help you discern the answers.

- *Was there anyone else who was directly affected by my offense other than the one offended person I am aware of?*
- *Was there anyone else who witnessed my offense?*
- *Who should know or needs to know what I did?*
- *How would the offended person be honored (or dishonored) if someone else hears my confession?*

Your motives are important when announcing your sin and repentance to people other than the offended. Some people are so honest and humble about themselves that they volunteer to give public testimony of how God granted them forgiveness when they repented from their sin. This can be encouraging and a positive example to others. However, take care that your confession to people other than the offended person gives glory to God, not to you. And, make sure that it honors the offended person without embarrassing them.

The *P* in the P.E.A.C.E. Principles stands for Protect all parties (see Chapter 2, *Biblical Foundations*). If you are going to confess your sin to people other than the person you offended, make sure you protect the one you offended. Do not expose them to shame or embarrassment. You can ask a coach about this. As part of your apology, you can also ask the offended themselves if they think there is anyone else you should or should not make a confession to regarding your offense toward them.

Q: I offended an individual while we were in a public meeting. Do I go to that person alone, or do I apologize publicly?

If the meeting is over, you should complete Stage One as normal and go to the person privately.

After you have confessed to the person privately, I would suggest that you also seriously consider making a confession to the group the next time you have a chance. This will show your honesty, humility, and honor of both the offended one and the group. Also, consider consulting the offended person before you confess to others (see the question above).

If the group does not meet together again soon (or not at all), then consider how you can communicate your contrition to the people who witnessed your offense. If it is a small group, you could go to them individually. If it is especially large, you could explore an appropriate way to communicate to all of them at once.

If you are still in the meeting and you catch yourself offending someone, I believe it's a valid option for you to go ahead and make your confession to the individual while the group is still in session.

Whatever option you choose, make sure you follow the guidelines for making a biblical confession.

Q: When should an offender not meet with the offended (or not meet alone) to confess?

If you are in the offender role, normally you should personally repent to the person you offended. But there are a few exceptions.

As I explained in an earlier question, you generally would not go and confess to a person you have sinned against only in your heart with sins like lust or jealousy. If the offended is not aware of your sin or not affected by it, ask yourself: Would they be honored if I confessed my sin to them?

There are cases when the offender has committed a physical or strongly emotional offense. Or, the offended has legitimate reason to be frightened or intimidated by the offender. In these cases, it may not be wise or loving to the offended for the offender to approach the offended alone, even if the offender has the good motive to repent.

In a case like that, how can a sincerely remorseful and repentant offender communicate honesty about their offense, humble themselves, and show honor to the offended? One possible way is to arrange for one or more silent witnesses to be present. These witnesses should be people who are trusted by the offended to "protect" them while the offender makes their confession. In cases of extreme offense, other forms of communication can be used that would not require the offender and offended to be in the same room.

Sometimes religious or cultural reasons make it inappropriate for the offender and offended to meet alone, such as age differences or when the parties are a man and a woman who aren't married. In this kind of situation, do what you can to apply the P.E.A.C.E. Principles and find an appropriate way for the offender to communicate humility, honesty, and honor to the offended person.

Q: Why is the initiator icon attached to this step? I thought the definition of an initiator is a person who is not part of the relational problem.

Let's say that you consider filling the initiator role for two people in a relational problem. Let's also say that you have some kind of professional or personal relationship with one or both of the parties. As you process the *Analyze*, *Evaluate*, and *Take the plank out of your eye* points, you may realize that you may have contributed somehow to the conflict between the two parties. In that case, you would need to make an apology to the appropriate person. I attached the initiator icon to this step for such cases.

Forgive

ROLES INVOLVED

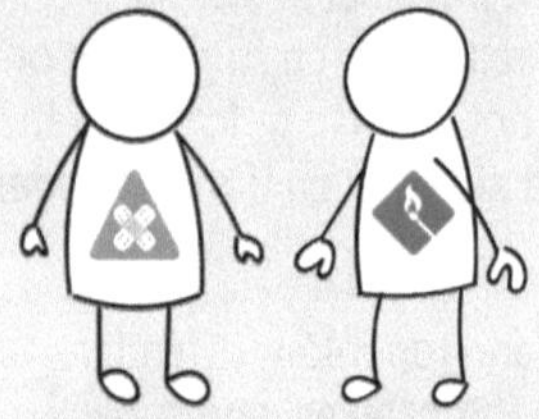

PURPOSE

To give you practical help on your journey through the process of forgiving someone who has offended you.

KEY QUESTIONS

Are you prepared to forgive the other party in your heart before God?

How can you prepare to grant forgiveness personally to the other party if they confess and repent to you?

As you begin this step, I assume you want to forgive the person who offended you, or at least that you are convinced that you should forgive them. So, I will focus on the practical aspects of forgiving. If you need biblical reasons or theological motivation to forgive, see the *Five Pillars of Peace Pursuit* in Chapter 2.

To review, our working definition of peace is when two people reach appropriate confession and forgiveness for their relational problem. So the *Forgive* point is absolutely essential to pursuing peace. You could say the *Forgive* and the *Repent of your part* steps of Stage One are the two sides of the coin of peace.

What does it mean to forgive a person?

Two common Bible words translated as "forgive" in English mean to show kindness and favor to graciously pardon, cancel, and release another person from grievances, complaints, sins, and debts (Ephesians 4:32, Colossians 3:13, Luke 17:3, Matthew 6:12, Luke 7:41–50). Because God graciously pardons, cancels, and releases us from our sins and debts against him that we can't repay, we are to do the same to other people. This is living out the gospel in community.

Forgiving with honesty, humility, and honor

To forgive, you need to be honest about the offense, to humble yourself, and to honor the offender. These principles are like a mirror image of similar ones in the *Repent of your part* step.

I'll start with the topic of honoring the offender as you forgive them. This concept is new to some people. To honor the offender when you forgive means you will treat them as a fellow human being and child of God created by the Father. You will show them the same love and dignity you would want them to show you if your roles were reversed. You won't seek revenge or hope the offender suffers shame or harm because of their offense to you. I don't say this is always easy to do.

To humble yourself when you forgive means you will give up your "right" to collect on the relational debt the offender owes to you.

To be honest about the offense you are forgiving means to call it sin, if it is sin. If it is not sin, call it something else, like a mistake, a misunderstanding, an oversight, or similar.

The suggestions I share below are practical applications of these principles of honesty, humility, and honor when you forgive.

Forgiveness in two directions

As the one who is offended, you forgive the offender in two ways: in your heart before God, and to the offender personally. You could describe the act of forgiving the person in your heart before God as vertical forgiveness. Horizontal forgiveness is when you personally grant your forgiveness to the offender. (I honestly don't remember where I first heard the terms *vertical* and *horizontal forgiveness*, but I am grateful to the person who coined them. May God bless them and their ministry.)

Two Dimensions of Forgiveness

Stage 1

Vertical forgiveness

Forgive the offender before God

Stage 2

Horizontal forgiveness

Grant forgiveness to the offender

The order of these two types of forgiveness is important. You forgive the offender in your heart as you meet with God at Stage One. Another way to say this is that you declare to God your forgiveness of the offender. That's why you can call this forgiveness on the vertical dimension. Your eyes and heart look upward to God. This is a clear biblical concept (Matthew 18:35, Mark 11:25). It is also practical. It can be really hard to grant forgiveness to someone in person if you haven't already forgiven them in your heart before God.

Even before the person apologizes to you, prepare your heart so you can say this to God: "Lord, I forgive the offender for what they did to me." Be as specific as you can. When you do this, your heart will be more ready and free to grant them forgiveness if they confess to you.

When you forgive someone in your heart when you meet with God before that person apologizes, you are obeying Ephesians 4:32, "forgiving one another, as God in Christ forgave you." When did God in Christ forgive you? Jesus suffered, died, and paid the penalty in your place for your sin long before you were born. He was already prepared to grant you forgiveness before you finally humbled yourself to repent and receive it. That's why you can, and should, do the same for the person who offended you.

After you have forgiven the offender in your heart at Stage One, the second way you forgive the offender is to grant them forgiveness personally at Stage Two if they repent (Luke 17:3–4).

By personally, I mean you declare your forgiveness to the offender directly, not through someone else. You can call this forgiveness on the horizontal dimension. I explain more about this in *The offended role at Stage Two* (Chapter 7).

How you can know when you have forgiven the offender in your heart

Forgiveness is a process that can take a short or long time. To start the process, you can pray prayers to God like the ones below.

> *"Lord, I want to forgive this person just as you in Christ forgave me."*

God in Christ forgave you long before you ever repented to him. He did it with grace, with mercy, and completely (Colossians 3:13). This prayer declares to God your good intention to forgive the offender in your heart in the same way before they repent to you, and even if they never repent to you.

> *"Lord, I want to see the offender through your eyes of grace and mercy."*

The offender is another of God's children. Your Heavenly Father loves that person as much as he loves you. The offender is valuable enough in God's eyes for Jesus to die for them. Ask God to give you his eyes and heart for them. As you forgive, you choose not to focus on the hurt they caused you. You choose not to look for other faults of theirs. You will see and appreciate whatever positive traits they may have.

> *"Lord, please help me renew my mind. I do not want to keep reliving the offense."*

Repeating the offense over and over in your mind is of no profit to you or anyone else. In fact, it is harmful to your mental, emotional, and spiritual health. It is also the opposite of the Bible command to let your mind dwell on things that are true, honorable, just, pure, lovely, commendable, excellent, and worthy of praise (Philippians 4:8). With this prayer you declare your intention to God and you ask for his help. Sometimes people need prayers from others to help heal memories of deep offenses.

> *"Lord, I do not want to remind the offender of the offense inappropriately."*

Let's say you have forgiven someone in your heart before God at Stage One, you have chosen to overlook the offense this time, and you have decided not to have a Stage Two conversation with them. Certainly, you would not bring up this same offense to them later. You overlooked it.

Now let's say that in another situation you decided to have a Stage Two conversation with the offender, they repented, and you granted them forgiveness on the horizontal level. In this case, you would also normally not bring up this offense to them again.

However, perhaps as part of their own mentoring or discipleship the offender may need to be reminded of this offense in the future. This should only be at the appropriate time and place, such as when you sense or observe that they are struggling with a similar temptation.

If you sense you should mention their offense again, first check your motive. Then, make sure you do it gently, out of love, and after reviewing the other points of Stage One. It's possible that you might not be the appropriate person to bring it up. It can be a sign that you probably have not completed the process of forgiveness if with an angry voice you say to the offender something like, "There you go again! You are acting just like you did last month [or five years ago]!"

> *"Lord, I do not want to tell others about the offense inappropriately."*

Of course, you never want to gossip about or slander the offender. However, there may be a time in the future when you should tell an appropriate person about the offense. Who might be appropriate to tell? It depends on the nature and severity of the offense.

Here's a question to ask if you feel you need to tell someone else about the offense: Is the person you are considering to tell about the offense someone who, because of their role, would need to know about the offender's fault in order to fulfill their legal, or organizational, or leadership responsibility? An example could be a spiritual leader or future employer. Of course, for serious offenses, you may need to inform police or other government agencies.

This also depends on your motive. Ask yourself questions like these:

Why am I considering telling a third person about the offense?

Who am I honoring, protecting, or blessing by telling another person?

In my pain or anger am I committing gossip or slander?

A Peace Pursuit coach, as I describe in this handbook, may be an appropriate person to tell about the offense as you go through Stage One. The coach could witness the prayers of forgiveness you make before God. Later, if doubts come from your conscience or accusations come from Satan about whether you forgave the offender in your heart before God, the coach can remind you that you did forgive the offender in prayer.

"Lord, I pray for your blessing of grace and mercy on the offender."

Praying for blessing on the offender is not the same thing as praying that they will recognize how much they hurt you, that they will receive conviction from the Holy Spirit about their sin, or that they will see the light and repent to you. To pray for blessing on them means praying for God's grace and mercy on them. When you can do this spontaneously and with sincerity, you will know your heart is growing in its understanding of the depth of forgiveness.

Let me repeat that forgiving can be a brief or prolonged process. In any case, you can begin by saying these prayers to God, even if you don't totally feel like they are true in your heart yet. If some time later you wonder if you have truly forgiven the offender, just ask yourself: Have all these prayers been answered in my life? If they have become true for you, or they are well on their way to becoming true, then that is proof you have forgiven the offender. You can then walk in the freedom and comfort of a clear conscience that you have indeed forgiven them.

Q: What does it look like to personally grant forgiveness?

When an offender confesses to you, simply say something like, "I forgive you for [the offense they have confessed]."

Be specific and honest about what you are forgiving them for. That way you both know that you have reached peace about that particular topic.

When an offender confesses to you, be careful not to say, "No worries," "That's OK," or any other phrase that minimizes the offense, especially if the Bible calls it sin. Sin is not OK. Jesus died for that sin. If the offender has taken the time and care to pray and prepare a biblical confession, it honors them when you accept their apology as seriously as they present it. It will also reinforce the conviction the Holy Spirit has made in their heart, which will encourage them to listen to the Holy Spirit again. I explain this more in depth in the section, *The offended role at Stage Two* (Chapter 7).

Q: What am I not doing when I forgive?

It's just as important to know what forgiveness is not, as it is to know what forgiveness is.

When you forgive, you are not:

- Denying that the offender committed the offense;
- Minimizing the hurt or cost the offender caused you;
- Communicating that the offense was acceptable;
- Proclaiming that the offender is free to repeat the offense;
- Excusing the offender from their responsibility;
- Blaming others for the offense instead of the offender;
- Promising that you will completely trust the offender in a similar situation in the future; or
- Negating the relational, legal, or organizational consequences of the offender's actions.

The offender may face consequences from others even if you personally forgive them. For example, if the offense is a crime, the offender may face punishment by law enforcement agencies. If they have seriously violated the ethics or values of a company or organization, they may need to be disciplined or dismissed.

Q: What if I don't want to forgive?

Jesus made two promises just after he taught his disciples to pray what is often called the Lord's Prayer in Matthew 6:9–13. The first is in verse 14: "For if you forgive others their trespasses [other translations use *sins* or *debts* for the word *trespasses*], your heavenly Father will also forgive you." That's a verse we love to memorize and claim.

The second promise is in the next verse: "But if you do not forgive others their trespasses [sins, debts], neither will your Father forgive your trespasses" (Matthew 6:15). That's the uncomfortable one we often try to ignore. Remember, both verses are promises. They both have the same grammatical structure: "if… then…" When God promises something, we can expect it to happen. It's sobering to think of the connection between our forgiveness of others and God's forgiveness of us.

The parable of the unforgiving servant is also sobering (Matthew 18:21–35). Through a story, Jesus teaches that the debts we claim from offenders are extremely small compared to our debt to God because of our sin. God is not pleased if we freely accept his forgiveness for our huge debts to him, but then withhold our forgiveness toward other people who have hurt us.

I am comforted by the fact that Jesus can sympathize with us because he was tempted in every way as we are (Hebrews 4:15). That means Jesus must have been tempted not to forgive Judas, the Pharisees, the Romans—and you and me. So when I am tempted not to forgive, I cry out to Jesus and ask him to give me the strength to overcome my weakness toward that temptation and to give me the grace to forgive the person I don't want to forgive.

Q: What if the offender hurt me so badly that I can't forgive?

I will not try to convince you that forgiveness is easy. If forgiveness were easy, I think we would do it naturally, and we wouldn't need handbooks on how to make peace.

Only God knows the extent of the pain in your heart caused by an offender. I can only say that God does not command you to do something that is impossible, if you depend on his help and grace. Forgiving a serious offense is a process that may take much time, prayer, and counsel. Remember, "with God all things are possible" (Matthew 19:26; see also Mark 10:27).

Q: What if the offender caused long-term effects on my life? I forgave them in my heart, but to be honest, it doesn't seem fair that they go free while I continue to suffer the painful consequences of what they did to me.

I have acknowledged throughout this step that forgiveness is not easy. Neither is enduring the pain you have suffered from another person's hurtful and damaging actions, especially if you have to live with those consequences the rest of your life.

Part of the beauty of the gospel is that it is in fact not "fair," if fairness means that every person should pay the penalty or get the punishment they deserve. If God were fair in that sense, then all of us deserve the death penalty because all of us have sinned enough to deserve it (Romans 3:23a, 6:23a; Ephesians 2:1). But the good news is that Jesus suffered, died, and rose again to pay the penalty for all of our sins (Romans 5:8), to reconcile us to God (2 Corinthians 5:18–19), and to give us eternal life (Romans 6:23b), no matter if our sins are more or fewer than another person's. Even though I have sinned much, much more than a multitude of people, I receive the same benefits of grace and forgiveness from God as they receive. It may not be "fair" for God to forgive me like that, but it is the truth of the gospel. And I am thankful for it.

Here is one woman's testimony.

> "I have realized that in our Father's gracious sovereignty, he has given me opportunities to identify with Jesus as I follow his example to endure sorrows while suffering unjustly. I receive it as a kind of affirmation of my growth in Christ that by the Father's grace I am able to forgive the offender and be mindful of God while suffering the consequences of that person's hurtful choices (1 Peter 2:19–22)."

As for the person who hurt you, they have access to the same grace and forgiveness from God as you and I do. If they are a sincere follower of Jesus, they should repent and do what they can to make amends with you to produce fruits in keeping with their repentance (Matthew 3:8, Hebrews 12:11). Of course, there may be things they can't fix.

If the offender is not a sincere follower of Jesus, or if they don't believe in him at all, you can choose to do what Jesus did when he was wrongly treated to the point of death. "When he was reviled, he did not revile in return; when he suffered, he did not threaten, but continued entrusting himself to him who judges justly" (1 Peter 2:23). You can identify with Jesus as you entrust the Father to judge the offender in a just way.

Q: What if the offender keeps repeating the offense and repenting? Do I have to forgive them each time?

Jesus' disciple Peter asked him this same question, in Matthew 18:21. Jesus' answer was essentially, "Yes." In Luke 17:3–4 Jesus also taught that we should forgive someone even if they keep sinning and repenting "seven times in a day."

We are to forgive as Christ forgave us (Colossians 3:13). Since Jesus doesn't limit the number of times he will forgive us when we repent, we shouldn't put a quota on our forgiveness of others. That's one way we demonstrate the gospel in real life.

However, this does not mean that you or others are prohibited from finding ways to help the offender grow in Christian maturity and transform their offensive habit into a godly one.

It also does not mean that you should not protect yourself from the offender habitually hurting you. You should seek help if the offense is physically or mentally harmful.

Q: Should I voluntarily offer forgiveness on the horizontal level even if the offender has not confessed, repented, or said sorry?

Jesus forgave at least two persons who as far as we know did not confess their sin: the paralytic in Mark 2:5 and the criminal next to him on the cross (Luke 23:42–43).

It takes much discernment and wisdom to voluntarily offer forgiveness to an offender who has not repented. You shouldn't do it in every case. However, I can think of two situations when it could be appropriate to declare your forgiveness of an offender before they repent.

Sometimes you will see in the news when victims of crimes publicly announce that they have forgiven unrepentant criminals. This can be a powerful testimony of God's love flowing from the hearts of those victims.

Here is a less high-profile situation. Let's say that you sense the offender in your relational problem appears genuinely sorry and contrite, but they also seem too ashamed, or embarrassed, or don't know how to come to you to repent. I think it might be appropriate for you to offer them your forgiveness.

However, I do not recommend that you voluntarily go to an offender who has not repented and say, "I forgive you" in circumstances like these:

- When the offender doesn't know they offended you and you haven't had a Stage Two conversation with them yet.
- When the offender knows you feel offended but you know they don't believe your feeling of offense is legitimate.
- When the offender knows they have offended you, but you have good evidence that they have decided not to repent to you or God.

Here's another way to look at this question. It can be considered a loving thing for you not to declare your forgiveness to an offender who has not repented. If you announce to an offender that you forgive them before they have repented to God or you, they might not repent to God or to you at all, and therefore miss the grace that God gives to the humble (James 4:6).

Q: What thoughts might hinder my motivation to forgive?

The Bible makes a connection between what we believe in our hearts with what we say and do. Here are just a few references: Jeremiah 17:5–8, Psalm 1, Matthew 12:33–35, and Luke 6:43–45. You can think of your beliefs about God, yourself, and others in your heart as "roots" that produce the "fruit" of your words, actions, inactions, and reactions. Here is a simple diagram to illustrate this analogy. This first, basic illustration is in the *Repent of your part* step, but the following diagrams are different.

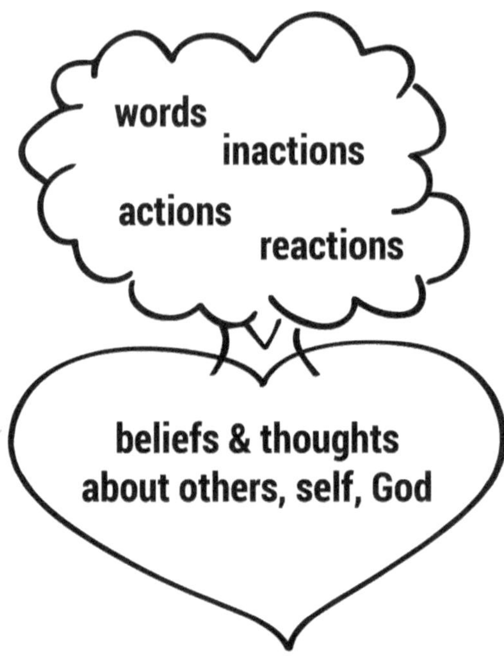

Over the years, I have coached many people who have struggled to forgive. Here are some common beliefs they identified in their hearts that hindered their forgiveness. These kinds of root thoughts often come from what they have heard and experienced in their family and culture. The heart diagram below is full of root beliefs that hinder forgiveness and can produce other fruit that does not lead to peace.

- *I have a right to be offended, irritated, and angry.*
- *What that person did to me is unforgivable.*
- *They should come to me to apologize before I forgive them in my heart.*
- *My relationship with my Heavenly Father will not be affected if I don't forgive that person.*
- *I can't forgive!*
- *Jesus does not understand my pain.*
- *I swear I will never forgive them!*

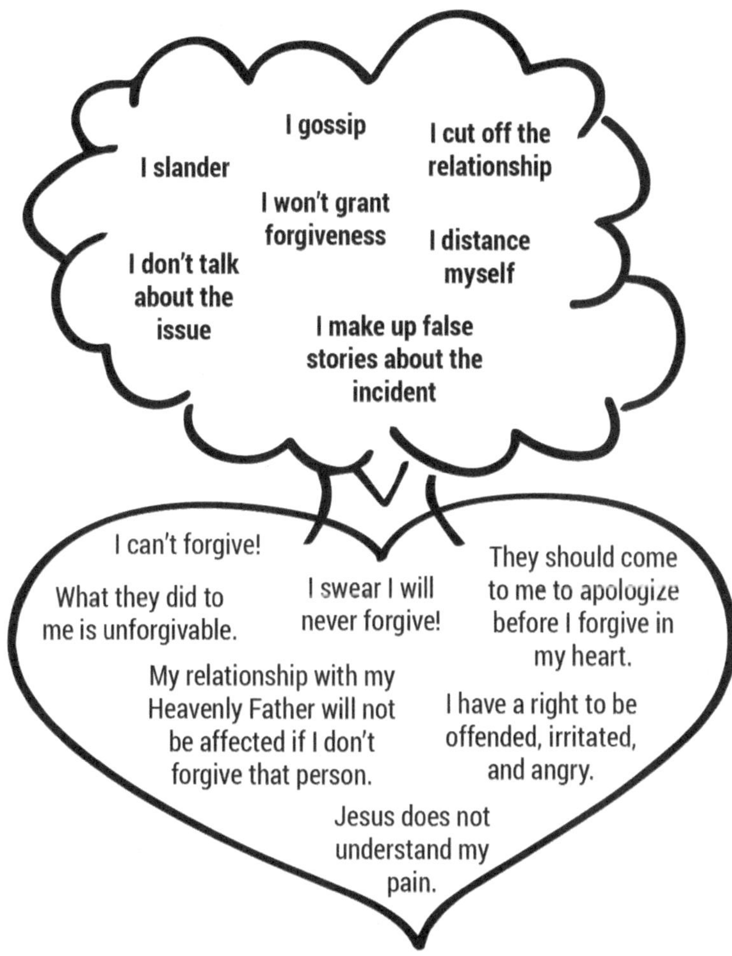

Here are some biblical truths that can address thoughts that hinder forgiveness (paraphrased):

- *I choose to forgive as God forgave me* (Colossians 3:13).
- *I could overlook this* (Proverbs 19:11).
- *While I was an enemy of God, Jesus died for me and reconciled me to God* (Romans 5:10).
- *I will be given grace and strength to forgive when I am tempted not to forgive* (1 Corinthians 10:13).
- *I choose to cover this offense with love* (1 Peter 4:8).
- *Jesus suffered the same way and still forgave* (Hebrews 4:15, Luke 23:34).

The diagram below shows how a heart full of biblical roots leads to "a harvest of righteousness...sown in peace by those who make peace" (James 3:18).

I don't gossip

I don't slander

I continue the relationship

I grant them forgiveness

I will talk about the issue (if appropriate)

I pray for blessing on them

I could overlook this.
Colossians 3:13
Proverbs 19:11

I choose to forgive as God forgave me.
Colossians 3:13

I choose to cover this with love.
1 Peter 4:8

While I was an enemy of God, Jesus died for me and reconciled me to God.
Romans 5:10

I will be given grace and strength to forgive.
1 Corinthians 10:13

Jesus suffered the same way and still forgave.
Hebrews 4:15
Luke 23:34

Q: Why is the offender icon attached to this point?

Let's say you consider yourself primarily in the offender role. While you process Stage One, you might think of some way the offended person has hurt you or offended you. Maybe the offense you are preparing to confess was your reaction to something they did to you, but they haven't yet apologized to you for that. You need to forgive them in your heart before God at Stage One before you meet with them at Stage Two to repent for your part.

Seek appropriate counsel (optional)

ROLES INVOLVED

PURPOSE

To consider whether you could benefit from wise and impartial coaching to help you process your role at Stage One.

KEY QUESTIONS

How might coaching or counsel from a wise and impartial person help you process Stage One more thoroughly?

Who might be an appropriate Peace Pursuit coach for you?

We all need wisdom to resolve conflicts biblically. If you are in the offended role or the offender role, or you are considering the initiator role, you have the option to seek wisdom from an impartial person to help you fulfill your role.

The Book of Proverbs has much to say about seeking wisdom. Here are some examples.

- "Let the wise hear and increase in learning, and the one who understands obtain guidance" (Proverbs 1:5).
- "The way of a fool is right in his own eyes, but a wise man listens to advice" (Proverbs 12:15).

- "Listen to advice and accept instruction, that you may gain wisdom in the future" (Proverbs 19:20).

With the motive to protect you from committing gossip, some teach that you should never talk to a third person about a relational problem. I understand the thought behind this teaching. Obviously, if you never speak to anyone about another person you will not commit the sin of gossip. On the other hand, you may miss out on receiving wisdom that will help you resolve your relational problem. I do not believe you are committing gossip or slander if you have right motives and seek wisdom from a person who has the qualities of a Peace Pursuit coach as I describe in this handbook.

Let me be clear that you are not required to consult a coach. However, I believe it is a biblical option for you, if you feel you need a wise and impartial person to help you process your Stage One role.

Sadly, some people misunderstand what I just said above. Some think that I say they are free to talk to anyone about a relational problem. That is not true. You should never talk to someone who:

- Is already partial to you
- Will be strongly tempted to become partial to you
- Has a reputation for gossip
- Is prejudiced against any party

Showing empathy is not the same as being partial. Of course, you can seek counsel from a coach who can empathize with your role in a conflict, as long as they can remain objective and impartial to you without prejudice toward any other parties. I realize you may have very few people in your life who might meet these standards.

Q: Who might be an appropriate Peace Pursuit coach for me?

I do not believe that a coach needs to be a pastor or licensed counselor. A coach's primary role is to ask you questions as you discover for yourself what God wants you to do in your Peace Pursuit role.

The person you go to as a coach is not required to know the Peace Pursuit Model. However, you should only choose a person to be your coach who has these characteristics:

- They are wise.
- They will not gossip.

- They will be objective toward you and any other party in your conflict.
- They are not afraid to lovingly speak the truth to you.

In other words, your coach needs to have biblical wisdom: "Wisdom from above is first pure, then peaceable, gentle, open to reason, full of mercy and good fruits, impartial and sincere" (James 3:17).

They also need spiritual maturity and the "power of discernment trained by constant practice to distinguish good from evil" (Hebrews 5:14).

If you say, "I don't know anyone like this," then you should definitely not talk to anyone at Stage One about your relational problem. Otherwise, you could tempt yourself or the person you talk to into becoming an aggravator. Please hear me clearly: only seek counsel from someone who has the characteristics of a coach as I have described. Otherwise, meet with God and complete Stage One by yourself.

Here is a small word of caution as you consider choosing a coach. You want someone who will listen to you, who will not preach at you, and who will only give their opinion of what you should do next in these kinds of situations:

- If you can't see the way forward yourself after you answer the questions of Stage One
- If they discern you still have planks in your eye and you don't see the situation clearly
- If they discern that you chose your next step based on wrong motives
- If they believe the next step you have chosen might do harm rather than good to you or others
- If they believe you aren't accurately understanding and applying scripture in the situation

Q: How could a coach help me?

A good coach will ask you questions that will supplement the Stage One questions in the Peace Pursuit Quick Start Guide.

Here are some other ways a coach can help you:

- A coach can be a witness that you have forgiven the offender in your heart before God when you pray through the *Forgive* step with them.
- You can practice your confession with a coach as you work on the *Repent of your part* step. They can also be a witness that you have repented before God in prayer for any part of the relational problem that you are aware was your fault.

- As you work through the *Prepare with love* step, you can role play with a coach what you are going to say to the other party before you meet with them at Stage Two.
- Of course, a coach can pray for you. They can pray for you as you meet with God and go through the steps of Stage One. And, if you proceed to Stage Two, they can pray for you while you have a conversation with the other party.
- A coach can also debrief with you after you return from your Stage Two meeting with the other party.
- When you are fearful or tempted not to follow through with the decision(s) you made in Stage One regarding how you will proceed toward peace, a coach can hold you accountable to take those steps.

Q: How do I ask someone to be my coach who is not familiar with the Peace Pursuit Model?

Let's say you want to ask Jules to coach you through your role at Stage One, and you have already asked for a convenient time to meet. Let's also assume that Jules has not heard of the Peace Pursuit Model of biblical peacemaking.

You could approach Jules and have a conversation like the example below. Of course, you can adapt this conversation to your own style.

YOU: Jules, thank you for taking the time to talk with me. Is this still a convenient time for you?

JULES: Yes, I'm happy to talk with you. How can I help?

YOU: Well, I have a relational problem with someone, and I'd like you to consider coaching me in my role as I go through Stage One of biblical peacemaking.

JULES: Your role at Stage One? What does that mean?

YOU: Let me explain. [You show Jules the Stage One roles in the Peace Pursuit Quick Start Guide].

See these four roles here? I consider myself to be primarily the one who has been offended by the other person. That's the triangle with bandages on it. So, I am in the offended role. I consider the other person to be in the offender role. That's the icon with a flaming match in it. I'd like you to consider filling the coach role for me. That's the icon that looks like a map. I am asking you to help me do what God wants me to do to get from where I am now to my destination of peace. I am going to meet with God and go through all the steps of Stage One that have my icon. I will ask you to help me with that.

JULES: OK, so exactly what do I have to do in this role?

YOU: As it says here in the Peace Pursuit Quick Start Guide, the main thing is for you to help me be as biblical and objective as possible about the problem and the other party while I decide what to do. As I meet with God, you would ask me questions that will help me discover what God wants me to do next. You don't have to come up with all the questions yourself. The Peace Pursuit Quick Start Guide has lots of questions in each step to stimulate my prayer and thinking.

I've been praying and working through these by myself, but I'm not sure about some things. I'd like to have a mature person like you by my side as I process them all.

JULES: I think I understand the coaching part. I mainly ask you questions from the Peace Pursuit Quick Start Guide. But it says here I am also to give you wise counsel. I'm not a pastor or licensed counselor.

YOU: I'm asking you to help because I believe you are mature and wise. I don't need a pastor or licensed counselor at this point. If for some reason I don't get enough light myself after we've gone through the coaching questions, I would welcome some wise advice from you based on your knowledge of me, the Bible, and your life experience.

Like it says here, I am also asking you to be impartial toward me and the other party, and not to gossip to anyone.

JULES: OK, I think I understand. Sorry to interrupt, but you said you are in the offended role and the other person is in the offender role. What if you have both offended each other?

YOU: Good question. I'll begin in the offended role because I feel that's my primary role at this point. As we go through all of the steps of Stage One for the offended role, I might discover that I have wrongly taken offense. Or, I may realize that I have also offended the other person. By the time I complete Stage One, I will know what to do, even if I am partly offended and partly an offender. But the important thing is for me to start the process in just one role.

Would you be willing to fill the coach role for me?

JULES: Yes, that sounds good. Let's pray and then you can tell me which Stage One step you want to begin with.

I trust that you see how simple and clear it can be to ask someone to coach you through the Peace Pursuit Quick Start Guide, even if they have never heard of the Peace Pursuit roles and stages.

Q: How do I ask someone to be my coach who already knows about the Peace Pursuit Model?

If you want Jules to be your coach and Jules is already familiar with the Peace Pursuit Model, you could begin the dialogue like this:

> *YOU: Jules, can we get together on Saturday morning? I'm in Stage One in a relational problem and I'd like you to fill the coach role as I go through the Peace Pursuit Quick Start Guide.*
>
> JULES: Sure!

When you meet with Jules on Saturday morning, you can do your normal greetings. Then you can start the coaching session like this:

> JULES: How about if I pray for the Lord's wisdom for you and me, and we get started?
>
> *YOU: That sounds great.*

After praying, Jules says:

> JULES: What is your role, and which of the Stage One steps of the Peace Pursuit Quick Start Guide do you want to begin with?
>
> *YOU: Well, I think I'm primarily the offender this time, and I'd like to start with the* Analyze *step, then move to the* Repent of your part *step. I will especially need your help with the* Prepare with love *step.*

As you can see, if you both know the Peace Pursuit roles and stages, you can begin practical steps toward resolving your relational problem in a matter of minutes.

Q: Do I have to make a formal arrangement with a coach?

You don't have to have a formal arrangement, but it is always fruitful to clarify legitimate roles. You need to make sure they understand their role and your expectations for them as a Peace Pursuit coach.

When you ask someone to be your Peace Pursuit coach, you communicate to them that you are serious about resolving your relational problem. You also ask them to help you decide your next steps in an impartial way within the bounds of the coach role. This will make your conversations with them more focused, and you will have a clear result in mind.

Here's another benefit of making expectations clear with a coach. Let's say you are in a particularly tense conflict with someone who has become fearful and suspicious of you. And, let's say they ask you in a challenging way who you might have talked to about your conflict. If you have spoken with a person who has the qualities of a Peace Pursuit coach, you can explain that role to the other party. You can also say to the other party that your motive was to honor them and God by talking with an impartial person who would help you process Stage One. The other party might be positively influenced by your integrity and your sincerity in trying to pursue peace. This might actually help rebuild trust with them.

To be honest, it is also possible that the other party may have lost so much trust in you that they might accuse you of the sin of gossip, even if you have seen an appropriate person to coach you. In that case, you just continue with the Peace Pursuit process as best you can.

Q: Does a coach have a role at Stage Two?

Your coach will not normally go with you when you go to the other party at Stage Two, except in exceptional cases which I mention in Chapter 7. You can certainly ask your coach to pray for you in another location during your Stage Two discussion with the other party.

It is also fruitful to debrief with your coach about what happened at Stage Two. It will bless your coach to hear about how you made peace. Or, if it turns out you are not reconciled with the other party at Stage Two, your coach can give you more help for what to do next.

Question your role

ROLES INVOLVED

PURPOSE

To reconsider your Peace Pursuit role in light of the other steps of Stage One. You want to complete this step before you finally decide whether to meet with the other person at Stage Two.

KEY QUESTIONS

Are you an appropriate person to approach the other party?

If you are not, who may be?

Protect all parties is the *P* of the P.E.A.C.E. Principles (see Chapter 2, *Biblical Foundations* in this handbook). To question your role is a practical application of this principle, whether you believe you are primarily the offended person or you are considering the initiator role.

Q: As the offended or the initiator, are there times when it is appropriate not to meet with the offender alone (or at all)?

If you are in the offended role, processing Stage One will help you decide whether to meet with the offender. If you decide to have that conversation, you would normally meet with the offender alone at Stage Two.

However, there are at least two situations where you should be especially careful about deciding to meet alone with the offender.

1. You lean toward having a conversation with the offender, but when you get to the *Question your role* step you realize that it would be potentially harmful to you if you met alone with the offender. By harmful, I mean if you have reason to believe there is a high probability that the offender will physically, emotionally, or mentally mistreat you if you "go and tell him his fault, between you and him alone" (Matthew 18:15).

   In an exceptional case like this, you could ask yourself, *Who else could appropriately go with me or for me?* Depending on the situation, this could be an impartial and trusted leader who has relational influence with the offender, or a person with some kind of spiritual or organizational authority. This person would fill the Peace Pursuit role of witness.

2. Because of significant cultural reasons, you realize that it would not be appropriate for you to be alone with the offender, such as a great age difference or as a man and a woman being alone who aren't married to each other. In that case, you would work out a culturally appropriate way to communicate with the offender.

If you are considering the role of initiator, the *Question your role* step gives you another opportunity to stop and ask God if you truly are an appropriate person to talk with one of the parties in a relational problem when you are not the offender or offended.

Q: What if I am in a position of leadership or I have some kind of authority over the offender?

Let's say you are a teacher, a parent, or an employer. Your student, child, or employee did something you expected them not to do, or didn't do something you expected them to do. Your expectation was legitimate, clearly understood, reasonable, and loving (see the *Analyze* step of Stage One). In this case, you need to decide if the offense is one of two types: a personal offense against you, or an offense against your position. Sometimes, it could be a combination of the two.

For example: your child fails to put into practice your legitimate, clearly understood, reasonable, and loving expectations about how to behave. I see this as an offense against your position as a parent, not a personal offense between two people who are peers or equals. I would consider this a parenting situation which requires a parent-to-child conversation rather than a personal peacemaking situation with you in the role of offended and the child in the role of offender.

Or, suppose you are a leader or supervisor and the person you lead or supervise isn't meeting your legitimate, clearly understood, and reasonable expectations for their task. You need to have a conversation with that person from your position of leadership. I don't think it is helpful for you to consider yourself in the offended role, as if you are in a personal peacemaking situation as peers.

Of course, I believe that you should apply the principles of Stage One before you have a conversation with anyone who has committed an offense against your position relative to them. This will prepare you to have an appropriate interaction with the person and can help prevent you from wrongly using your authority position.

If what the offender has done is a combination of offenses against you personally and against your position, do your best to separate those as you complete the *Analyze* and *Evaluate* steps of Stage One.

Search your heart

ROLES INVOLVED

PURPOSE

To check the motives behind your decision to have (or not to have) a Stage Two conversation with the other person.

KEY QUESTION

How could you explain in biblical terms your motives behind your decision either to have a conversation with the other party about this problem, or not to talk with them about it? Ask God to reveal your heart motives to you.

I have mentioned the subject of motives in other points of Stage One, but I have made this a separate step because it is so important whatever your Peace Pursuit role.

Verses 23 and 24 in Psalm 139 are part of a prayer in which you ask God to search your heart to see if there is anything offensive in it. Sometimes the word *offensive* in this verse is translated as *wicked, grievous, hurtful,* or *evil*. If you are not careful, these kinds of motives can wrongly influence your decision to meet with the other person or to not meet with them.

Q: What are good and bad motives for meeting with the other party at Stage Two?

If you are in the offended role or initiator role and you decide to have a conversation with a person you believe is in the offender role, your motives for that decision should include:

- Love for the offender
- Love for people their offense may have affected
- Love for people their offense may affect in the future
- Love for the glory of God among his children

Do not go to the offender with these or similar motives:

- To shame them
- To punish them
- To "teach them a lesson"

If you are in the offender role, don't go and confess to the offended if you aren't truly contrite.

Also, don't go:

- Just to clear your own conscience
- Just because someone else told you to
- Just to "move on"
- Just because it is the "right thing to do"

Whatever your role, take care that none of these inappropriate reasons are part of your motivation for you not to meet with the other person:

- Lack of humility on your part
- Unfounded fear of the other person's potential response
- Lack of care or love for the other person

Consider your responsibility

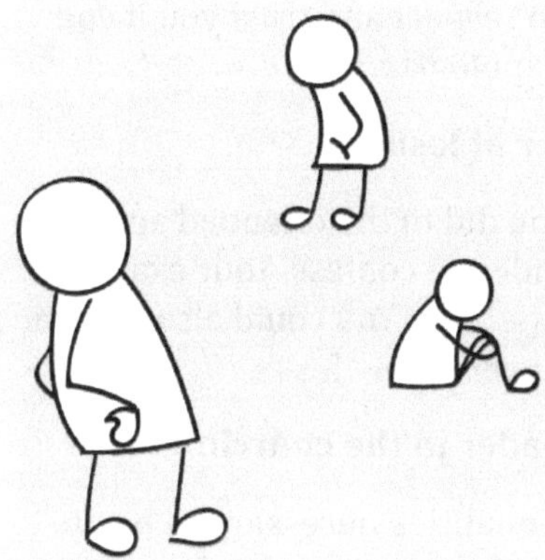

ROLES INVOVLED

PURPOSE

To consider what might happen or not happen if you don't have a Stage Two conversation with the other party.

KEY QUESTION

What are the real or potential consequences for you, the other party, and others if you don't meet with them?

If you are in the offender role and you don't meet with the offended person to confess to them, you face some potential consequences:

You risk your intimacy with God.

If you knowingly ignore God's commands to pursue peace (Matthew 5:23–24, James 5:16, Romans 12:18), your willful disobedience will affect your communion with him. Your heart might get used to disobeying God's other commands as well.

You risk your relationship with the offended.

It will possibly be harder for them to respect and trust you if you don't admit you offended them and apologize.

You risk your witness as a follower of Jesus.

Let's say other people know what you did to the offended and they know you have not gone to the offended to confess. Your example will potentially discourage other Christians. You could also become a stumbling block to people who don't yet follow Jesus.

You risk your qualification as a leader in the church.

1 Timothy 3:1–13 lists some of the qualities necessary to be an overseer in the church. Included are these traits: a leader must be respectable, above reproach, well thought of, and have a good reputation with those outside the church. If you don't make peace with someone you have offended, you are likely to lose the respect of others, you open yourself to legitimate reproach (criticism/ blame), and you could rightly be called a hypocrite by those outside the church.

Assume you are in the offended or initiator role and you have met with God and completed all of the points of Stage One thoroughly and in good faith.

Let's say the *Analyze* and *Evaluate* points have convinced you that what the offender did is serious enough to approach them about. You have searched your heart and you believe love is your motive to have that conversation. But, let's say you are hesitant to talk with the offender because you are afraid of making a mistake, or you fear the offender's potential reaction.

Let me encourage you not to let fear keep you from talking with the offender if the other steps of Stage One indicate that you should have a conversation with them. You may be the first person in the offender's life who has cared enough to go through all of the points of Stage One and tried to lovingly win them (Matthew 18:15), gently restore them (Galatians 6:1–2), and rescue them from death (James 5:19–20).

Prepare with love

ROLES INVOLVED

PURPOSE

If you are ready to process this step, you have made your decision to meet with the other party at Stage Two. The purpose of this step is for you to prepare carefully and prayerfully for that conversation.

KEY QUESTIONS

How would you want to be approached if you were in the role of the other person?

Have you reviewed your motive and plan for talking with them?

Whatever your role, you want to try to create an environment for your Stage Two conversation where the other person would most likely respond to you and do their part to make peace. Here are some tips for you to think about as you prepare.

- Envision yourself in the place of the other party. When and where would you want to be approached if you were in their role? How would you want to be spoken to? When you think of their personality, culture, and spiritual gifting, what kinds of words and body language would communicate best to them? These types of questions are an application of considering the other person's interests more important than your own (Philippians 2:3–4).

- Plan a time that is convenient for the other party so that your conversation will not be rushed.
- Choose a place that is convenient for the other party and will be quiet with no distractions from noise or people.
- Practice what you are going to say before you meet. Sometimes when I am coaching someone, they tell me something like this: "When I meet with the person, I'm going to say such-and-such." It is good for them to think this way and to envision what that conversation might look like. However, my advice to them and to you is not just to imagine what you will say, but actually practice as if you are in a dress rehearsal for a play. If you find it helpful, write down notes to help you focus.

If you role play with a coach, they can help you see how clearly you communicate what you were hoping for the other person to understand. This can help if you are nervous or if your relational problem evokes strong emotions. Sometimes the words that actually come out of your mouth when you practice might be different than what you intended when you initially prepared in your mind. It is good to get that difference sorted out at Stage One before you go to Stage Two.

If you have met with God and completed all the steps of Stage One, you are ready to make your final preparations for Stage Two.

Keep these things in mind, depending on your role:

If you are in the offender role, prepare so that your confession is honest about your offense, shows humility, and is honoring to the offended. Consider the offended party's personality, culture, spiritual gifting, and their tendency toward truth or grace.

If you are in the offended role, prepare so that you have adequately analyzed and evaluated the issue. State your unmet expectations clearly. Use biblical terms if you believe the issue involves sin.

If you are in the initiator role, add an extra measure of caution and tentativeness to your preparation.

Now go to your role at Stage Two in Chapter 7 for ideas about how you can make arrangements with the other party to have your conversation.

7. STAGE TWO: IF APPROPRIATE, MEET WITH THE OTHER PERSON

 **Make sure you prayerfully and thoughtfully complete Stage One for your role before you continue!**

STAGE TWO OVERVIEW

A conversation, not a confrontation

Stage Two normally involves two people who converse or communicate in the way, place, and time which will create the most effective environment for appropriate confession and forgiveness. *How* this environment is created can depend on cultural norms and various circumstances. I will briefly address a few of these circumstances and cultural norms below, but first I need to clarify an important point.

Many people in the offended or initiator role have admitted to me that they have been hesitant to talk with an offender because they didn't want to "confront" him. The majority of native English speakers I have talked with think and feel that to confront is something negative.

There is good reason for them to think and feel this way. The Oxford Dictionary (oxfordictionaries.com) defines the verb confront as "come face to face (with someone) with hostile or argumentative intent." A sub-definition is "compel (someone) to face or consider something, *especially by way of accusation*" [emphasis mine].

Let me be clear here. The first meeting at Stage Two is not a time when the offended or an initiator "confronts" the offender, in the way the Oxford Dictionary and so many native English speakers define that word. If you are the offended or initiator and you process Stage One sincerely and completely, *how* you approach the offender at Stage Two (time, place, words, body language) should feel to them more like a conversation than a confrontation.

Of course, the purpose of an offended or initiator having a Stage Two conversation with an offender is to discuss the offender's presumed fault, sin, or offense. Popular English versions of Matthew 18:15 translate this encounter as "point out their fault, just between the two of you" (NIV), "tell him his fault, between you and him alone" (ESV), and "show him his fault in private" (NASB). Even if the sin of the offender is serious, you can "point out" or "tell him" or "show him" the problem with a cool head and warm heart in a calm, rational way. The more your Stage Two meeting feels to the offender like a conversation rather than a confrontation, the more likely he is to listen to you, the more likely you are to "win" (NASB, NIV) or "gain" (ESV) your brother (Matthew 18:15), and the more likely you will be able to "restore him in a spirit of gentleness" (Galatians 6:1–2). This is why I urge you to meet with God prayerfully, thoughtfully, and sincerely and complete all the steps of Stage One before you meet with the offender at Stage Two.

How circumstances can affect Stage Two

As we saw above, in Matthew 18:15 Jesus uses a phrase that is translated, "just between the two of you," "between you and him alone," and "in private" to describe an interaction between an assumed offended person and a supposed offender, or between a person in the initiator role and a supposed offender. I believe a possible reason Jesus chose to use those particular words was to show us a way to create a safe environment where the supposed offender would most likely listen to someone who cared enough to gently and calmly approach him with the motive of restoring him to right relationship with God and his community without shaming him, embarrassing him, or exposing him to potential gossip. With those same motives and principles in mind, we say that a Stage Two interaction normally involves two people.

However, I doubt that in Matthew 18:15 Jesus meant to institute a legalistic practice to be followed in every case, every time, without exception. Jesus demonstrated by his words and actions that he valued people more than procedures. I believe that there are circumstances where the biblical values of love, wisdom, and protecting the vulnerable should take priority over the practice of an initiator or offended person meeting alone with the offender. I'll give two examples.

Protect all parties

The *P* in the P.E.A.C.E. Principles stands for Protect all parties. If you are in the offended role, there may be times you need to protect yourself from a particularly violent or powerful offender. Examples could be physical, sexual, emotional, or mental misconduct. In such cases, it is simply not wise or loving for you to meet alone. In cases of serious maltreatment, consult with specialists in that field. Also, review again the *Question your role* step of Stage One. Perhaps you should not be a person who approaches the offender at all.

Consider the nature of the offense

If an offender's sin affects many people, if it is particularly grave or dangerous, or if it tempts people to slander the name of Christ and his sincere followers, it is conceivable for you in the initiator role to go to the offender with an appropriate person who has also completed Stage One. Again, the key here is to create the environment where the offender is most likely to listen to you.

Cultural factors and Stage Two

This handbook is about helping two sincere followers of Jesus apply the biblical principles of honor, honesty, and humility to reach appropriate confession and forgiveness to resolve a relational problem between the two of them. It is not meant to be an exhaustive treatment of the cultural factors which affect how people of different faiths or worldviews deal with conflicts. However, since all of us can be affected by the culture around us, I want to share two observations I have made based on many years of helping Christians from a number of ethnic and national backgrounds make peace with each other.

Don't ignore culture

Some people make the mistake of ignoring cultural differences when approaching Stage Two. This is not wise or loving. If you don't try to understand the other person's culture, you might be tempted to wrongly judge their values or behavior as sin, just because they are different from yours. When you appreciate another person's social values and background, you are more able to distinguish legitimate offenses from simple cultural differences. The *Analyze, Take the plank out of your eye,* and *Prepare with love* steps of Stage One can help you make those distinctions.

Don't use culture as an excuse to avoid honesty, honor, and humility in confession and forgiveness at Stage Two

In some cultures, factors such as differences in age, gender, education, marital status, or social position may hinder two Christians from meeting alone for a peacemaking conversation at Stage Two. Or, at least these customs might make it extremely unlikely that a supposed offender would listen to an initiator or an offended person in a conversation where the two are alone. Of course, you need to keep these cultural factors in mind as you consider how to create the best environment for the two parties to reach appropriate confession and forgiveness.

At the same time, be aware that to combine all three biblical values of honesty, humility, and honor to achieve appropriate confession and forgiveness between two people is counter-cultural in virtually every human society. Sometimes a person may hinder your peacemaking efforts by playing the "cultural trump card" and communicate to you verbally or non-verbally something like, "We don't resolve conflicts that way in my culture [or family or church]." When I encounter situations like this, I try to have a respectful discussion with the person. By the end of our conversation, we usually discover together that their culture's way of dealing with conflict is actually weak in or lacks one or more of the biblical values of honesty, humility, and honor, just like virtually every other culture in the world, including mine.

When both parties in a relational problem are followers of Jesus, they should follow biblical commands and values to reach appropriate confession and forgiveness, whether their culture is labeled guilt-innocence, honor-shame, Northern, Southern, Eastern, or Western. The offender and offended both need to humble themselves, not preserve their own pride or humiliate the other person. They both need to be honest about offenses given and received, not hide them or deny them. And, they each need to promote the other person's honor, not protect their own.

An exceptional Stage Two: going alone with somebody

To review, at Stage One, one person meets with God. At Stage Two, normally two people meet together alone. However, let's say you are in the offended role or the initiator role and that you think you are in an exceptional situation. For example, you believe you need to take someone else along when you talk with the offender for the first time because of a legitimate cultural reason such as when you and the offender are of the opposite sex.

In a case like that, I recommend you do what you can to make that conversation seem like a one-to-one conversation, just between you and the offender. I call this "going alone with somebody." You could call it Stage 2.1. This is not a Stage Three situation, which you would normally consider only after trying more than one Stage Two conversations.

Though it can be awkward, when you arrange a meeting with the offender, I advise that you communicate to them your intention to bring someone along who will not participate in your conversation, but whose presence would enable your meeting with them to be culturally appropriate.

If at all possible, make sure the person you want to bring along is someone who is respected and trusted by the offender, and who will remain silent while you and the offender discuss your relational problem "just between the two of you." This arrangement allows you and the offender to interact just between yourselves even though there is someone else in the room. That's why I describe this idea as "going alone with somebody," or Stage 2.1.

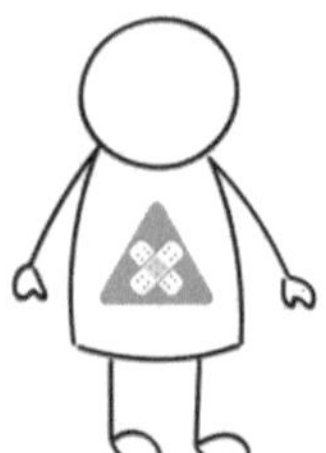

THE OFFENDED ROLE AT STAGE TWO

Before you move on to Stage Two, make sure you have completed Stage One in the offended role.

Let's review how you reached Peace Pursuit Stage Two. You felt some kind of offense by another person. This put you in the Peace

Pursuit offended role and the other person in the offender role. While you met with God during Stage One, you had two biblical choices. In this case, you chose Option 2.

Offended Role

Complete Stage 1: Meet with God. You will then decide whether or not to have a conversation with the offender.

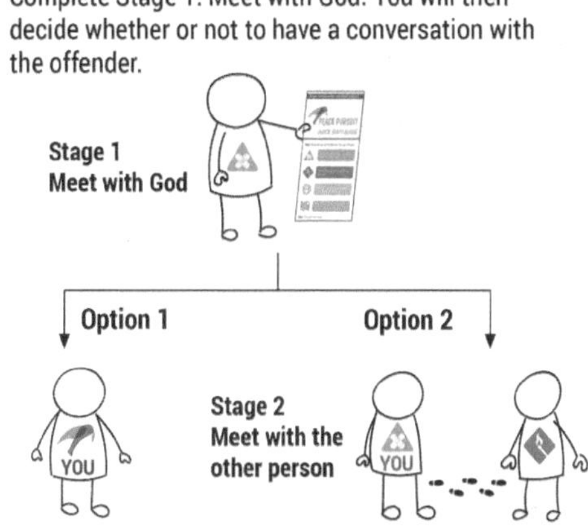

I will forgive in my heart, overlook the offense, and not have a conversation with the person at this time.

I will forgive in my heart and have a peacemaking conversation with the person.

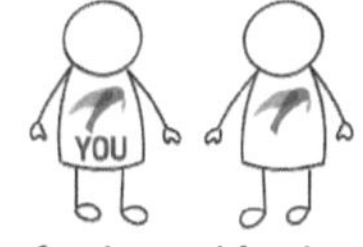

Confession and forgiveness, as appropriate

Remember that the goal of your Stage Two conversation with the offender is to arrive at appropriate confession and forgiveness, the "Bounce of Peace." Always patiently listen to the offender's responses to what you bring up to them. If they apologize, grant them your forgiveness. Repent of any part you may have had in the situation. Then celebrate together that you have made peace.

It is possible that when you talk with the offender you will find out that you were mistaken in your understanding of some part of the situation. You might find out you were wrong about the offender's words or actions or the context of your perceived offense. Don't let this possibility discourage you from having a Stage Two conversation. If you have done Stage One as well as you can, and if you have approached them at Stage Two like I describe here, the person you thought was the offender will probably still thank you for caring enough to talk with them.

In an ideal conversation, the offender will believe the best and trust you have come with good motives. They will humble themselves, they will rejoice in the truth of what you have brought them, they will repent with godly sorrow, they will receive your forgiveness, they will thank you and thank God for you, they will try to make right anything their sin has caused, and they will forgive you for anything you may confess to them.

Q: How do I prepare for and arrange a conversation with the offender?

For many people, just knowing how to get a conversation started with an offender is a huge step toward making peace. If you are convinced you are the appropriate person to talk with the offender and have prepared by completing all the steps of Stage One, you are ready to approach the offender in love. Preparing in love means you will practice how you are going to bring up the subject with the offender. Choose a time and place that will be convenient for them. You want to create an environment for them to be ready to hear what you want to share. You will approach them with an attitude like you would want to be approached with if you were in their shoes.

As you think and pray about the best time and environment for your Stage Two conversation, you can choose to bring up the subject during a meal, an informal time together, special meeting you have arranged, or some other context. Again, the important thing is to create a situation where you and the other person will be as calm and prepared to listen to each other as possible.

If at all possible, arrange your Stage Two meeting by talking in person, by video call, or by voice call. Using these forms of communication can show that you value your personal relationship with the offender and may lower tension. Email and texting can be perceived as impersonal and unfeeling.

Here are a few ideas about how you could bring up the idea of a conversation with the offender. Of course, you would say these in your own words and after you have made appropriate greetings.

> *"Neal, do you have a few minutes to talk sometime soon? I'd like to ask you about what I heard you say to me the other day."*
>
> *"Katrina, can we discuss the project we are working on? I'd like to clarify with you what you understand our individual responsibilities in the project to be."*

> *"Nancy, can we have a chat about the church picnic last weekend? I wonder if I misunderstood something you did there."*

Notice that none of these examples say, "I want to come and show you your fault," or "I want to rebuke you for your sin toward me," or "I need to confront you about something." These examples use tentative and non-accusing language, but they still include a clear statement that you want to talk about something the person said, did, or did not do.

Tips for the offended role at Stage Two

These are some practical ideas for how to act and speak when you meet with the offender at Stage Two. This is not a legalistic formula. It is simply a list of things to remember during your conversation. These tips are outlined in the Peace Pursuit Quick Start Guide as well.

Review your preparation from Stage One

Look back at the Stage One process to remind yourself of the reasons why you are having this conversation. Make sure you have completed the *Prepare with love* point.

Approach in love

Arrange a time and place that will be quiet and convenient for the offender. Enter the conversation with the attitude you would want to be approached with if your roles were reversed. Remember that the Holy Spirit is the one who convicts them of sin (Matthew 7:12, Galatians 6:1, Proverbs 25:8–12).

Use God-honoring speech

Speak calmly and respectfully. Avoid accusatory words. Control your eyes, face, arms, hands, and posture so that your body language does not appear angry, challenging, or threatening. State any offenses with clear, biblical terms as much as possible (Ephesians 4:29; Proverbs 15:1; 25:11–12).

Speak with "I" statements when you first share your thoughts and feelings about the situation

For example, you can begin with "I" statements like these:

> *"I was [confused / hurt / surprised / offended] during our conversation the other day."*

> *"I would like to share how I perceived the situation when we last interacted."*
>
> *"Here's how I felt after we last talked."*

Confess with genuine sorrow

If you have contributed to the problem in some way, confess and repent for your fault. Review the *Repent of your part* step of Stage One (Chapter 6) before you go (2 Corinthians 7:8–11).

Listen

Be quick to hear, slow to speak, and slow to anger. Give your sincere attention to their responses. Do not interrupt them or speak over them (James 1:19, Proverbs 18:17). As you politely discuss the issue, clarify and correct any misunderstanding of facts from your perspective or theirs.

Grant forgiveness

If the offender repents, give them your forgiveness. Review the *Forgive* point of Stage One (Luke 17:3–4).

Q: What are some ways the offender might respond to me when I have a conversation with them in the offended role?

Even when you prayerfully complete Stage One and approach an offender in a respectful and appropriate manner, they could respond in a variety of ways. It is good for you to know these possibilities so that you are not surprised by any of them. Here are some common examples.

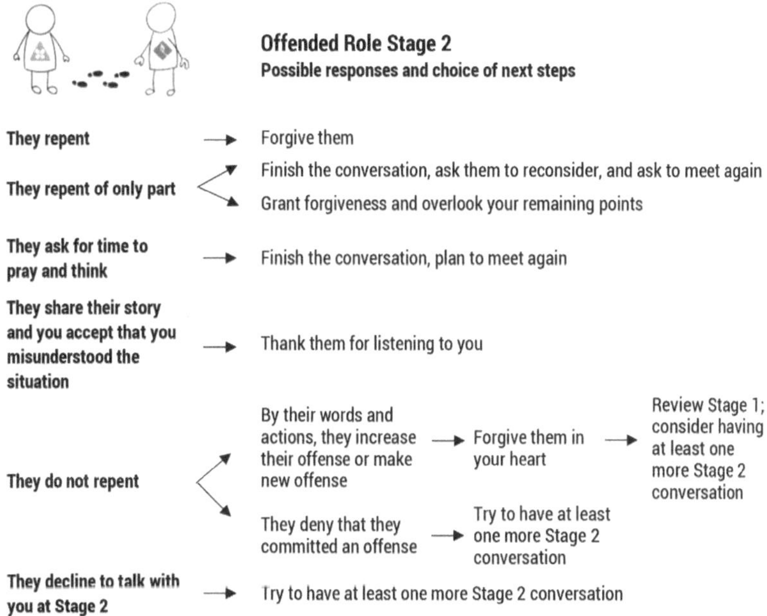

- **They could receive what you have shown them and repent to you.** You would then grant them personal forgiveness. Then together you could thank God that you reached peace.
- **They could decide to hear what you have to say, but repent of only part of what you have shown them.** Then you will have two more choices, depending on how serious you consider the offenses they do not confess. (Remember, in the *Analyze* point of Stage One you prioritized the offenses you wanted to talk about with the offender.)
    - You can ask if they will take some time to pray and think about what you've brought up to them and agree to have a follow-up conversation with them.
    - You can grant them forgiveness for what they have confessed and you can decide to overlook the remaining points.
- **They could ask for time to pray and process what you have said to them.** Sometimes the offender will be completely surprised at what you bring up. They may need time to consider thoughtfully and prayerfully what you have presented to them. They may even want to consult a coach to help them process what you have brought to them. It's loving for you to give them time and space, and not to make them feel pressured to repent to you immediately. Ask them to agree with you on a time and place when you will continue this conversation.

- **They could respectfully explain where they believe you have misunderstood the situation.** You could be convinced by their explanation and accept that you did indeed misunderstand the situation. Then you would thank the person for their time and patience to hear you out.
- **They could hear all you have to say, but not repent of what you have shared with them.** If they simply deny they committed an offense, try to have another Stage Two conversation later. If by their words or actions during your conversation they increase their offense toward you or make a new offense, forgive them in your heart, review Stage One, and consider having another Stage Two conversation with them.
- **They could decide not to hear what you have to say.** You could then choose to have another conversation with them later after you have thought and prayed more about the situation.

Q: What if the offender really has committed an offense but does not confess or apologize to me?

This is a sad situation, especially if you have met with God and completed Stage One in good faith before you talk with them at Stage Two. Ask God to help you maintain your forgiveness of the offender in your heart. This helps deter you from bitterness or holding a grudge. Be comforted and encouraged that even if they don't apologize to you, you will have done what depends on you to be at peace (Romans 12:18).

You may wish to ask them to have another Stage Two conversation. If they don't accept their fault a second time (or if they refuse to have a second conversation with you), you have the option of moving to Peace Pursuit Stage Three.

Q: What if the offender's confession isn't like I wanted it to be?

The Golden Rule, Matthew 7:12, applies here: "Whatever you wish that others would do to you, do also to them." Receive their apology like you would want a person you have offended to receive your imperfect confession.

Maybe the offender has not prepared a well-rounded confession like I describe in *Repent of your part* (Chapter 6). If you sense they are sincerely sorry and are basically addressing the offense you have in mind, grant them forgiveness as specifically as you can.

Q: How many times should I repeat Stage Two?

How many times you need to meet at Stage Two depends on how willing both you and the other party are to look at the situation with eyes of truth and a heart of grace.

During your first Stage Two conversation, the offender might ask you for time to thoughtfully pray about what you have brought them. They could meet with God in the offender role using the Peace Pursuit Quick Start Guide. Then, they would arrange to meet with you again to clarify with you any remaining misunderstandings and/or appropriately repent for their fault you have shown them. You will then grant them forgiveness. In this example, you will reach peace in two Stage Two conversations.

However, Stage Two may need more than two conversations between you and the offender. That is not a bad or shameful situation. It doesn't mean you are failing at peacemaking. Remember, you are having a conversation with them for the goal of mutual understanding and appropriate confession and forgiveness. In fact, having more than two discussions may bring a clearer and deeper peace between you.

Let's say that you don't reach peace after multiple Stage Two conversations, and you are sincerely convinced that the offender needs to repent. The Bible calls this "not listening" on the part of the offender (Matthew 18:15–17). If that is the case, you should seriously consider moving to Stage Three and ask an appropriate person to help you and the other party move toward peace.

Q: What if I approach the offender in an inappropriate way?

If you meet with God and process Stage One prayerfully and completely, you'll likely not find yourself in this position.

However, if for some reason you do decide to go to the offender when you don't have legitimate reason to, or if you go to them with a wrong attitude or manner, you should confess and repent of your lack of love and kindness to them.

Q: Are there cases when I can take someone else along the first time I talk to the offender about their offense?

In the introduction to Stage Two, I mentioned a few exceptions to the principle of the two parties conversing alone. If you haven't read that introduction, please do so before you continue.

There are many benefits of talking with the offender alone. Since only you and the offender are involved, talking with the offender alone protects them from these possibilities:

- The potential for being a victim of gossip
- Interference by aggravators
- Shame and embarrassment in front of others

Also, if you and the offender can make peace without involving anyone else, the next time you have a relational problem you are likely to resolve it just between the two of you again. This will keep you from falling into the habit of bringing others in to help you make peace every time there is an offense between you.

If you complete Stage One and conclude that you should have a conversation with the offender at Stage Two, Matthew 18:15 clearly directs you to speak with the offender alone or in private.

Ask yourself questions like these if you do not want to talk with the offender alone the first time you bring up the subject with them.

- What approach will "win" or "gain" the offender (Matthew 18:15) and "gently restore" them (Galatians 6:1) while at the same time protect them from potential gossip, from interference by aggravators, and from undeserved shame and embarrassment?
- What would you want done if you were in the offender's place? Would you want an offended person or initiator to come alone to you, or would you want them to bring someone else along?

There are some cautions to consider before you take someone else along:

- If you decide not to do Stage Two alone, you raise the potential for gossip and for the shame and embarrassment of the offender. If you come to the offender with someone else without talking to the offender alone first, you may create fear in them, or make them defensive. Neither of these reactions is likely to make them more willing to listen to you.
- The offender may ask you, "Why didn't you come to me alone like the Bible says to do in Matthew 18:15?" Be prepared to answer this question with wise, loving, and godly reasons.

Q: A person has approached me to talk about my relationship with someone else. They are concerned that I am offended and have not made peace with the other person. How should I respond?

If the person coming to you has prayerfully completed Stage One in the Peace Pursuit initiator role, it means they care for you very much. I advise that you listen to their concern for you and explain your perspective. After your conversation, you can decide for yourself if it is appropriate to begin Stage One in the offended role in relation to the person who offended you.

If the person who has approached you has not completed Stage One in the initiator role, you can still respectfully listen to what they have to say and decide if you want to fill the offended role.

THE OFFENDER ROLE AT STAGE TWO

When you know or believe you have sinned against or offended someone, complete Stage One before you go to apologize to them.

When I introduced the offender role earlier, I said there are three common scenarios for that role.

1. You are aware that you are an offender. No one has approached you yet to talk about the situation.

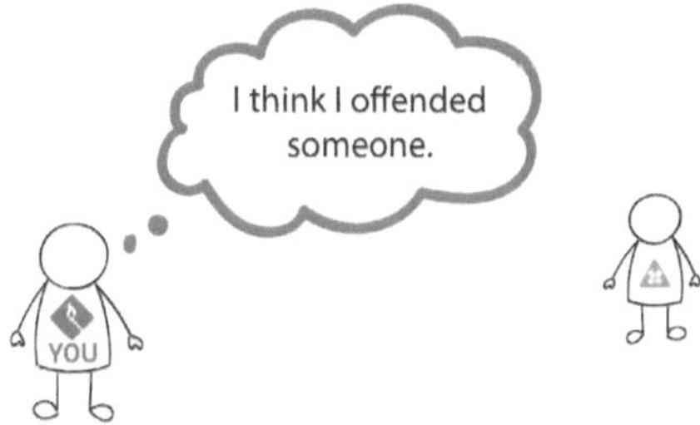

2. You have been approached by someone who feels they have been offended by you. This puts you in the offender role.

3. You have been approached by someone who is taking the initiator role and who believes you are in the offender role.

Since you've read this far, you are already familiar with the biblical choices and responsibilities of the offender role (see Chapter 5). Here, I will only repeat essential points as we look at the offender role at Stage Two.

Offender role scenario 1

You are aware that you are an offender. No one has approached you yet to talk about the situation.

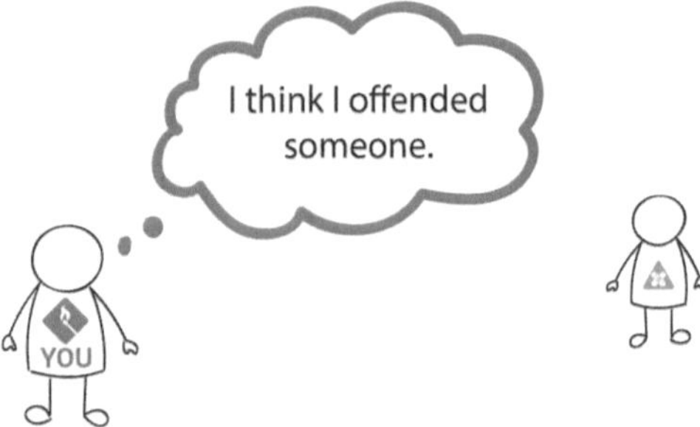

At Stage Two, approach the offended with love to confess your fault with honesty, humility, and honor. To approach them with love means you'll choose a time and place that is appropriate and convenient for the offended person. You'll use words and tone of voice that you would want someone to use with you if your roles were reversed. Ideally, the offended will grant you forgiveness and you will achieve peace. You can then start to rebuild your relationship with the offended.

Here is what this scenario looks like. First, complete the Peace Pursuit Quick Start Guide in the offender role at Stage One. Then meet with the person to apologize to them.

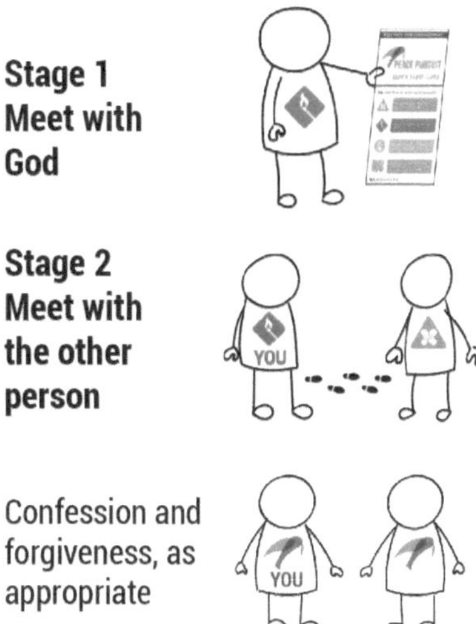

Q: How do I start a conversation with the offended person?

Let's say you had a disagreement with Richard two days ago. You perceived from his body language and heard from his voice that he was offended by your words and actions. Since then, you have realized you were primarily in the offender role because of how you treated or responded to him (even if you still disagree with him over the content or subject of your argument). Let's say you have completed Stage One and now you want to apologize to him for the way you interacted with him. Think and pray about when and where it would be best for him for you to talk together. Depending on the situation, you might need to set up an appointment for a convenient time to meet in person or make a call. You could say something like this:

> *"Richard, do you have a few minutes sometime soon? I'd like to apologize for how I behaved toward you during our discussion the other day."*

With these two simple sentences you already show honesty, humility, and honor to Richard, even before you've made your apology. If you begin your conversation like this, it will probably melt some of the ice between you. Richard will likely be open to listen to you and forgive you. He might even be pleasantly surprised by your approach to him if he's never received a proper apology from someone before.

This is a much better way to bring up the subject with Richard than if you said something vague like, "Richard, can we get together and talk?" Remember that Richard's last memory of you was your conversation in which you offended him. He may be wary of talking with you, because you haven't told him what you want to talk about. He may be wondering if you are just going to continue offending him, or if you are going to blame him for something. So, make your intentions clear from the start.

Q: I sense I have offended someone, but I'm not sure they are actually offended. How do I start a conversation with them?

You want to make a gentle, tentative exploration of whether you offended them or not. Choose your words carefully so that you don't come across as accusing them of something or being defensive yourself. This is one of the rare situations when it is appropriate to use a phrase like, "if I offended you." (I strongly recommend not saying "if I offended you" in a case where you are sure you offended them or they have told you that they are offended.)

Here are some possible introductions for a conversation with someone you think you might have offended. After you make appropriate greetings, you could say something like these examples. Of course, you would adapt them to your situation.

- *"Tracy, may I ask you how you received my words and actions today? I am wondering how I came across to you."*
- *"Patricia, it seems that our interactions have become shorter and less frequent lately. I value our communication, and I am just wondering if I have done something to harm our relationship. Would you mind if we talked about this?"*
- *"Henry, I noticed the other day when we were talking that your countenance changed somewhat after I shared my opinion. May I ask if something I said or the way I said it that bothered [upset / frustrated / offended] you?"*

Like with any Stage Two interaction, you should choose a time and place that is convenient for them to have a quiet, uninterrupted conversation.

Q: Is it OK for me to bring up the other person's offenses toward me in the same conversation when I am apologizing to them?

Naturally, you don't want to appear like you are confessing your part in a conflict just to manipulate the other person into admitting their fault. On the other hand, if you value your relationship and want to speak truth in love, you can consider at least bringing up to them how you feel they also offended you.

To prepare for this situation, I suggest that you pray and process Stage One twice. Vew yourself first in the offender role, and then a second time in the offended role. Try as hard as you can to separate your offenses to them and their offenses to you as you process the *Analyze*, *Evaluate*, *Take the plank out of your eye*, and *Forgive* steps.

Also ask yourself, "Was their offense possibly a reaction to what I first did to them?" In other words, did you start it? If yours was the first fault in what became a series of back-and-forth mutual offenses between you, then the humblest road for you is to take responsibility, admit your fault, and overlook their reaction.

To be clear about your intentions for talking with the other party when you feel there are mutual offenses between you, you could say something like this when you are arranging the time and place for the conversation:

> *"Alison, I would like to have a time where we talk about our relationship. I know I have done some things to offend you, and I want to apologize to you for them. I would also like to share how I have perceived your interactions with me. Would that be OK?"*

Here is some encouragement for you, from my personal experience and from observing others. If you have prepared well at Stage One and you have arranged a time and place to meet at Stage Two that is convenient and appropriate for the other party, most of the time they will not only listen to your apology and forgive you, they will probably humble themselves to some degree and admit at least part of their contribution to the conflict.

Q: Are there situations when I might take someone else along when I want to apologize to the offended?

Sometimes an offended person might not trust you enough to be alone with you, even when you want to apologize to them. In that case, you can offer to bring another person with you when you apologize to the offended. I believe this is legitimate if the person who comes with you does not speak for you and only silently observes your apology and the offended person's response.

For example, let's say you have offended Deborah and you know she does not want to be alone with you. You could try to find someone who you are sure that Deborah trusts to protect her. For example, you could say something like this to Deborah:

> *"Deborah, I would like to come and sincerely apologize to you. Is it OK if I bring someone we both trust along to be with us while I apologize? I'd like someone to hold me accountable for confessing and repenting to you in the appropriate way. If you agree, let's discuss who might be appropriate to be with us during our conversation."*

If Deborah agrees to this idea, you can contact the person you both have decided on and ask them to be a silent witness for you.

If Deborah will not accept anyone else to be present, and still won't allow you to come alone, you could offer her your confession by internet video, by voice call, or in writing. If she accepts none of those options, you can rest in the fact that you have done what you can in good faith to make peace with her, as much as it depends on you (Romans 12:18).

Q: What if the offended person does not grant me forgiveness when I apologize, even if I've done Stage One well?

It's possible the offended wants to forgive you, but at the same time they may still be very affected by the nature or depth of your offense. They may need time to heal somewhat before they are able to have the spiritual strength and emotional capacity to forgive you in their heart and then grant you forgiveness in person. In this case, you will probably just have to be patient and bear with this consequence of your offense until they are ready to go through the forgiveness process.

In rare cases, the offended might choose not to grant you forgiveness at all. If you have done Stage One well, and if you have apologized with honesty, humility, and honor, then you can rest in the knowledge that you have obeyed Romans 12:18. That is, you've done everything in your power, as far as it depends on you, to be at peace with them. If they don't forgive you in their heart before God, or if they don't grant you forgiveness personally, that is a problem they have in their relationship with God. You are likely not the best person to discuss that topic with them.

Offender role scenario 2

You have been approached by someone who feels they have been offended by you. This puts you in the offender role.

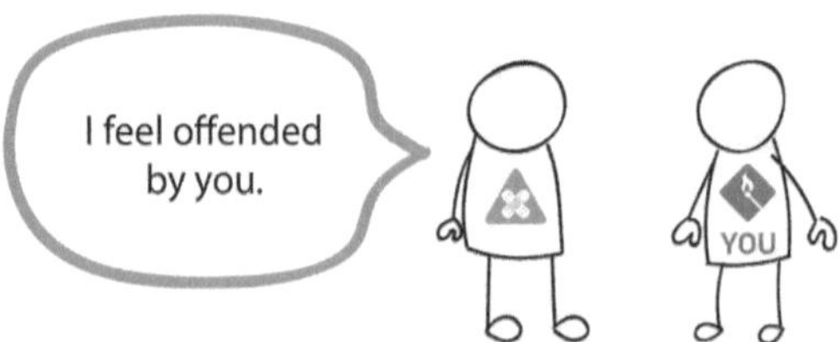

You have three good options to choose from when a person who feels offended by you comes to talk with you about their feeling of offense. You could also choose a bad option.

Let's say Bob feels he has been offended by you and approaches you to talk about it.

Good option 1

Receive what the offended says and confess to them.

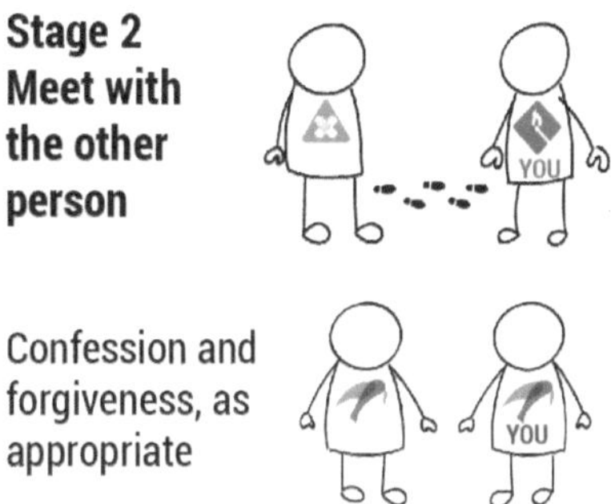

If you receive what Bob shares and you are convinced you are at fault, you could respond like this.

> *"Bob, thank you for coming to me with this. I appreciate the care you have taken to come to me. I see that what you have shown me is true, and I repent of [specific offense]."*

Good option 2

Listen to the offended and ask for some time to process on your own what they have said to you.

You could respond in a way similar to this:

> *"Bob, thank you for bringing this up to me. I'd like some time to spend with God praying and thinking about what you've said. Can we meet together again two days from now?"*

If Bob is a reasonable and sincere follower of Jesus, he would likely understand and agree with your request. You would then keep your word to meet with God at Stage One in the offender role and contact Bob to make an appointment to meet with him in two days.

Good option 3

Listen to the offended and discuss any misunderstandings right then.

You could calmly and respectfully respond like this:

> *"Bob, thank you for sharing your thoughts and feelings. I don't quite see things as you do at the moment. I want to understand your perspective, and I'd like to share mine with you, as well. May we talk this through some more right now?*

Again, if Bob is a reasonable person and follower of the Prince of Peace, he will agree to your request. (If Bob met with God and completed all the points of Stage One before coming to you, he will have planned for time for you two to continue your conversation.) You would then respectfully listen and respond in a godly way as Bob shares more. You may then confess whatever amount of Bob's perceived offense that you can receive in good conscience. If you believe that some or all of Bob's feeling of offense is not legitimate, you would patiently and respectfully explain your perspective.

A bad option

Refuse to listen at least once to the offended person.

You could choose to make unbiblical responses like these: "I don't want to hear this!" or "What do you mean I have offended you? You offended me!" or "I'm offended that you would call me the offender!"

This choice could lead to a number of consequences for you. Your relationships with God and with the other party could be negatively affected. And, your faith community might need to become involved in the resolution of your conflict.

Offender role scenario 3

You have been approached by someone who is taking the initiator role and who believes you are in the offender role.

You have two good options when a person approaches you to talk about your role in a conflict when they are not one of the parties. You can also choose a bad option.

Let's say Kathy believes you have offended Bianca and does not think you have approached Bianca to apologize. Kathy sees herself in the initiator role, and she sees you in the offender role. She approaches you to talk about your relationship with Bianca.

Good option 1

Listen to the initiator and accept the offender role right away.

You could respond to Kathy in this way:

> *"Kathy, thank you for coming to me with this. I appreciate the care you have for me and my relationship with Bianca. I see that what you have shown me is true. I will now meet with God at Stage One in the offender role and prepare to apologize to Bianca."*

You would then complete Stage One in the offender role and arrange an appropriate time and place with Bianca to confess to her at Stage Two.

Good option 2

Listen to the initiator and inform them you will take some time to process sincerely and prayerfully what they have said to you:

> *"Kathy, thank you for bringing this up to me. I would like some time to spend with God praying and thinking about what you've said. Can we meet together again two days from now?"*

You would then complete Stage One in the offender role. After that, you would contact Kathy to have another conversation. During that talk, you would inform Kathy that you believe you should repent to Bianca, or you would respectfully explain to Kathy how you see the situation differently than she does.

A bad option

Refuse to listen at least once to an initiator.

You could make bad responses to Kathy, like "This is none of your business!" or "Who do you think you are to say I am at fault?"

This choice could lead to a number of consequences for you. Your relationships with God and with the other party could be negatively affected. And, your faith community might need to become involved in the resolution of your conflict.

Tips for the offender role at Stage Two

Here's some advice for you to keep in mind when someone wants to talk with you in the offender role at Stage Two. These tips are also outlined in the Peace Pursuit Quick Start Guide.

Believe the best

Unless you have good reason to believe otherwise, trust that the person has come out of love for you and with a godly attitude. Believe the best even if they don't approach you at a time, place, or in a manner that you feel is right (1 Corinthians 13:7).

Listen

Give your ear to the person patiently, attentively, sincerely, and completely before you respond. God may be speaking to you through them (James 1:19, Proverbs 18:17, Proverbs 25:12).

Humble yourself

God will give you grace if you humble yourself and seriously consider what the person says, even if it feels uncomfortable to you. Ask yourself, "What might God be trying to teach me here?" (James 4:6).

Rejoice in the truth

There may be some truth in whatever you are being approached about, even if it is a small part. Love rejoices in the truth (1 Corinthians 13:6).

Repent with godly sorrow

Genuinely acknowledge, confess, and renounce with biblical terms any sin you can admit to. Make a commitment to change. See the *Repent of your part* step of Stage One (Chapter 6) for how to humble yourself, how to be honest about your offense, and how to honor the one you offended (2 Corinthians 7:8–11, Proverbs 28:13).

Receive forgiveness and cleansing from God

If you truly repent, be assured you are cleansed and forgiven by God (1 John 1:9).

Receive forgiveness from the other party

If the person you offended forgives you, receive that as grace as well.

Give thanks

Thank the person for taking the time, trouble, and potential risk to approach you. Thank God for sending them to you (1 Thessalonians 5:18).

Grant forgiveness

If the other person repents of any offense toward you in the same conversation, grant them your personal forgiveness (Luke 17:3–4). See the *Forgive* step of Stage One (Chapter 6).

Make right any wrongs you can

Embrace the consequences of your offense and do what you can to repair the practical and relational damage you caused. Of course, depending on your offense, this can take time, effort, and expense (Matthew 3:8, Hebrews 12:11, Acts 26:20, Galatians 6:7–8).

Q: I feel I have been wrongly accused by someone. How should I respond?

Calmly, respectfully, and patiently explain your perspective of the situation to the person.

Remember that Jesus did not respond in an ungodly way even when he was falsely accused of offenses that eventually led to his death (1 Peter 2:21–23, 1 Peter 3:15–17).

Sometimes in the normal course of life a person might feel hurt or offended by an action or decision you have had to make because of your responsibilities as a leader or person others are accountable to. For example, let's say Phil doesn't like a decision you had to make that affected him and he comes to you saying he is offended by your decision. Let's also say that after you listened to Phil, you met with God at Stage One to weigh what Phil has brought to you. If you are convinced that you did the right thing in an appropriate way, you can express sadness and regret that Phil was hurt by your actions without taking on undue blame or shame on yourself.

If Phil insists you are guilty but you are sure you are innocent, you can suggest that you and he get help from an appropriate person. You can suggest you two meet with someone you both trust who will fill the role of witness or mediator at Stage Three.

However, consider the possibility that you may have done the right thing, but you did it in an inappropriate way. For example, maybe you were not kind, gentle, or patient when you fulfilled your duty or responsibility toward Phil. In that case, you would repent of the way that you acted, not necessarily what you did.

THE INITIATOR ROLE AT STAGE TWO

Before you move on to Stage Two, make sure you have completed Stage One in the initiator role.

Let's review the description of the initiator role and how you got to this stage in the Peace Pursuit process. To be in the initiator role, you are not personally hurt or angered by the supposed offender. In other words, you are not in the offended role. You are a third party in one of these situations:

1. You observed with your own eyes or ears a conflict between a supposed offender and another person.

2. You strongly sense there is conflict between two people and you do not believe either of them is seeking peace. You are not sure who is the primary offender or offended person.

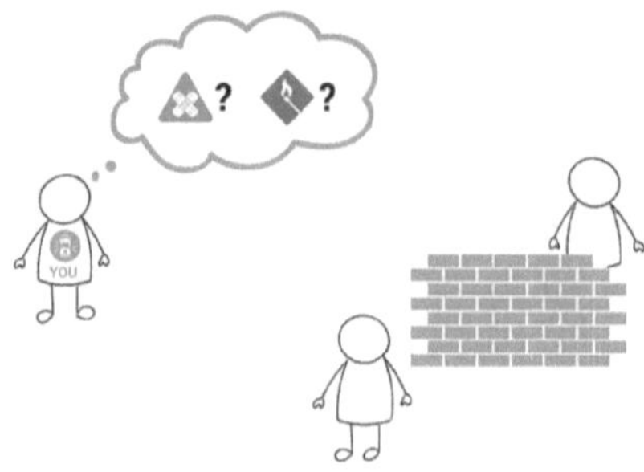

3. You sense that a supposed offender has sinned against God, but has not yet repented to him. The person's sin may or may not have apparent consequences for other people.

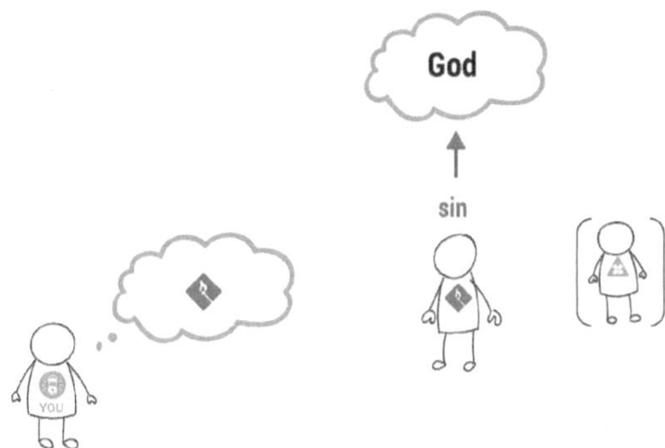

The main reason to consider filling the role of initiator is because you care for both parties' relationship with God and with other people, though you will likely focus on the supposed offender.

Here is what you were meant to do before you arrived at Stage Two. (If you haven't done these things, go back and complete Stage One in the initiator role.)

- You confirmed that the two parties indeed are not working toward peace between themselves.
- You discerned which of the two persons is likely to be the primary offender. Or, if you couldn't tell which one is the primary offender, you decided which party you think will most likely listen to you.
- You met with God first. After you fully completed Peace Pursuit Stage One, you were convinced you are an appropriate person to be an initiator, and you were prepared to have a conversation with one of the parties (usually the supposed offender).

What does an initiator do at Stage Two?

If you've done everything I explained in the preceding section, here are the next steps for you in the initiator role. In this situation, you would be approaching the supposed offender.

- Arrange a time and place that is convenient for the supposed offender to have a conversation with you. You

want to create an environment where the offender is most likely to listen to you. The place should be quiet and free from interruptions.
- Speak with them alone at Stage Two with a tentative, loving attitude like how you would want to be approached if you were in the offender's role. This conversation should feel to them more like a conversation than a confrontation.
- Respectfully discuss the issue with the offender, and clarify and correct any misunderstanding of facts.
- Encourage them to process Stage One in the offender role. During Stage One, they would prepare to have a conversation with the offended person.

At this point your role as initiator is complete. However, it is possible that this party might ask you to transition to the role of coach for them when they process the optional step, *Seek appropriate counsel* in Stage One. See the coach role section in Chapter 5.

Q: I believe I should be an initiator and I have completed Stage One as best I can. How can I initiate a conversation with the person I believe is the primary offender?

If at all possible, arrange your Stage Two meeting by talking in person, by video call, or by voice call. Using these forms of communication can show that you value your personal relationship with the supposed offender and may lower tension. Email and texting can be perceived as impersonal and unfeeling.

After you have made appropriate greetings, you could begin your conversation with something like the examples below. Maybe these examples will feel too direct to you, but remember that you would only approach the offender after you have completed Stage One. That means you have already prayed and processed the situation from a number of angles. And, it means you believe that the loving thing for the person (and for others) is for you to speak with them. Of course, you would communicate one of these ideas in your own words and in as relaxed a context as possible. You want the supposed offender to feel like your meeting is a conversation, not a confrontation.

- *"Jim, do you have a few minutes to talk? I'd like to ask you about what I heard you say when you spoke to Arthur the other day."*
- *"Elizabeth, I've noticed recently that you and Cindy don't seem to be as warm and congenial with each other as you have normally been. Would you mind if I talked with you about it?"*

- *"Naomi, can I talk with you about the church anniversary celebration last week? I saw you do a couple of things and I would like to see if I understood the situation correctly."*
- *"Alfred, do you mind if I bring something up? I've noticed that when you and Carl are in the same room, you both seem to avoid each other. I know it may be personal, but I just wanted to check as a brother to see if you think you need to do any peacemaking with Carl."*

Q: In the initiator role, if I have a Stage Two conversation with the person I believe to be the primary offender, what are some ways they might respond?

Even when you prayerfully complete Stage One in the initiator role and approach a person properly, they could respond in a variety of ways. Here are some common examples.

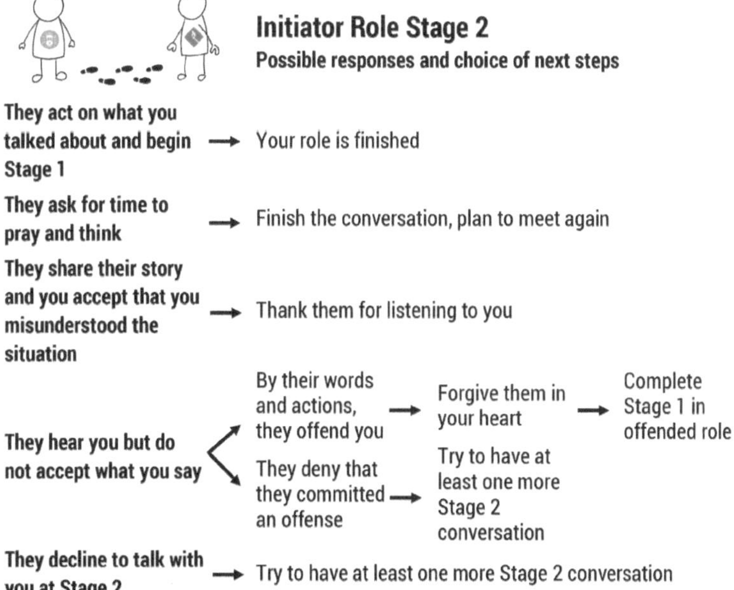

- **They could receive and act on what you have shown them.** Your role as initiator is then complete. They would process Stage One to prepare to have a conversation with the offended alone at Stage Two. When the offender processes the optional *Seek appropriate counsel* step of Stage One, they may want to consult a different person as a coach. Or, they might ask you to switch roles and become their coach. This is appropriate, as long as you and the offender keep in mind the description and responsibilities of the coach role at Stage One.

- **They could thank you for coming to them and ask for some time to think and pray about what you have said.** They could then arrange a time for you to meet again.
- **They could decide to hear what you have to say, but they could respectfully explain and convince you that you have misunderstood the situation.** If you are convinced by your conversation with them that in fact you did indeed misunderstand the situation, then thank the person for their time and patience to listen to you.
- **They could listen to all you have to say, but they do not accept it. They do not repent to God or the other person.** Let's assume you sincerely believe you have an accurate understanding of the facts of the situation. You may then decide to bring the subject up with the offender more than once at Stage Two.
- **They could decide not to hear what you have to say at all.** Why wouldn't a person want to hear you? One possible reason is that they challenge the idea of you filling the role of initiator. They might respond to you in one of these ways:
    - "Who do you think you are to talk to me about this?"
    - "You are meddling in other people's business!"
    - "If that person is offended, they should come to me in person. They should read Matthew 18:15."
- **If their words or actions during your conversation are offensive to you, forgive them in your heart.** You can then choose the offended role and complete Stage One.

In any of these or similar cases, you would calmly explain that you prayerfully completed Peace Pursuit Stage One and that you believe you have a biblical role in helping them become reconciled to the offended person and to God. If they still don't want to hear you out, you would consider approaching them again. If they don't listen to you after several conversations, you would review the *Question your role* point of Stage One. You might think of an appropriate person who you could bring along in the witness role and attempt to meet with the offender at Stage Three.

Q: I am in the initiator role, and I have completed Stage One. I believe it is appropriate for me to have a Stage Two conversation with the person I think is the primarily offended person. How would I introduce the topic to that person?

Normally, you would only fill the role of initiator with an offended person who you know well, who trusts you, and/or who is a person under your care. In this role, your purpose is to gently and appropriately encourage the offended person to forgive the offender in their heart and process Stage One in the offended role, if necessary.

Below are sample ways you could begin a Stage Two conversation in the initiator role with a person you believe is the primary offended one. These are carefully worded, and they are based on the assumption that you have completed Stage One in the initiator role.

> *"Stephanie, I understand that Karen did not do what she promised last week, and that has cost you extra time and effort. I have heard you mention this several times in various conversations. As a friend, can I ask how your heart is feeling toward Karen?"*
>
> *"William, as a friend, I am wondering how you are doing in your relationship with Peter. I noticed that your facial expression changed after he said something to you the other day, and it seems that you are avoiding him since then. I am not trying to meddle; I'm just checking to see if you need to do any peacemaking with Peter."*
>
> *"Elena, when we were together in our Bible study last week, Bethany announced to the group that you are expecting your first grandchild. I noticed that you gave a visible reaction of surprise and you looked toward Bethany. This week, you seemed very quiet during Bible study and you didn't appear to interact with Bethany at all. I don't mean to pry, but as a friend, I am wondering if Bethany's announcement of your news last week has affected your relationship with her."*

The main purposes for these kinds of introductions are:

- To show that you care for the offended person's relationship with God and their relationship with the supposed offender
- To share with the offended person that you have noticed one or more reactions or changes in their behavior that could possibly be connected to a feeling of offense toward the supposed offender
- To provide the offended person a safe, non-confrontational environment to reflect on the perceived offense, if necessary

Q: How might the offended person respond when I approach them in the initiator role?

Like in any other Stage Two situation, the person you have a conversation with could respond in a variety of ways.

- **They could say they don't have a problem with the supposed offender.** It's possible that this is true, and they could tell you that the behavior you noticed in them was for different reasons. If they really aren't offended, don't try to convince them they should be. For example, don't say something like, "Well, if I was in your place, I would be offended. What they did to you was rude, unloving, and disrespectful."

- **They could deny that they have a problem with the offender, when in fact they were offended and have not yet forgiven the offender in their heart.** Depending on how close a relationship you have with the offended and how much discernment you have about the situation, you can choose to tentatively explore more with them. Or, you could choose to leave the topic for now and continue to observe their relationship with the offender.
- **They could admit that they were offended and have not yet forgiven the offender.** It is possible that they will thank you for your care and interest in their relationship with God and with the offender. This is when you can encourage them to choose their role and go through Stage 1 and meet with God in the Peace Pursuit Quick Start Guide. When the offended agrees to go through the Quick Start Guide, your role as initiator is finished. However, when they come to the *Seek appropriate counsel* step of Stage One, they might ask you to be their coach. You would then have the choice to transition into that role.

8. STAGE THREE: YOU AND THE OTHER PERSON MEET WITH SOMEONE ELSE

Stage 3 and the roles of witness and mediator are based on principles from these and other Bible passages: Matthew 7:12, Proverbs 18:17, 1 Timothy 5:19, and Matthew 18:16.

As I wrote in the Introduction (Chapter 1), we have heard many testimonies from those who regularly use the Peace Pursuit Model, and based on those testimonies and our personal experience, we believe that if each party fulfills their Peace Pursuit role, the great majority of relational problems between sincere followers of Jesus can be resolved in Peace Pursuit Stages One and Two. I showed the pie chart below to illustrate our belief.

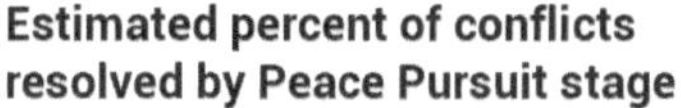

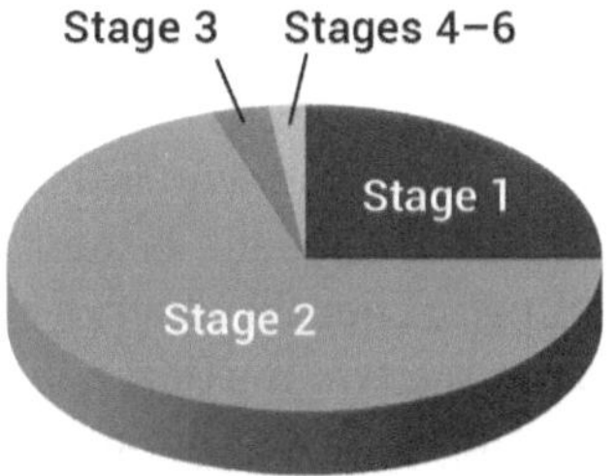

However, there may be occasions in your life when you and another party somehow don't reach appropriate confession and forgiveness at Stage Two. You might need to ask an appropriate person whose presence in your conversation will help the two of you achieve peace with each other. An appropriate person is someone who fills the Peace Pursuit role of witness or mediator. I describe both of these roles in this chapter.

When you add a third person to the peacemaking process, you move from Stage Two (two people) to Stage Three (three people). In a positive sense, when you move to Stage Three, you demonstrate that you and the other party value your relationships with God and with each other. You are sincere and want to get to peace. If you and the other party can agree on an appropriate person to fill the role of witness or mediator, you will very likely reach peace at Stage Three and you will not need to go further.

As I explain here in Stage Three, I am assuming that you and the other party have already had more than one Stage Two conversation and have not reached peace. Personally, you believe you need to move to Stage Three and you choose to involve a third person in your next conversation. You then have two possible situations. The first is for you and the other party to agree to invite or accept a third person into your conversation. This is usually the preferable option, if possible. The second option is when you unilaterally decide to bring a third person along while you have a Stage Three conversation with the other party.

THE WITNESS ROLE

I use the term witness to describe three Peace Pursuit sub-roles:

- **Observing witness.** A person who is asked by one or both parties in a conflict to be present in their Peace Pursuit Stage Three meeting to silently observe and note the interaction between the two parties.
- **Eye witness.** A person who personally heard with their own ears or saw with their own eyes the offense(s) between the two parties.
- **Character witness.** A person who can give an accurate and unbiased report of the normal character, moral qualities, and reputation of one or both parties apart from the present conflict.

The observing witness

For the sake of example, let's say you and another person did not reach peace after more than one Stage Two conversation. You could arrange for an observing witness to be present while you and the other party interact during a Stage Three conversation.

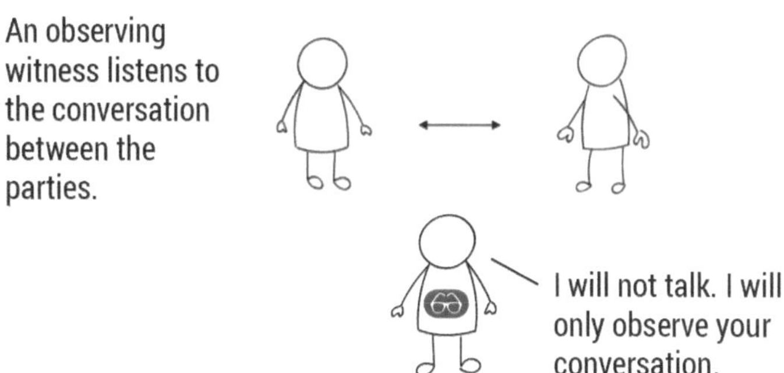

An observing witness pays attention to how well you and the other party use godly communication principles such as respect, patience, gentleness, and self-control. Normally, the observing witness is silent and stays in the background. In fact, you could also call this person a silent witness. This means the observing witness does not guide your discussion or make comments unless you and the other party agree that the witness can speak. This arrangement allows you and the other person to interact just between yourselves in a Stage Three conversation even though there is someone else in the room.

If you believe you need to move to Stage Three and involve an observing witness, I advise that you discuss the idea with the other party. It's best if you and the other party can agree on a person you both trust and respect to be an observing witness in your next conversation.

The observing witness role is less formal and requires less skill than the mediator role, which you will see later. The observing witness should take at least mental notes so that after your conversation they can debrief with you (and with the other party, if they agree). If you and the other party agree, I recommend that the observing witness take written notes, in order to record significant exact quotes from you and the other person.

Of course, I know that moving from Stage Two to Stage Three can be awkward. The reality is you have a choice between two potentially uncomfortable situations. You can choose to leave your relational problem stuck at Stage Two. Or, you can choose to pursue peace further and take a positive step forward, even if it feels awkward.

Q: How do we ask someone to fill the role of observing witness for us?

For an example, let's say that you and Barbara have a relational problem, but you haven't been able to achieve peace after more than one Stage Two conversation. Let's also assume that both of you are sincere and want to continue to pursue peace in good faith. And, let's say you and Barbara agree that Consuelo would be an appropriate person to fill the role of observing witness as you two continue talking together. When you make your request to Consuelo, you would clarify for her exactly what you are asking her to do, what you are not asking her to do, and what kind of time commitment you are asking her to make.

You, or Barbara, or both of you could ask for Consuelo's help and clarify your expectations for her role like this:

> *YOU: "Consuelo, I have a request for you to consider. Barbara and I have a relational problem we are trying to work through to reach appropriate confession and forgiveness. We aren't quite there yet, and we think we need someone to help us. Barbara and I agreed that we would like to ask you to observe our next conversation as a witness of how we communicate with each other.*
>
> *"We are not asking you to guide our discussion or to judge who is right or wrong. We believe your silent presence will help ensure that we communicate with each other in a respectful and godly way. However, at the end of our discussion, we may ask you to share your observations of how we each communicated. Would you be available to meet with us for 90 minutes sometime soon?"*

If you ask for Consuelo's help like this, you will have communicated to Consuelo that both you and Barbara want her as an observing witness, and you have explained to Consuelo exactly what you expect of her in terms of her role and time commitment. This will give her the information she needs to make a wise decision whether to accept the role of observing witness for you and Barbara.

The eye witness

An eye witness is a person who saw the offense with their own eyes or heard it with their own ears. (Of course, in many cases, there is no eye witness to the offense.)

Sometimes when two parties meet alone at Stage Two an offender says to an offended, "It's your word against mine, one valid opinion against another." If you are in the offended or initiator role, and an offender has repeatedly denied their offense at Stage Two, you have the option to bring an eye witness and move the process to Stage Three. An eye witness adds another person's word to the equation. If you are in the offended role, an eye witness's testimony, combined with your prayerful Stage One preparation, might help the offender be open to listening to you at Stage Three.

An eye witness explains to the two parties what they saw and heard regarding the conflict.

I saw and heard the offense.

I believe any eye witness you bring to a Stage Three conversation should go through the appropriate points of Peace Pursuit Stage One themselves. They should take great care to be impartial.

By the way, if you are an eye witness to an offender's actions that don't directly involve you, and no one else seems to be talking with the offender about it, you can then consider filling the role of Peace Pursuit initiator and begin the peacemaking process at Stage One.

Leviticus 5:1 describes the responsibility of an eye witness: "If anyone sins because they do not speak up when they hear a public charge to testify regarding something they have seen or learned about, they will be held responsible" (NIV). This speaks to anyone who knows of an offense that reveals the need for peacemaking, but who doesn't act on it. So, if you have information about a conflict that would be helpful for its resolution, you should share that information with those who are in an appropriate peacemaking role. I do not believe you are gossiping if you fill the role of eye witness in this way.

The character witness

A character witness normally is asked to come in at Peace Pursuit Stage Four (see Chapter 10), but I mention the role here to compare it to the other witness roles. A character witness gives impartial testimony about the integrity and general moral uprightness of one of the parties. This can help the person in the Peace Pursuit leader role at Stage Four who has been given authority to make a judgment of the case come to a well-informed opinion about the two parties and their conflict.

Imagine a conflict that reached an impasse after Stage Two and there has been no progress for some time at Stage Three. Let's assume that peace is blocked because the offender continues to deny they committed the offense or otherwise doesn't listen to whoever is presenting them with their sins or faults. Let's assume there is no eye witness. The offender keeps saying to the offended, "It's your word against mine."

If the person in the leader role at Stage Four cannot discern which of the parties is most likely to be telling the truth, there is a way to help break the stalemate. They can seek out other persons of honesty and integrity who know one or both parties well. In other words, the leader can ask for testimony by one or more character witnesses. With appropriate discretion, the leader briefly explains the case and then asks these persons to give a character reference for one or both of the parties. If done appropriately, this is not gossip or slander.

Calling on a character witness when needed is an application of the *P* in the P.E.A.C.E. Principles: Protect all parties. The testimony of a character witness can protect an offended person from an offender who is illegitimately blocking the peacemaking process. Just as important, it can also protect a supposed offender from being the victim of false accusations by a person acting in the offended or initiator role.

I have been in the leader role at Stage Four conflicts when I needed to request character witnesses. In some cases, character witnesses confirmed that the offender had a pattern of resisting peacemakers and denying similar offenses in other relationships. In other cases, it came to light that the offended person made false or baseless accusations against the presumed offender. In all these instances, the testimony of character witnesses was invaluable to reach peace or help us clearly identify who was blocking the peace process.

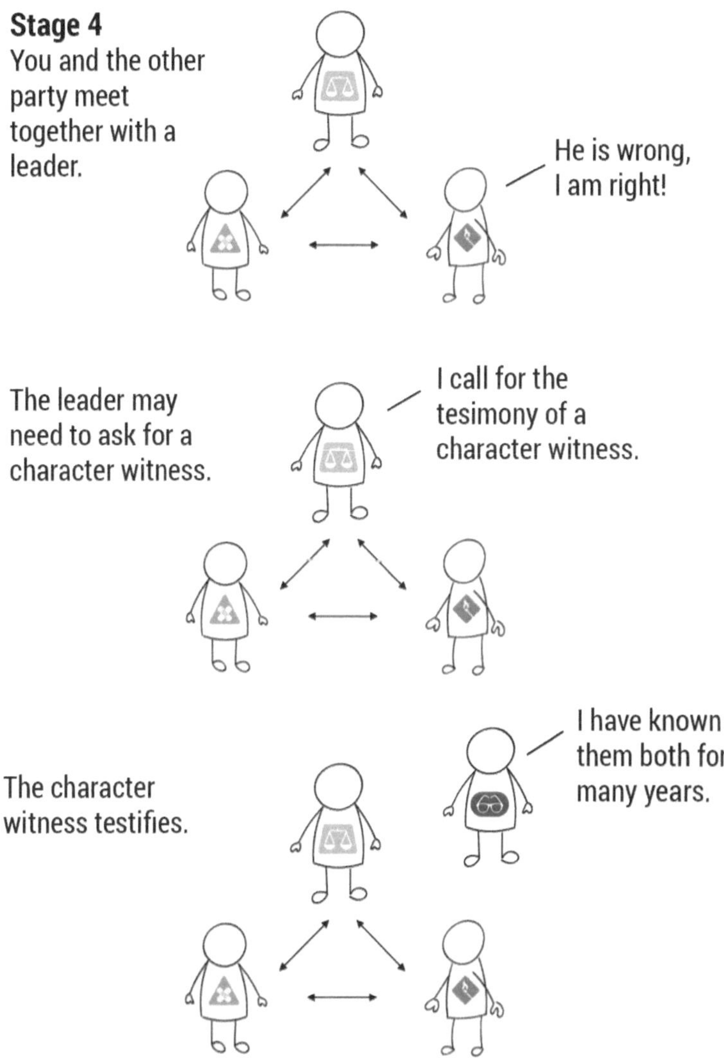

Q: What should I be careful about in my role as a witness?

The role of witness is not to be taken lightly. The Bible has serious warnings for those who do not share information they should, for those who are false witnesses, and for those who are partial. If you agree to be any type of witness, you must speak the truth about the issues and persons involved without partiality or prejudice (Proverbs 19:5 and 24:28).

THE MEDIATOR ROLE

If two people are not able to get to peace even after multiple conversations at Stage Two, they can then ask a mediator to help them in the peacemaking process at Stage Three.

I use the term *mediator* for a person who both parties agree in good faith will actively assist them in reaching peace at Peace Pursuit Stage Three. The mediator role icon is a bridge. A mediator builds a bridge of communication for the two parties to work out peace between themselves. You could also call the person in the mediator role a facilitator. The mediator role is different than the witness role in that a mediator actively facilitates the conversation between the two parties.

Q: What characteristics should a mediator have?

You do not need to be a professionally trained counselor or attorney to be a Peace Pursuit mediator for interpersonal conflicts. This is especially true when the conflict is between sincere Jesus followers. However, you should aim to have characteristics like these:

- **You need to be a good listener.** Good listening for a mediator means you go beyond warmth, empathy, and feeding back the speakers' words to show that you heard them. Be able to clearly summarize and synthesize each party's perspective in your own words. You want each one to respond to your synthesis like this: "Yes, that's what I mean! You understand what I am trying to say!" The better you are able to do this, the more confidence they will have in the process and in your ability to be impartial. The more confidence the parties have in you and the process, the higher the probability they will reach peace.
- **You need to be impartial.** I prefer to use the word impartial instead of the word neutral when I describe a mediator. To be neutral is not bad, of course. To me, the word neutral means that I am passive and take no side. On the other hand, being impartial means that while I do not favor either party, I am equally for both sides. I proactively help both of them to be reconciled to God and to each other. If you prefer, you can use the word *objective* in place of *impartial*.

- **You need confidence in God and the Peace Pursuit process.** God wants the parties to get to peace even more than you or they do. It's his will for them. As a mediator, you provide the environment where the Word of God is sown and watered, and God gives the growth. If the hearts of the two parties are open, they will hear the voice of the Holy Spirit speaking to them. As you remind them of these things, you will communicate confidence to the parties (and to yourself). This will strengthen their faith that God is at work in the process. When you trust God in the process, it also takes the pressure off of you. You won't feel like the outcome depends on your performance. When you and all the parties are walking in the Spirit, no procedural "mistake" you might make as mediator is beyond repair.

Q: What should I do if someone asks me to be a mediator at Stage Three?

If someone asks you if you will go along with them to talk with another person about a conflict between the two of them, I strongly advise you to clarify with that person which of the two parties is in which Peace Pursuit role, and which role they want you to fill. If either person is not familiar with the Peace Pursuit Model, introduce the model to them. Ask the person these questions:

- Which role are they in?
- Which role do they believe the other person is in?
- Which Peace Pursuit role are they are asking you to fill? In other words, do they want you to be a Peace Pursuit witness or a mediator?
- Do both parties want you to fill the Peace Pursuit role of mediator?

Please do all you can to ensure that you and the two parties have clear agreement about your role before you accept a request to help them.

SEVEN PHASES OF MEDIATION

Now, I will walk you through the process I normally follow when I am asked to mediate a relational conflict between professing Jesus followers. You may notice that other models of mediation follow similar principles and practices. However, you will also see that since Peace Pursuit Stage Three is built on the biblical foundations of Stage One and Stage Two, there will be some differences with other models of mediation.

Like at every stage of the Peace Pursuit Model, my primary purpose at Stage Three is to help the two parties reach our definition of peace: appropriate confession and forgiveness. That's why I spend most of the time in my role as a mediator helping the two parties individually prepare their hearts and minds for them to have a calm and godly conversation at Stage Three. I focus on reconciling their relational problem before they try to resolve their differences of opinion over material, organizational, or financial issues, either with my help or the help of other resource people.

Below are the Peace Pursuit Seven Phases of Stage Three. I see these phases as a sequence which has some flexibility. I do not think of the process as a legalistic checklist. You can adapt it to your situation.

In the illustrations, I am represented by the mediator icon.

Mediation Phase 1: Clarify expectations

I clarify everyone's expectations of the peacemaking process and my role in it.

PHASE 1

Mediator clarifies everyone's role and expectations of the process (time commitment, communication guidelines, etc.) either separately or together.

Each party willingly accepts the mediator and agrees to the process.

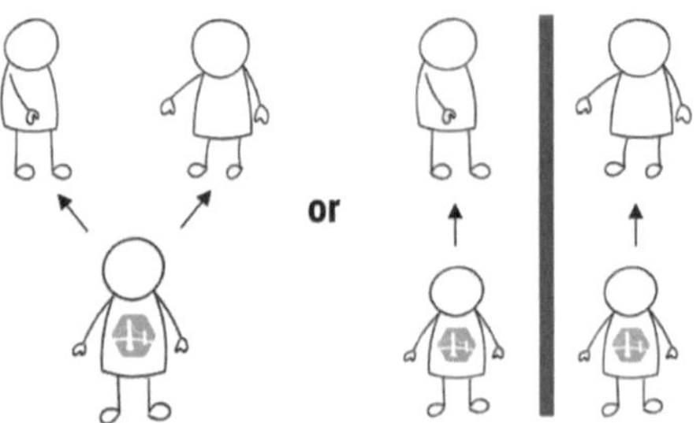

My goal in this first phase of mediation is to build personal trust between each party and me, and to build their confidence in the Peace Pursuit process. This lowers their fear level and increases their faith and hope that they will make progress toward peace.

1. **Before I meet with each party, I ask them each to read carefully through the Peace Pursuit Quick Start Guide, Biblical Foundations, and the Peace Pursuit Model pages at PeacePursuit.org.**

2. **I meet with each party individually or together to clarify my role and their expectations for the process.** If possible, I do this in person. The next best way is by video call. Audio call is my third choice, but that is still acceptable. I try to use email only for arranging appointments or sending written documents I want them to read. (However,

I do ask the parties to give me any emails that they have exchanged related to their conflict.) I assure each party that we are at Peace Pursuit Stage Three and that I am in the mediator role as defined in this handbook. I clarify that I am not in the role of judge or spiritual authority and that we are not at Peace Pursuit Stage Four, in which the two parties would meet with a leader.

3. **I affirm my commitment to follow the P.E.A.C.E. Principles** (see Chapter 2, *Biblical Foundations* in this handbook), **to be objective about the issues, and to be impartial to each person involved.** I pledge not to favor either side. I declare that I am equally on the side of both parties. I explain that my purpose is to actively help each of them make peace with God and reach appropriate confession and forgiveness with each other.

4. **I ask each party to confirm that they are freely willing for me to be the mediator and that they trust my character, my competence, and the process I am using.** I hear from them that they have willingly assented to me and the Peace Pursuit Model. This affirms to them and me that they have ownership in the process. No one is forcing me or my model on them.

5. **I explain to them the next step in mediation is for me to fill the role of Peace Pursuit coach for each party separately as they go back and process *Stage One: Meet with God.*** If either one tells me they have already completed Stage One, I still review it with them. As mediator, I need to know how they see themselves, the issues, and the other party.

6. **I assure each one that I will not bring them together with the other party until I am convinced that both they and the other party have prayerfully and sincerely met with God and completed Stage One in good faith.**

7. **I estimate how many Stage One coaching sessions I will have with each party, and how long the actual mediation meeting will last.** I confirm with each party their commitment that they will invest the time and effort

necessary in the process, and that they will be responsible to keep coaching appointments.

8. **I explain the communication principles we will expect of each other for the mediation meeting, and ask the parties to agree to them.** Each party commits to use godly speech, to show respect for each other, to show respect for me and the process, and to stay in the meeting for its entirety. They will have the option to ask me to pause the meeting for a private conference with me, if they feel it is necessary. I also can ask for a private conference with either one of them. (However, because I coach each party through Stage One before we meet at Stage Three, I have rarely needed private conferences during a mediation time.)
9. **I ask each party to identify and confirm who in their life would fill the Peace Pursuit leader role** (an elder, deacon, pastor, ministry team leader, person they are accountable to in spiritual matters, etc.). In the rare case that they don't reach peace during Stage Three, their next step would be for them to move to Stage Four. As a matter of principle, if either party cannot name a leader, authority, or person they are accountable to in spiritual matters, I decline to fill the role of mediator. (I have found little success in peacemaking with a person who says, "I am accountable only to God.") I offer to be an observing witness in case they go to Stage Four and the leader needs my testimony about how the parties interacted at Stage Three.

Earlier I described a mediator as a bridge person who facilitates an environment where the two parties can resolve the conflict themselves. What I've said above may sound like I am being directive with the parties and telling them what to do. In one sense I am, and in another I am not. By the time the parties need a Stage Three mediator, they often have lost hope for peace and are discouraged. They don't know what else to do. By assuring them that I am for both of them and by giving each one clear next steps, I try to communicate hope and confidence that they can get to peace. Almost every time, both parties are encouraged that an impartial person with skill and experience is there to help. Once I have established their trust and built up their hope level, I transition back to the coach role and point each party to Stage One.

Mediation Phase 2: Each party completes *Stage One: Meet with God*

PHASE 2

Each party prayerfully, sincerely, and separately processes Stage 1 in the **PEACE PURSUIT *QUICK START GUIDE***.

I have found that in almost every case where two people need help at Stage Three, it is because one or both of them did not do Peace Pursuit Stage One and/or Stage Two thoroughly. So, after I clarify my role and the process of Stage Three, I have each of them complete or review Stage One alone.

This speeds up the mediation process and allows each one to focus on a common framework and vocabulary to discuss the issues, attitudes, feelings, and principles involved in their relational problem.

Mediation Phase 3: Mediator meets with each party

I coach each party through the key questions of each point of Stage One before we meet all together at Stage Three.

Note: I am extremely careful not to share inappropriately with either party what the other person is working on in their own Stage One process.

PHASE 3

Mediator transitions to **coach** role and helps each party separately process and review Stage 1 in the **PEACE PURSUIT *QUICK START GUIDE***.

This phase continues until the mediator is convinced that each party has prayerfully and sincerely met with God and completed Stage 1 for their role.

I do not bring the two parties together to talk about the conflict until I am assured that each has fully completed Stage One in good faith. This can take some time over multiple sessions. That is why before I accept a request to mediate a conflict at Stage Three, I ensure that the parties have set aside enough time for me to personally coach them through Stage One before we three meet together.

In the coach role, I hear both sides separately and observe how each one is processing Stage One. This helps me understand what each party feels are the most important issues and offenses. Then I give appropriate coaching and counsel on which of those issues would be fruitful to address when the two meet. I offer them my counsel only when they can't answer Stage One questions for themselves or if I discern they have a blind spot.

It is important for me to help the parties separate professional disagreements from personal offenses. Their professional disagreements over policies, procedures, or programs may never be reconciled, but personal offenses (especially words, actions, inactions, and reactions the Bible calls sin) must be appropriately confessed and forgiven.

While coaching each party separately at Stage One, I witness and affirm each individual's prayers of forgiveness of the other party to God, as appropriate. I also witness and affirm any prayers of repentance to God they need to make. I help them prepare and practice a biblical confession they will make to the other party, if they need to confess anything.

Some may ask, "Why do you wait to arrange a mediation meeting with the three of you until you are satisfied that each party has completed Stage One?" Remember that I am usually asked to mediate at Stage Three because one or both of the parties did not do Peace Pursuit Stage One and/or Stage Two thoroughly. At the very least, they are not communicating with each other in a healthy way, and at worst, they have lost total trust in each other. So, the more thoroughly they do Stage One with an experienced and focused coach, the better prepared they will be—mentally, spiritually, and emotionally—to meet with the other party at Stage Three. If they are going to invest time and emotional energy in a mediation meeting, I want that meeting to be as effective as possible.

In my experience, coaching the parties individually through Stage One can take half or three-quarters of the total time set aside for the whole Stage Three mediation process. Of course, how long Stage One takes for each party depends on how deep and prolonged the conflict has been and how open each party is to hearing and obeying the Holy Spirit through each of the steps for their role.

In other words, in the total time planned for mediation, the parties and I only meet all together the last quarter or half. This is because in most cases the reason that the two parties cannot agree on practical, organizational, or financial issues is because one or both have offended the other by how they have interacted personally. Often, they have violated one or more of the "one another" verses or God's expectations for specific people (see the *Analyze* step of Stage One). After they deal with the interpersonal offenses between them, the practical problems and decisions are much easier for them to sort out either among themselves or with some help from resource persons.

Occasionally another trusted and competent Peace Pursuit coach will coach one of the parties instead of me. I will then debrief with that coach before we continue.

Mediation Phase 4: Bring the two parties together

When both parties have done Stage One thoroughly and in good faith, they are ready, and usually eager, to meet each other. Their meeting will look as much like a Stage Two conversation as possible, though I will be with them.

Before we start, I review my role in the meeting and the communication principles we will follow.

I have the parties affirm their trust in my discernment to move back and forth between these mediator sub-roles as necessary:

- **An observer** who only makes comments about the process
- **A monitor** who only intervenes when the parties violate their agreed-upon and understood norms of conversation
- **A guide** who leads the discussion process

You can picture these sub-roles on a sliding scale. As you move to the right, the more influence the mediator has in the conversation.

I remain an observer in the background unless I feel I should:

- Clarify a point of miscommunication between them;
- Focus them back on a topic they have strayed from; or
- Encourage them to move forward if they reach an awkward moment of silence.

PHASE 4

Mediator brings the two parties together to discuss their offenses and reach appropriate confession and forgiveness.

As necessary, the mediator moves back and forth between the sub-roles of observer, monitor, and guide.

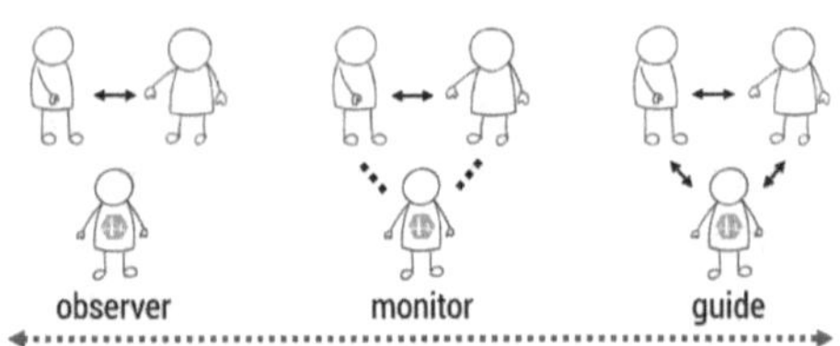

The parties will almost always reach appropriate confession and forgiveness if they and the mediator fulfill their Peace Pursuit roles.

Thank the Lord for his grace. Bless you two for loving the Lord and each other to make peace.

Usually one or both parties have already asked me if they can be the first to confess their part in the conflict to the other person. They want to outdo one another in showing honor (Romans 12:10). Once in a while, neither party volunteers to go first. In those cases, before the meeting I choose whose confession would most likely move the process forward soonest and ask them to confess first.

I give each party plenty of time to share their hearts after they have confessed and forgiven each other. In other words, they keep talking after they reach the Bounce of Peace. Normally, this is the part where they are able to calmly and rationally explain the context of the offenses they committed. Sometimes the parties need to ask each other for clarification of something the other said or wrote. Often, the two will make good progress toward rebuilding their relationship even while this meeting continues, though I don't impose that expectation on anyone.

Mediation Phase 5: The parties discuss practical issues

Almost always, once the two parties have completed the spiritual transaction of confession and forgiveness, they are ready to discuss any professional disagreements or practical implications of their conflict. Sometimes, practical issues which were so important evaporate once they've made peace on the relational level.

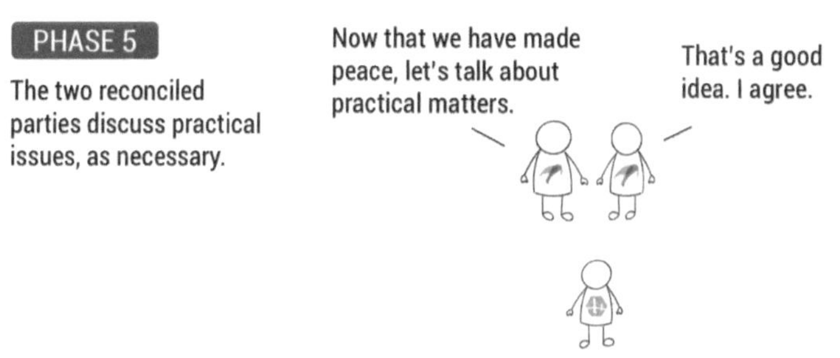

I ask the parties if they want me to stay with them while they discuss the practical issues, or if they now trust each other enough that they don't need me or someone else to be with them.

Mediation Phase 6: Celebration

To bring closure to the mediation, I like to celebrate in some way with the two peacemakers. I review and affirm the steps of honesty, humility, and honor they took to make peace and then give a prayer of thanksgiving to God. If we are all in the same location, we then have a meal or light refreshments.

Mediation Phase 7: The mediator summarizes

I write a summary of the peacemaking process and the reconciliation meeting, and send it to each party. My summary records that I witnessed the two parties reach appropriate confession and forgiveness over specific topics at a specific time and place.

PHASE 7

Mediator writes a summary of the peacemaking process and sends it to the parties.

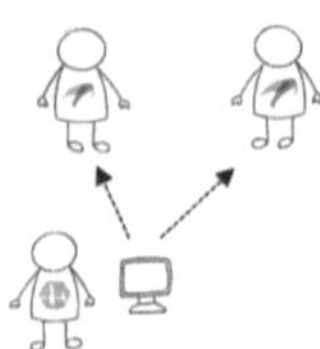

This summary is helpful for the two parties to have as a reminder for themselves and any other person who needs to know that they reached peace.

Q: What should I be careful about when I am in the mediator role?

- Make sure both parties want you and trust you as a mediator. Your ability to help them get to peace is very much tied to the amount of trust each of them has in the process and in your ability to be impartial. I do not recommend you take on this role if either one of the parties does not trust your competence as a conversation facilitator or your ability to be impartial.
- Clarify expectations with each party concerning your role, their role, the stages of the peacemaking process, their commitment to invest time and energy into the process, and communication principles for the mediation meeting.
- Plan sufficient time for yourself and the parties for each phase of the mediation process.
- Don't talk too much when you coach each party at Stage One or during the mediation meeting at Stage Three. When you coach them at Stage One, you want them to hear God's voice more than yours. In the mediation meeting, you want them to hear each other's voices more than yours.
- When you review Stage One with each party alone, don't talk with party A and then tell party B what party A wants to say to them, or vice versa.
- Don't make a judgment of who is right and wrong, unless both parties ask you to.
- In the mediation meeting, ensure as much as possible that the environment is calm, quiet, and there will be no interruptions. Remind the two parties of their agreed guidelines for speaking and listening to each other.

- Focus on reconciling the relational problem—reaching appropriate confession and forgiveness—before moving to practical issues.

Q: Is Stage Three possible if the parties and/or the mediator are not physically present with each other?

Of course, it is normal and preferable to have the two parties and the mediator in the same room. Sometimes that is not possible. Thankfully, the internet creates a way for two people to make peace without delaying until they can be in the same location. I have mediated Stage Three meetings by internet video when I and the two parties were in two, and even three, different locations.

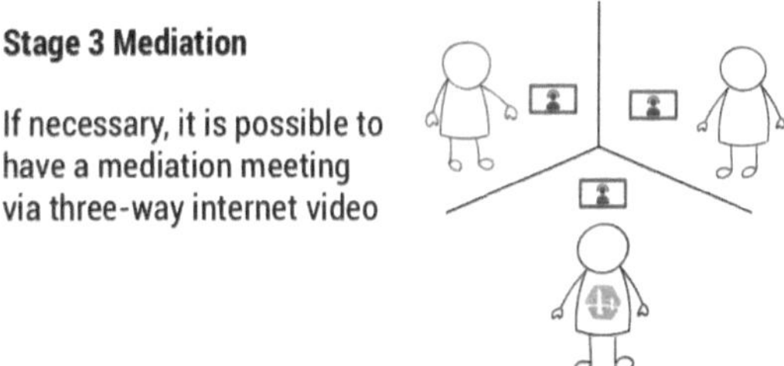

However, I only agree to do internet-based mediations under these conditions:

- Gathering the two parties and me together in the same location would mean a huge delay or expense. The parties and I decide what a huge delay or expense means on a case-by-case basis.
- I am convinced that each party is so well prepared that they can communicate effectively despite the awkwardness of a virtual meeting. That means I have been able to sufficiently coach each party through Stage One, either in person or by internet video.
- The technology we will use provides consistent and good-quality video as well as audio between all parties.

HOW TO ASK SOMEONE TO FILL THE ROLE OF MEDIATOR AT STAGE THREE

I'll walk you through an example of how you could ask someone to mediate for you and the other party at Stage Three. For this example, it does not matter if you were in the Peace Pursuit role of offender or offended at the beginning of the process.

Let's say you want to make peace with Alex. You've completed *Stage One: Meet with God*. You've met alone with Alex at Stage Two more than once, but you haven't reached peace. You think you need more help than a person in the role of observing witness would provide.

You could invite a person you both trust and respect to take on the Peace Pursuit mediator role to help you two continue your conversation toward peace. If Alex sincerely wants to make peace with you, this will likely be a mutually agreeable step.

For example, you could bring up the idea to Alex like this:

> *"Alex, you and I have met to try to resolve our conflict more than once at Stage Two. But we haven't been able to come to peace yet. How about if we ask someone to help us work this through? We can choose someone who we both know will be wise, impartial, and trustworthy."*

If Alex agrees, then you can discuss who that person might be. Together, look for these traits in a person you know in common:

- You and Alex both trust this person to be impartial
- You and Alex are confident that this person has the skill to facilitate your discussion
- This person is available and can provide enough time to meet with you

You and Alex should also agree what expectations you will have for this person as they help you two have a healthy, godly conversation. Once you and Alex agree who might help you and clarify your expectations for that person, then you or Alex (or both of you) can contact that person to request their help.

Let's say you and Alex agree that Matthew would be a good person to fill the Peace Pursuit mediator role during Stage Three conversations between you. Here are two examples of how you and/or Alex could approach Matthew. In the first example, Matthew does not know about the Peace Pursuit Model. In the second, he is familiar with the Peace Pursuit concepts and terms.

Scenario 1

Even if Matthew is not familiar with Peace Pursuit, you can still ask him to help you and Alex apply the Peace Pursuit Model to resolve your conflict. In this example, it would take you less than two minutes to explain to Matthew exactly what you want him to do for you.

"Matthew, I have a request for you to consider. Alex and I have a conflict. We've met together several times, but we haven't arrived at peace yet.

"We are looking for someone to help us who we both trust is mature and impartial. We also need someone who is able to facilitate our discussion in an objective way so that each of us feels safe, respected, and heard by the other. Alex and I both think you are that kind of person.

"We would like to ask you to help us get to the place where Alex and I have appropriately confessed and forgiven the offenses between us. We would ask you to meet with each of us privately to review our perspectives of the problem and to help each of us see the situation from God's perspective, as well. Then, you would facilitate a meeting between Alex and me with the goal for us to have a godly discussion and reach appropriate confession and forgiveness. So, we are asking you to have at least three meetings: once alone with me, once alone with Alex, and once with us together. Depending on how well Alex and I prepare, we may need more meetings.

"I have some helpful Bible-based materials that clearly lay out what Alex and I need to do to move forward, and some suggested procedures for how you could help us. I can send those to you.

"Would you be available to help us?"

Assuming that Matthew agrees, you would ask him to become familiar with the Peace Pursuit Quick Start Guide available at PeacePursuit.org. You would explain the Peace Pursuit mediator role to him in more detail, as described in this handbook.

Scenario 2

Let's say Matthew is already familiar with the roles and stages of the Peace Pursuit Model. You and/or Alex could explain your situation to Matthew and ask him to help in less than a minute:

> *"Alex and I are in a peacemaking situation and we are using the Peace Pursuit Model. We have had several Stage Two conversations, but we haven't gotten to peace. Matthew, we'd now like to ask you to fill the role of mediator for us at Stage Three. Would you be available to help us?"*

When you and Alex discuss who might mediate for you, keep in mind that a person in the Peace Pursuit mediator role is not acting as a judge with authority. Their job is to create an environment for you and Alex to have a safe, respectful, and rational conversation about your conflict with the goal of getting you to appropriate confession and forgiveness.

Q: What if we two parties can't agree on a person to help us?

If you can't agree on someone to help you, it may be because one of you does not sincerely want to get to peace. Assuming you are the one who wants to make peace and it is Alex who is resisting, you have a couple of options.

Option 1

You can decide that you have done enough. To get to this point you have already done much to pursue peace. You have completed Peace Pursuit Stage One in good faith, you have had multiple Stage Two conversations with Alex, and you have tried to agree with Alex on an appropriate person who could help you two get to peace. You could say to yourself and God, "Since I have done all these things in good faith, I have obeyed Romans 12:18 and done everything in my power to be at peace with Alex." However, I advise that before you decide you've done enough, review Stage One for your role and meet with God one more time.

Keep in mind that there are implications and consequences if you decide to stop the peacemaking process with Alex at this stage. You must maintain forgiveness toward Alex in your heart before God, and you must not talk to anyone about Alex inappropriately. And, you may still have to live with or work with Alex.

Option 2

You can decide to keep pursuing peace with Alex. Normally, this means you would have a conversation with whoever is Alex's spiritual leader or a person Alex is accountable to. In other words, you would move to Peace Pursuit *Stage Four: You and the other party meet with a leader.*

You would explain to the leader of Alex all that you have done so far:

- You have completed in good faith Peace Pursuit Stage One.

- You tried multiple times to reconcile with Alex at Stage Two.
- You attempted to agree with Alex on an impartial and competent person to help you reach peace at Stage Three.

You would then encourage the person who is Alex's spiritual leader to fulfill their Peace Pursuit role at Stage Four (see Chapter 10).

Q: What if the other party won't accept the idea of asking someone to help us reach peace at Stage Three?

If Alex does not agree with the idea of another person helping you two get to peace, you have the same two options as in the question just above. You can choose to stop the process, being aware of and accepting the implications. Or, you can move to Stage Four and approach Alex's spiritual leader.

Q: What if peace is not reached at Stage Three?

In my experience, the vast majority of conflicts between sincere Jesus followers can be resolved if each party fills their role in good faith at Peace Pursuit Stages One and Two. Occasionally you might need to move to Stage Three. Before you move to a higher stage, try to ensure that both parties have completed Stage One thoughtfully, with prayer, and in good faith.

If you ever need to go to further stages, it is important to process them in a prayerful, careful, and biblical way. See Chapter 9 of this handbook for an introduction to the higher stages.

9. EXTRAORDINARY SITUATIONS: A BRIEF INTRODUCTION

The majority of this handbook focuses on Peace Pursuit Stages One and Two because if both parties in a conflict do the hard work (and *heart* work) to fulfill their Peace Pursuit roles in those two stages, they will normally reach appropriate confession and forgiveness without needing to go further. If for some reason the parties choose to go to Peace Pursuit Stage Three, they will almost always achieve peace there.

Therefore, the need to move to Stage Four and beyond is very rare, as illustrated by this chart.

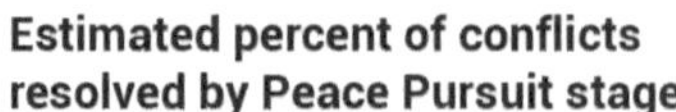

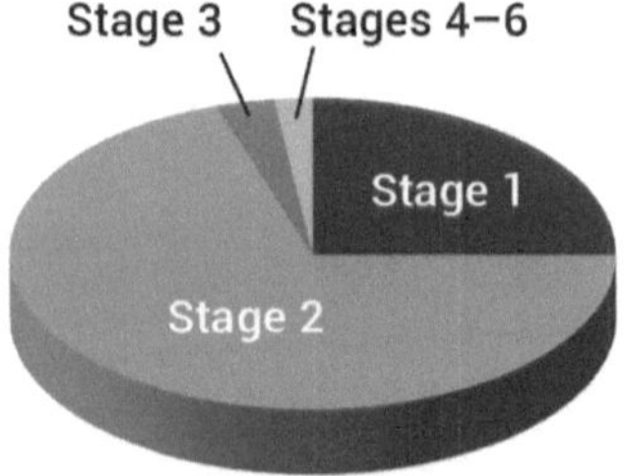

STAGES FOUR, FIVE, AND SIX

This handbook is not the place for a detailed explanation of the higher stages. However, I want to give you a very brief introduction to the essential principles of Stages Four, Five, and Six. How these principles are applied in a certain church or Christian ministry depends on its specific values and organizational structure.

I have seen that there are generally two types of situations which lead to Stage Four and beyond.

- When the Peace Pursuit Model as I have described in this handbook has been followed by all persons involved, it is rare for a peacemaking process to move beyond Stage Three. The reason to go to higher stages has almost always been because one or more of the parties has been spiritually blind, spiritually deaf, or in some way resistant to godly, wise, caring, and patient love on the part of sisters and brothers in the Lord who have gently brought him or her through the previous three stages. Normally, at Stage Four and beyond, it becomes clear to all which party or parties have been hindering their reconciliation with God and with other people.
- I have been asked to give advice in complicated cases where the Peace Pursuit Model has not been followed. Often, the peacemaking process is frozen and there is little or no agreement on what to do next. Sometimes, the situation has been unnecessarily escalated to the point where persons with assumed and/or legitimate authority get involved. In other cases, persons with legitimate authority are not fulfilling the responsibility associated with their position. To prevent further unnecessary escalation, relational damage, discouragement, and unfruitful expenditure of time and emotional energy, my normal counsel in these cases is to roll back the process to Peace Pursuit Stage One, identify legitimate roles for all involved, and proceed from there.

TRY TO REACH PEACE AT THE LOWEST STAGE POSSIBLE

There is a folk proverb that says, "Fools rush in where angels fear to tread." Please don't rush into the higher stages.

The Peace Pursuit Model is designed so that you reach relational reconciliation at the lowest possible stage. Stage One involves one person. Stage Two involves two people. Stage Three involves three people. You see where this is going. The higher the stage, the more people become involved.

To involve more people when necessary and appropriate is a good thing. However, you need to know that it has consequences and potential risks.

Here are a few risks and consequences when more persons than the two parties are involved in the peace process:

- The more people you get involved, the greater the possibility for someone to fall into the aggravator role.
- More people involved means more potential for gossip, embarrassment, or shame for one or both parties.
- The investment of other people's valuable resources like time and emotional energy increases.
- The two parties are in control of the peacemaking process through Stage Three. They can choose to involve a coach or coaches, witnesses, or a mediator. From Stage Four and beyond, a leader guides the process.

So, before you jump to a new stage, do what you can to make sure each party has fulfilled their legitimate Peace Pursuit role in the previous stages. Almost every time I am asked to mediate a conflict at Peace Pursuit Stage Three, I discover that one or both parties had not completed their role in Peace Pursuit Stage One and/or Stage Two. That's why, when I accept the mediator role, I bring each party back to Stage One and coach them individually through their role before I bring the parties together.

The good news is that if you find yourself in a legitimate role in a peacemaking situation beyond Stage Three and everyone involved applies the Peace Pursuit Model, the fruit of so many prayers and so much effort can be a God-honoring reconciliation where everyone is blessed (Peace Pursuit Pillar 5).

10. STAGE FOUR: YOU AND THE OTHER PARTY MEET WITH A LEADER

Stage Four and the leader role are based on principles from these and other Bible passages: Matthew 7:12, Hebrews 13:17, 1 Peter 5:1–4, 1 Corinthians 6:1–8, 1 Thessalonians 5:14, 2 Timothy 4:2, Hebrews 5:14, and Matthew 18:17a.

At Stage Four, the two parties talk with each other in the presence of a recognized spiritual leader who has the authority to care for the supposed offender in matters of godliness and Christian character. If the two parties do not reach peace, the leader makes a prayerful, thoughtful, and impartial judgment concerning the conflict.

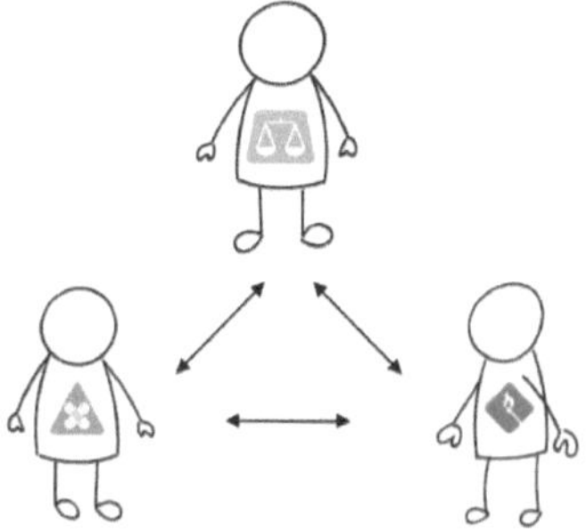

The leader considers these things:

- The interaction between the offended person and the supposed offender
- The nature of the offense(s)
- Appropriate input from credible witnesses or mediators

All persons involved should respect and submit to the leader's decision. Depending on the response of both parties and the nature of the offense(s) between them, the leader approves a discipleship plan for the offender under their care. The leader can appoint a mentor to guide the offender through Stage Five.

The process above is basically the same when the scenario involves an initiator and a supposed offender.

THE LEADER ROLE

You can fill the Peace Pursuit leader role if you are in the position of *recognized spiritual leader* in relation to one or both of the parties in a conflict. Of course, in certain models of church government, recognized spiritual leadership can reside in more than one individual, such as in a board of elders or church staff team. When I refer to the Peace Pursuit role of leader, I mean whatever model of leadership is recognized in your particular spiritual community or organization, whether it is an individual or a group.

It is essential for each party in a conflict to identify who their spiritual leader is before the Peace Pursuit process moves to Stage Four. I believe that they should communicate this to each other even before they begin Stage Three.

By the term *spiritual leader*, I refer to a person (or persons) whose biblical role is to keep watch over your soul. They will answer to God for how well they watch over you.

Various Bible words for this role are translated as overseer (1 Timothy 3:1), leader (Hebrews 13:17), elder (Titus 1:5), and shepherd (1 Peter 5:2). Churches and Christian ministry organizations use these and other names for persons who function in this role. These persons are in a position of authority to which you and I are to submit and obey in spiritual and character matters (Hebrews 13:17, 1 Peter 5:5).

By the word *recognized,* I mean the combination of all three of the following points:

- Someone else has called, appointed, or affirmed them for this biblical leadership role. They did not create or claim the position themselves (Acts 14:23, Titus 1:5).
- The person in leadership has consciously accepted this role and is sincerely committed to fulfill their responsibility of caring for souls (1 Peter 5:1–4).
- The one whose soul is being cared for acknowledges that they are to submit to and obey the leader(s) in matters of godliness and character (Hebrews 13:17, 1 Peter 5:5).

In other words, the leader is *recognized* by people "above" them, the leader *recognizes* the responsibility they have taken on for their role of caring for the follower, and the follower *recognizes* the leader's authority.

For a simple illustration of what I mean by these three points, let's look at an imaginary situation. Noah is a new believer in Jesus. A friend recommends that he join Fellowship Community Church (FCC), which is led by Pastor Smith.

Noah reaches out to Pastor Smith and asks what it means to be a member of FCC. Pastor Smith explains:

> "FCC is part of a group of churches which recognized me as qualified to be a minister. This group of churches oversees me and I report to them about my personal life and ministry. I am also accountable to the FCC elder team, which is elected by the congregation and which called me as pastor. I love the members of FCC and I take seriously my responsibility for their soul care. I care for the flock by teaching, preaching, praying, visiting, and counseling.
>
> "When a person joins FCC, they commit to give a portion of their time, effort, and finances to serve the other members and the mission of FCC. They also commit to follow my biblical teaching and counsel, and to submit to my leading and authority in spiritual matters."

After thinking and praying, Noah decides to join FCC. One Sunday, Pastor Smith leads a time to receive a group of new members, including Noah. Pastor Smith reminds the congregation and the new members who he is responsible to and who he is responsible for.

He describes the responsibilities of new members, including their agreement to follow his spiritual leadership when they join FCC. At this time, Noah publicly commits himself to membership.

This brief story contains all three aspects of recognized spiritual leadership I mentioned above.

- Pastor Smith was commissioned by a network of churches and is accountable to the FCC elder team which called him. He did not unilaterally declare himself to be the leader of the FCC congregation.
- Pastor Smith embraces and takes seriously his role of caring for the souls of his church members, including Noah.
- Noah publicly accepted Pastor Smith's authority as his spiritual leader during the Sunday worship service.

Now, let's say that sometime later Noah has a conflict with another believer which somehow escalates to Peace Pursuit Stage Four. In this case, it would be appropriate for Pastor Smith to fill the Peace Pursuit leader role in relation to Noah.

What the leader does at Stage Four

The icon for the Peace Pursuit leader role is a set of scales. The leader impartially listens to the facts and testimonies regarding the two sides of a conflict, and decides the degree to which each one has the weight of truth.

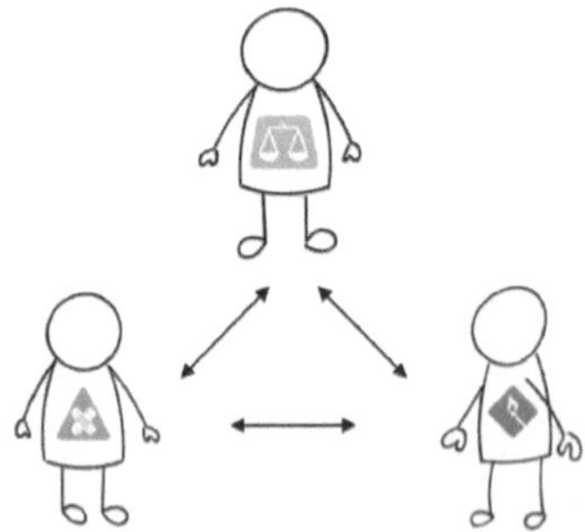

Here is an outline of what the leader does at Stage Four.

- Listen to each party's story, including how they processed Stages One, Two, and Three.
- Observe how the two parties interact with each other.

- Hear testimonies from any character witnesses, observing witnesses, or eye witnesses.
- Ask the two parties clarifying questions.
- Give the two parties an opportunity to reconcile in the presence of the leader.

If the two parties don't reach peace during this meeting, the leader continues with these steps:

- Discern which party (or parties) has been hindering peace so far.
- Make an impartial judgment regarding which party (or parties) needs to repent and/or forgive the other party.
- Determine appropriate follow-up steps for one or both parties.
- Approve a mentor for the offender, as needed.

The last two points include the leader's discerning whether an offender needs a Peace Pursuit Stage Five program of counseling, training in righteousness, or similar discipleship. If the leader decides the offender needs such a program, the leader approves both the program and the mentor who would minister to the offender during that process. Please see Stage Five.

The process above is basically the same when the two persons who meet with the leader are in the roles of initiator and supposed offender.

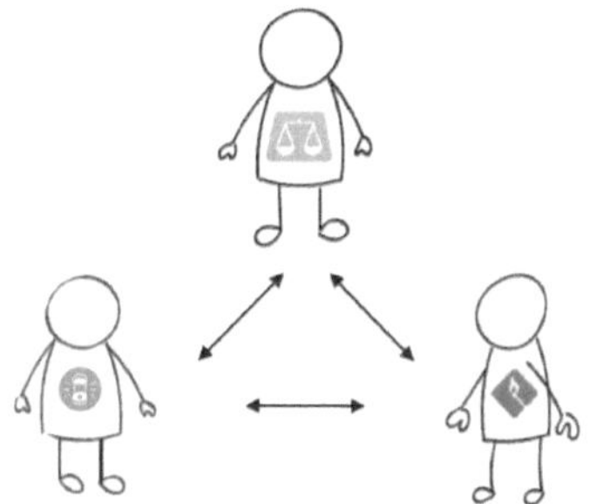

The definition of *authority* in the Peace Pursuit leader role

I gave a brief scriptural introduction to the topic of authority in my explanation of the term *recognized spiritual leadership* above.

Because this is such a critical and debated concept, I will expand on it more here.

Let me start by saying that I am well aware of these facts:

- In many Christian circles, the term *authority* in relation to spiritual leadership has fallen out of favor. Of course, one major reason is the increasing revelation that some spiritual authority figures have crushed vulnerable souls instead of caring for them. This horrible hypocrisy needs to be exposed and appropriate confession, forgiveness, and restitution needs to be made.
- Around the world, there are hundreds of thousands of men and women in authority positions in churches and ministries who *do not* abuse individuals and who *do not* lord it over or treat the flock under their care in a domineering way (1 Peter 5:3).
- There is a wide spectrum of understanding and practice regarding the concepts of spiritual leadership, accountability, and authority among the tens of thousands of Christian church traditions, associations, denominations, and ministries in the world.
- Individuals bring their personal definitions of leadership, accountability, and authority with them when they join a church, a Christian organization, or a ministry team. If their definitions are different than those of the group they join, there is a potential for anything from mutually frustrating misunderstandings to painful, prolonged struggles during a peacemaking situation.

While doing Peace Pursuit training, consulting, and coaching with Christian leaders and followers from many countries and cultures, I have heard varied definitions for the English words *accountability* and *authority* in relation to a person's spiritual life and character. Below are three of the most common examples I have heard. I have written these examples as if I am the person who is being held accountable and/or who is under authority.

1. Some say that for me to be *accountable* to a person means that I have agreed to report to or share with them about some area or areas of my life and character. They are free to ask me questions, comment, and give advice about those areas,

but I am not required to submit to or act on their opinion or counsel. I can decide to "take or leave" what they say.

2. Most would agree that for me to be under a person's *authority* means I am required to obey and submit to their care, advice, counsel, teaching, and correction in matters of biblical character and behavior, even when I disagree with them.

3. Some define the word *accountability* in the same way as the description of *authority* in point two above. For them, the two words accountability and authority are synonyms. So, for me to be accountable to a person means I submit to, obey, and put into practice their teaching, counsel, and correction even if I don't agree with them.

Your personal definition of the words *accountability* and *authority* may even be different from the examples above. If you are in any kind of formal or informal Christian ministry, I urge you to at least clarify your understanding of the principles behind those terms with those you minister with and minister to, even if your definitions of those words are different from theirs.

With that background, I can now say that in the Peace Pursuit Model, the leader role is filled by a person in a position of authority in the sense of example definition number two above. At Stage Four, the leader makes a careful, wise, prayerful, loving, grace-filled, truth-filled, warm-hearted, and cool-headed judgment of the situation. The party who is under the authority of the leader is expected to submit to that judgment.

Q: What if it is not clear who is in the Peace Pursuit Stage Four leader role of one or both parties?

Do your best to identify who that person might be. If it is still unclear, try to find a mature, biblically literate, impartial, and objective person who is "wise enough to settle a dispute" between Christians (1 Corinthians 6:5). Then confirm that the party or parties will submit to a Stage Four judgment made by that person.

Q: I am in the position of Peace Pursuit Stage Four leader. Can I also fill other Peace Pursuit roles at different stages in the same conflict?

Yes, you could potentially and legitimately fill other Peace Pursuit roles at different stages in one conflict.

However, at every point along the way, it is essential that everyone involved is clear about which Peace Pursuit stage the process is in and which Peace Pursuit role you are filling.

In other words, at all times make it clear which single "hat" you are wearing and be careful to comply with the responsibilities of each Peace Pursuit role as described in this handbook.

SOME POSSIBLE OUTCOMES OF STAGE FOUR

Here are the basic possible outcomes of Stage Four, in descending order of frequency. The most common outcome is number one; the least common is number four.

1. The supposed offender receives and accepts revelation regarding his sin. He repents in godly sorrow for everything that has been shown him about his behavior. He then submits to the leader's decision about a Stage Five discipleship program.
2. The supposed offender admits only some fault or repents for only part of what has been shown him, but still submits to the leader's decision about a Stage Five discipleship program.
3. The supposed offender refuses or denies everything that has been shown him about his behavior. The leader then creates a Stage Five discipleship plan for the offender and the leader appeals to the offender to humbly accept the discipleship program. If the offender refuses the Stage Five discipleship plan, the leader can decide to move directly to Peace Pursuit Stage Six.
4. The leader discerns that the supposed offender has been wrongly accused by the other party and/or others who have been aggravators in the process. If the accuser and/or aggravators are also persons under the care of the leader, the leader corrects them and urges them to repent to God and the person they wrongly accused. If the accuser and/or aggravators are not under the leader's authority, the leader then decides whether to fill the role of initiator and begins to process Peace Pursuit Stage One in relation to those persons.

11. STAGE FIVE: AN APPROVED MENTOR MEETS WITH THE OFFENDER

Stage Five and the mentor role are based on principles from these and other Bible passages: Matthew 7:12, 2 Corinthians 7:10–11, Matthew 3:8, Ephesians 4:21–32, Colossians 3:12, 2 Timothy 2:22–26, Romans 16:17a, 2 Timothy 3:16–17, 1 Thessalonians 5:14, 2 Timothy 4:2, and Galatians 6:1–2.

Stage Five is a loving and costly investment of time and resources in the life of an offender by his faith community. With love, care, and patience, a mentor approved by the leader helps the offender complete the discipleship plan which was decided by the leader at the conclusion of Stage Four. It is possible that the leader could fill the Stage Five mentor role themselves.

Each Stage Five discipleship program is uniquely crafted for the individual involved. The scope and specific details of the program depend on the offender's response to Stage Four and the type and depth of his offense or offenses.

The goals of a Stage Five discipleship plan include the offender's reconciliation with God and with any offended person or persons. The plan is also meant to create a healthy environment for the offender's needed spiritual and emotional healing, renewal of mind, fruits of repentance, training in righteousness, and, if appropriate, his upgrading in ministry skills.

If the offender was in some kind of ministry or spiritual service prior to Stage Five, the leader may decide to relieve the offender from part or all of those responsibilities until the offender completes Stage Five.

THE MENTOR ROLE

To fill the Peace Pursuit mentor role, you accept responsibility to oversee the discipleship program of the offender at Peace Pursuit Stage Five which was determined by the offender's leader. You may or may not have had another Peace Pursuit role in the process up to this point.

You walk alongside the offender to help him reconcile with God and with any offended persons. You also oversee his spiritual growth to produce fruit in keeping with repentance for the offense or offenses that caused the need for Stage Four.

During Stage Five, you are also responsible to keep the leader of the offender informed of the offender's progress toward the stated goals of the discipleship process.

Q: What do you mean by "approved mentor"?

The leader is responsible for the spiritual care of the offender, so if the leader does not personally fill the mentor role at Stage Five, it is important for the leader to have wise discernment and approve who should fill that role.

Keep in mind that if the peacemaking process reaches Stage Five, it us usually because the offender was spiritually dull, blind, deaf, or willfully resistant through Stages Two, Three, and Four. The offender needs a mentor to watch over and care for him who understands and who will address the specific problems that created this Stage Five situation. The leader needs to be able to trust that the mentor will focus on those topics with the offender and that the mentor will regularly inform the leader of the offender's progress in those areas.

You can fill the approved mentor role of Peace Pursuit Stage Five if you have these characteristics:

- You are able to be both compassionate and impartial toward the offender.
- You clearly understand and accept the leader's rationale of the need for and the nature of the offender's Stage Five discipleship program.
- You commit to focus on what the leader believes are the offender's areas of need and the desired outcomes.
- You commit to regularly inform the leader about the offender's progress in the discipleship plan.
- You have sufficient time and energy to fill this role.

Q: What are some possible outcomes of Stage Five?

Stage Five is considered to be over in either of these two situations:

- The offender appropriately completes the discipleship program as expected. The leader confirms that the offender has reconciled with any other persons as needed and that the offender has shown evidence of fruit in keeping with repentance. If the offender had previously been in a ministry role before Stage Five, the leader may choose to reinstate him or help him find another ministry role.
- Or, the offender does not fully accept and/or fully complete the discipleship plan. This normally reveals the offender's true heart attitude and likely means that the offender does not recognize the authority of the leader, the spiritual community, and/or the authority of God in his life. The leader and the offender's spiritual community should try again to persuade the offender to listen to wise and mature counsel. If the offender refuses to listen and heed loving, patient, and wise counsel, the leader can create an alternative discipleship program or move the process to Stage Six.

12. STAGE SIX: THE LEADER MEETS WITH THE OFFENDER

Stage Six is based on principles from these and other Bible passages: Matthew 7:12, 1 Corinthians 5:9–13, 2 Thessalonians 3:14–15, Titus 3:10, Ephesians 5:3–5, 2 Timothy 3:5, and Matthew 18:17b.

Let me remind you of the P.E.A.C.E. Principles:

P = Protect all parties

E = Expose truth and error

A = Act in love toward all parties

C = Complete peace between persons and between persons and God

E = Exclude inappropriate persons and behavior

In the rare case when the offender does not accept or complete the Stage Five discipleship plan, the leader meets with the offender at Stage Six to give him one more opportunity to heed wise counsel and accept the loving grace and care of the community. The leader tries to persuade, to implore, and to urge the offender to be reconciled to God and other people, as necessary and appropriate (2 Corinthians 5:20). This is an application of the *P* in the P.E.A.C.E. Principles: Protect all parties. The leader meets with the offender at Stage Six to protect the offender from his own harmful and unwise decisions. Stage Six also protects the spiritual community from the bad example and influence of an unrepentant offender.

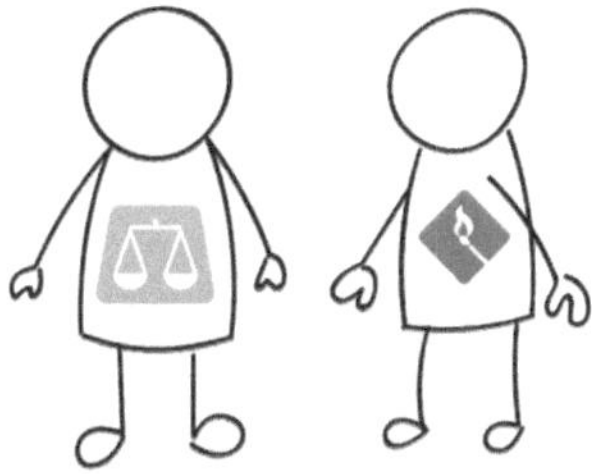

If the offender finally decides to heed wisdom and repent, he can enter (or reenter) a Stage Five discipleship program.

However, the offender may refuse to heed the leader's pleas and reject the wise and gracious love of the community. It is heart-breaking and sobering to witness an offender remain unrepentant or unsubmissive to wise judgment and patient, loving discipleship. The next step is agonizing for a leader. With great sadness, the leader formally dismisses the offender from the community. When done in a patient, biblical manner, dismissing an unrepentant offender is one last act of love to convince the offender to reconcile with God and people. It also gives him one more opportunity to see and feel the consequences of his chosen actions. Churches, ministry teams, and Christian organizations have different ways of processing an unrepentant offender's exit from their community, based on their particular values and structure.

After Stage Six, the community should continue to pray that the offender would come to his senses like the prodigal son in Luke 15:11–32. If the offender returns with godly sorrow and fruits of repentance, he may reapply to join the community.

THE LEADER ROLE AT STAGE SIX

Stage Six is as much about the leader (or leaders) as it is about the offender. A loving, caring, patient, and wise leader will neither rush into Stage Six nor shrink back from it. You could say that Stage Six is an expression of the *A* in the P.E.A.C.E. Principles: Act in love toward all parties. The leader must love the offender enough to be filled with both the truth and grace necessary to do a difficult thing for the purpose of reconciling the offender to God. Loving the offender also means having the courage to face potential backlash from the offender or criticism by others.

When leadership applies Stage Six with prayerful preparation and in a loving manner, the rest of the sheep under their care can feel loved, protected, and encouraged by a shepherd whose life is an example of obedience to biblical peacemaking principles. The community will also be reminded of the wisdom and importance of making peace in their own lives at the lowest possible stage.

EPILOGUE

In a parable in Luke 12:35–48, Jesus said that much will be required of the person to whom much has been given. Whether you have read through this handbook completely or you have looked at just a few topics, you have been given much to help you take biblical and practical steps toward resolving a relational problem. I believe the Prince of Peace requires you to act on what you have been given.

As you put into practice what you have read here, remember Peace Pursuit Pillar 5: Everyone is blessed when you pursue peace biblically. You are even a blessing when you pass along tools like Peace Pursuit to others and when you share your own testimony of peacemaking, as appropriate.

I want to invite you to visit our PeacePursuit.org website often. We periodically update our resources and add new ones to better equip you.

Blessed are you, peacemaker, for you will be called a child of God (Matthew 5:9, NIV).

THE PEACE PURSUIT QUICK START GUIDE

The Peace Pursuit Quick Start Guide immediately helps you take the first steps in resolving a relational problem. It walks you through the four primary Peace Pursuit roles of offended, offender, initiator, and coach and the two basic Peace Pursuit stages:

- **Stage One: Meet with God; and**
- **Stage Two: If appropriate, meet with the other person.**

Experience shows that if you and the other party prayerfully, sincerely, and completely fulfill your chosen role at Stages One and Two, you will reach appropriate confession and forgiveness in the vast majority of situations.

As you become familiar with the Peace Pursuit Model you will gain the confidence to use the Quick Start Guide to help yourself and others reach appropriate confession and forgiveness.

Available at PeacePursuit.org

Download various formats of the Quick Start Guide in multiple languages to print and/or view on your computer or handheld device. You may wish to keep a copy of the Quick Start Guide in your Bible or on your mobile device for quick access.

The Peace Pursuit Quick Start Guide is available at no cost and may be freely distributed.

ACKNOWLEDGEMENTS

I am grateful to God for a number of people who have impacted my growth in spiritual life and ministry over the decades. I want to acknowledge just a few of those who made significant contributions to my foundational understanding and practice of biblical peacemaking.

In the 1970s and 1980s, Dr. Ron Rand was one of my key pastors and a mentor when I was a new Christian in my university years. His teaching on keeping short accounts and keeping a "good report" in relationships by confessing and forgiving had an early and deep effect on me. Ron has been an outstanding example of how to make the teaching of difficult subjects like peacemaking both visual and memorable. Ron is the founder of Upbuilding Ministries (upbuildingministries.org).

Dr. Gary Sweeten was also one of my pastors in the 1970s and 1980s. From Gary's training I learned healthy listening skills and how to combine rational thinking with Scriptural truth and Holy Spirit-led discernment. Gary is the founder of Sweeten Life Systems (sweetenlife.com).

In the 1970s I was introduced to the writings of Dr. Jay Adams. His books on biblical counseling and his *Handbook of Church Discipline* have helped inform some of what I include in the Peace Pursuit Model.

Dick Scoggins was a wise and caring mentor for me for well over a decade beginning in the 1990s. Dick personally guided me through a number of peacemaking situations in my own life and ministry. His teaching and examples from his experience planted a number of seeds which I nurtured and grafted into various parts of the Peace Pursuit Model. His website: dickscoggins.com.

In the early 2000s, I came across Ken Sande's *The Peacemaker: A Biblical Guide to Resolving Personal Conflict.* I have highly recommended it ever since. Mr. Sande founded Peacemaker

Ministries (peacemaker.net), whose training I have benefitted from. He is the founder of Relational Wisdom 360 (rw360.org).

I also acknowledge the hundreds of individuals I have interacted with around the world since the 1980s who have significantly contributed to the development of the Peace Pursuit Model and continue to do so. Blessed are those peacemakers.

Special thanks

My dear wife, Laura, has been a gracious, patient, and encouraging partner as the Peace Pursuit Model has taken shape over the years.

I am in debt to fellow peace pursuer Bob Peckham for his encouragement and his editing, which brought clarity and fluidity to the text of this handbook. He is an invaluable "iron sharpening iron" friend and encourager. Bob coined the phrase "Bounce of Peace."

I am thankful to Dick Steward for his decades of experience as a pastor and counselor which he brought to the manuscript. Dick's valuable insights helped to make this handbook more user-friendly.

About the author

John Shindeldecker developed The Peace Pursuit Handbook based on decades of experience helping to resolve interpersonal conflicts among Christians. He is the creator of The Peace Pursuit Model™ and the founder of PeacePursuit.org.

John and his wife, Laura, have a passion for helping people to be reconciled to God and to each other as they follow Jesus, the Prince of Peace.

As part of their international ministry of equipping Christian leaders, they train and mentor others who share their passion for biblical peacemaking.

John and Laura collaborate with a growing number of individuals, churches, and international ministries who use the Peace Pursuit Model. Their ministry has taken them to more than 20 countries to train expatriates and local people.

Made in United States
Troutdale, OR
01/09/2025